ACTUALIZING TALENT

Also available from Cassell:

Joan Freeman: *Gifted Children Growing Up*
Diane Montgomery: *Educating the Able*
Martin Booth, John Furlong and Margaret Wilkin: *Partnership in Initial Teacher Training*

Actualizing Talent
A Lifelong Challenge

Edited by
Joan Freeman,
Pieter Span and
Harald Wagner

CASSELL

Cassell
Wellington House   215 Park Avenue South
125 Strand   New York
London WC2R 0BB   NY 10003

© Joan Freeman, Pieter Span and Harald Wagner 1995

All rights reserved. No part of this publication may be reproduced or transmitted in any form or by any means, electronic or mechanical including photocopying, recording or any information storage or retrieval system, without prior permission in writing from the publishers.

British Library Cataloguing-in-Publication Data
A catalogue record for this book is available from the British Library.

ISBN 0-304-33293-3

Typeset by Mayhew Typesetting, Rhayader, Powys
Printed and bound in Great Britain by Redwood Books, Trowbridge, Wiltshire

Contents

About the Contributors		vi
Abstracts of the Chapters		viii
Preface		xi
Part 1	**The Origins of Talent**	1
1	Review of Current Thinking on the Development of Talent *Joan Freeman*	3
2	Where Talent Begins *Joan Freeman*	20
3	What Can We Learn from the Lives of Geniuses? *Michael Howe*	33
4	Psychosocial Dimensions of Talent: Some Major Issues *Ulrike Stedtnitz*	42
Part 2	**The Processes of High-level Learning**	57
5	Acquiring High-level Learning Skills: A Perspective from Instructional Psychology *Erik De Corte*	59
6	Self-regulated Learning by Talented Children *Pieter Span*	72
7	Talent: The Ability to Become an Expert *Jan Elshout*	87
Part 3	**High-level Achievement**	97
8	Actualizing Creative Intelligence *Arthur J. Cropley*	99
9	The Emergence of Pictorial Talents *Norman H. Freeman*	115
10	Identification and Development of Talent in Young Athletes *Stephen Rowley*	128
11	Complementary Approaches to Talent Development *Harald Wagner*	144
12	Talent, Plasticity and Ageing: A Behavioural Management Approach *Peter G. Heymans and Gerard M. Brugman*	158
13	Towards a Policy for Actualizing Talent *Joan Freeman*	174
Name Index		193
Subject Index		196

About the Contributors

Gerard M. Brugman is attached to the Department of Developmental Psychology of the University of Utrecht, The Netherlands. His recent publications cover a broad range of topics within psycho-gerontology, including cognition, wisdom, epistemic knowledge, moral thinking and plasticity.

Arthur J. Cropley became Professor of Psychology at the University of Hamburg, Germany, after working at the University of New England (NSW, Australia) and the University of Regina, Sasketchewan, Canada. He is the author of a number of publications on the subjects of creativity, life-long learning, and the adaptation of immigrants. He is founding editor of the *European Journal for High Ability*.

Erik De Corte is Professor of Psychology at the University of Leuven, Belgium, and President of the European Association for Learning and Instruction (EARLI).

Jan Elshout is Professor of Cognitive Psychology at the University of Amsterdam, The Netherlands. His present research interests include the relationship between intelligence and metacognition, and the associative structure of numbers.

Joan Freeman is Professor in the Faculty of Social Science and Education at Middlesex University, UK, and also Honorary Lecturer at the Institute of Education, University of London. She has researched and published widely on the development of high-level abilities, notably her 14-year comparison study of gifted and non-gifted children growing up in Britain. She is a Fellow of the British Psychological Society, and was founder president of the European Council for High Ability (ECHA).

Norman H. Freeman is Reader in Psychology at the University of Bristol. He is a Fellow of the British Psychological Society, and was elected Scholar at Jesus College, Cambridge University. His extensive research often includes international collaboration, and has resulted in a wide range of publications, especially on pictorial representation. He is currently working on early speech disorders and the pre-schooler's 'theory of mind'.

Peter G. Heymans is Professor of Lifespan Developmental Psychology at the University of Utrecht, The Netherlands. His research interests are social development and modelling developmental processes over the lifespan. He is currently directing research on developmental tasks aimed at the identification of general characteristics of interaction episodes generating 'development'.

Michael Howe is Professor of Psychology at Exeter University, UK. He is researching the backgrounds of successful young musicians, and is the author of a number of books on exceptional abilities, human learning and remembering.

Stephen Rowley is Senior Consultant for Sporting Bodymind, a management consultancy which works with business and sport. He was the Director of the

Training of Young Athletes (TOYA) study, a longitudinal survey conducted at the Institute of Child Health, London. He has published widely on academic and practical interests in the psychology of sport, but has more recently pursued an interest in the role of the family with children of high ability, in which he recently completed his PhD.

Pieter Span is Professor Emeritus of Psychology at the University of Utrecht, The Netherlands. His major investigations have been into individual differences in the development of cognitive styles, with particular reference to the highly able. He has edited a variety of scientific research journals and handbooks. He was co-founder of the European Association for Learning and Instruction (EARLI) and of the European Council for High Ability (ECHA). He has a private practice for highly able children.

Ulrike Stedtnitz has a private practice in Zürich, Switzerland, for highly able children. She also specializes in ability assessments, seminars, coaching and consultation with individuals and organizations. She studied behavioural science in California, and completed her PhD on giftedness in children in the USA. She directed the first ECHA conference in Zürich.

Harald Wagner is Director of *Bildung und Begabung*, Bonn, Germany, a non-profit-making association which finds, stimulates and supports highly able secondary school pupils; it organizes four annual nationwide competitions in mathematics, foreign languages and art design, as well as residential summer programmes. He was Assistant Professor in Developmental Psychology at the University of Hamburg, and coordinator of talent searches and educational programmes.

Abstracts of the Chapters

1 Review of Current Thinking on the Development of Talent *Joan Freeman*

Provision for the talented usually depends less on resources than on political and social attitudes. Its definition is likely to remain a problem because of its complexity; therefore it is more valuable to study its development within the context of opportunity. Studies of the talented are often flawed, follow-ups are rare and cross-cultural research is minimal. Separated-twin studies are throwing new scientific light on old genetic–environment questions, although some believe that almost any child can be taught to be a talented achiever. The essential difference between the talented and others is their ability to learn, and the essential difference between potential and achievement is the learning which leads to expertise. New evidence shows that a foundation of early learning is vital for advanced development, especially language interaction with adults, and some very early precocity has been found to continue through life. Gender is often the single most important variable in achievement. While the talented do have emotional vulnerabilities, such as the effects of stereotyping, they are less likely to have emotional problems than others. To enable talented people to function at their best throughout life calls for access to the means to learn and practise within their chosen domain.

2 Where Talent Begins *Joan Freeman*

The beginnings of talent, the abilities and attitudes for learning, are ready to be developed at birth. New research using both naturalistic observation and laboratory investigations has shown that the cognitive attributes of mastery motivation, attention, memory and overall developmental advancement are excellent indications of future talent – all overlapping and affected by emotional development. Vital social influences centre on the development of language, and hence cognition. Babies, like older individuals, need tutoring, material provision and encouragement to practise specific skills, provided along with love without 'strings'. But the spark of originality that produces great works and ideas is as yet impossible to predict.

3 What Can We Learn from the Lives of Geniuses? *Michael Howe*

Studying the lives of geniuses and other people who have made creative achievements provides insights into the ways in which able people make progress that are hidden when we are able to take only brief glimpses of people's lives. Geniuses tend to be alike in certain respects, but in other ways they vary greatly. Some have come from wealthy backgrounds but others began life in poor families; some have had stable and structured families but others have experienced unstable and changeable early lives; some have been child prodigies and have made creative contributions early in life, but others have shown no special promise in childhood and produced no special achievement until comparatively late in life. The later part of the chapter examines two issues that biographical information about geniuses identifies as being important – first, practice and preparation, and secondly, family background – and further explores their contribution to the acquisition of high abilities.

4 Psychosocial Dimensions of Talent: Some Major Issues *Ulrike Stedtnitz*

Recent investigations of the development of talent have focused on the intricate relationship between affect and cognition, within a dynamic interplay of the individual and his/her environment. This chapter offers a brief overview of current research on psychosocial aspects of high ability, including personality dimensions, aspects of development, the socio-cultural environment and the special aspects of some subgroups. Research methodology has often been too undifferentiated and insensitive to offer real help to practitioners in diagnosis and therapy. Consideration is given to some neglected topics which relate to psychosocial aspects of the development of ability over the life-span, such as personality development and mentoring. It is to be hoped that attention to this area will increase in the future, as the elderly population is already growing dramatically, particularly in the industrialized nations, demanding innovative provision.

5 Acquiring High-level Learning Skills: A Perspective from Instructional Psychology *Erik De Corte*

Research findings from instructional psychology have had a substantial impact on mainstream psychological understanding of cognition, learning and development, but their relevance to the study of the development of high ability has been largely unrecognized. This chapter attempts to bring the two areas together with regard to the acquisition of high-level learning skills. Discussion is presented on how the emergent knowledge, both theoretical and empirical, on the processes of learning can be used for intervention in education, to design powerful teaching–learning environments. This is illustrated with the teacher-mediated computer-supported learning environment, CSILE (Computer-Supported Intentional Learning Environments).

6 Self-regulated Learning by Talented Children *Pieter Span*

The development of self-regulated learning depends on the acquisition of what the author terms 'meta-activities' as an aspect of information-processing in highly able youngsters. In comparison with more averagely able children, the highly able acquire these intellectual skills earlier in life, with more ease, and take them to a higher level. The variable most responsible for this difference is intelligence. Meta-activities are examined here in the context of research, and guidance is offered on how they could be improved. Special attention is paid to Vygotsky's cultural-historical theory, which indicates that meta-activities do not develop spontaneously, but have to be actively mediated by adults through interaction with babies and children. In school, for example, teachers can use this theory to help pupils to better ways of learning through cooperative teaching–learning interactions, and by guiding the pupils' reflections on their cognitive activities. Given that a fundamental goal of education is the transition of the control of learning from teachers to pupils, improved meta-activities should be a major outcome of the school experience.

7 Talent: The Ability to Become an Expert *Jan Elshout*

Excellence in any field is highly correlated with expertise. Expertise is a late stage in a person's skill and knowledge development, taking 5000 and more hours of hard work and learning to attain. At this stage a vast fund of conceptual, procedural and strategic knowledge has been built up that is flexibly organized to allow for fast, automatic and error-free processing (e.g. fast recognition), as well as slower deliberate processing based on deep understanding. Both are prerequisites for creative problem-solving. Research with persons in creative professions shows that, above a certain high level, non-cognitive personal traits contribute more to reaching the highest levels of expertise than intellectual factors. This may be understood from the high human costs involved in striving for high expertise. Talent, in general, may be defined as that combination of traits (e.g. persistence *and* fast learning) that make going the full course of knowledge development worthwhile for a person. Intelligence is important for the initial development of expertise. After a certain phase, domain-specific expertise takes over the various roles of intelligence. Only a change of domain will reinstate the importance of intelligence as measured by tests.

8 Actualizing Creative Intelligence *Arthur J. Cropley*

Talent can be thought of not only as involving actual high-level performance, but also as potential for such performance in many areas other than the intellectual. Its realization depends on both cognitive skills (in the intellectual field) and technical skills (in sport, music, etc.), as well as factors such as motivation and self-image. 'True' talent also requires creativity. These psychological domains interact to produce exceptional performances. The actualization of unusual potentials in these areas depends on favourable circumstances, and can be facilitated by adoption of appropriate measures.

9 The Emergence of Pictorial Talents *Norman H. Freeman*

Until recently, talent in the pictorial domain was identified entirely with studio work, stressing inspiration and spontaneous creativity in pictorial production. Recent evidence, however, places emphasis on children's tenacity in undertaking their own pictorial research, including descriptions of the sorts of discoveries children make. It is also now recognized that, in finding out for themselves, children develop their own theories of pictures. Consequently, emphasis is given to another kind of pictorial talent, that which is expressed through the roles of critic and intelligent spectator. Both aspects of pictorial talent – picture and theory production – rest on biological foundations that are common to all members of our species, the signs of differentiation being readily identifiable. However, educators differ widely in their recommendations of how to work with aspiring artists and art critics in fostering a high 'visual literacy'.

10 Identification and Development of Talent in Young Athletes *Stephen Rowley*

The identification of talent in sport has gained in importance over the years, as performance standards have continued to improve, and the age at which younger athletes reach the top has significantly reduced. Consequently, the training of many young athletes has become more systematic and more demanding. Yet little is really known about how children are socialized into sport, how talent is identified and at what age. Research in this area is reviewed, including the results of a 3-year longitudinal study (TOYA) involving 453 young athletes aged 8 to 16 years. This investigated the ways in which the children began participating in sport, who identified their potential and why they increased their involvement to start intensive training. Particular attention was paid to the role of parents in actualizing talent, and the effect age-appropriate thresholds of intensive training had on the children's emotional well-being.

11 Complementary Approaches to Talent Development *Harald Wagner*

The development of inherent potential into high achievement at all ages requires optimal support from the environment. Effective measures should incorporate inspiration, choice, challenge, incentives, counselling and cooperation. Particularly in the first six years of life, parents play a crucial role in talent development. Later on, the highly able need additional out-of-school provision for their special needs. A description of some of the most effective types of programmes are given, e.g. competitions, self-help groups, long-term weekend courses, residential summer programmes and science training programmes.

12 Talent, Plasticity and Ageing: A Behavioural Management Approach *Peter G. Heymans and Gerard M. Brugman*

Behavioural plasticity is to be found in the relationship between the person and the immediate environment. The model of behavioural plasticity presented here, the Behavioural Management Model (BeM-model), describes the potential of an individual to hold steady his or her previous high level of functioning, whether competence or talent, or to improve on it, when internal or external changes take place. It conceptualizes individuals as active, goal-directed problem-solvers, who create configurations of behaviours on the basis of internal and external resources within given situational constraints. The model is illustrated here with case studies, and some informed guesses are made about the usefulness of the BeM-model in the context of talent.

13 Towards a Policy for Actualizing Talent *Joan Freeman*

Coherent educational policies designed to enable people of all ages to fulfil their potential to the highest levels are rare. Unfortunately, the consequent lack of specific help has a cumulative effect, especially for those who do not have the means to help themselves. The talented are different because of their special capacities to learn more quickly and deeply, which means that they have special educational and psychological needs. Planning for these needs should include appropriate provision, both in and out of school, and should involve administrators, parents and teachers, as well as the individuals concerned. It should also include special training for teachers, both pre- and post-qualification, in techniques of enriching normal classroom teaching, monitoring and assessment procedures. A suggested change of educational direction, which would help develop high ability, is towards the flexible acquisition and use of meaningful knowledge, with encouragement to use this creatively.

Preface

The study of talent is part of the study of individual differences. It is not difficult to conclude that those who are high achievers are the ones who have had adequate provision to learn and develop their talent potential. The fewer avoidable frustrations there are in learning, and the more appropriate that process is for the learner, the happier that person will be to learn and keep on learning throughout life. The learning and coping skills of individuals determine how well they can take advantage of whatever they have access to. For exceptionally high-level achievement, such matters as emotional stability and self-confidence can be as important as the mastery of actual skills and knowledge.

Because of its concern with lifelong development, this selection of papers on the development and maintenance of talent aims to take ideas and information further than the currently available literature, which is usually limited to children at school. The text is based in psychology, using information from different areas of theory, research and practice, and drawing out ideas for application. Beginning with the vital first few months of life, consideration is given as to how development may be continued from its approximate peak to old age. This theme of continuity of development appears throughout the chapters, with a special focus in each one. Although the term 'gifted' does appear, the broader implications of 'talent' or 'high ability' are preferred. This is because of the stereotypical meaning of gifted and its usual association with an exceptionally high IQ, as well as expectations of emotional and other problems. Whatever term is used, the real concern here is with the development of abilities to exceptionally high levels (compared to the majority of people), not only in relation to the individual's life, but also to the prosperity and welfare of the community.

The major conclusion drawn from this collection of papers is that individuals with the potential for excellent performance have somewhat different needs from others with regard to their lifelong learning, practice and emotional development. Informed help, in the framework of understanding and practical provision, is necessary to fully actualize their talents. This text takes both a theoretical and an applied approach to the development of talent across the life-span, both generally and in particular aspects, such as the production and appreciation of fine art, creativity and sport. It concludes with an outline of a policy for talent development, with reference to efforts by individuals, government and industry. Support for the promotion of talent is not only a question of money: attitudes often have to be changed to encourage excellence.

LIFELONG DEVELOPMENT

Research data from psychology, the social sciences, neurobiology and medicine suggest that the quality of an individual's early life has a considerable influence on the development of that person's brain and mind. Those early conditions, which include sensory stimulation, appear to be closely related to skills and health in adult life. The key to improvement in all educational development lies in the use of flexible systems of care and teaching for the different needs of individuals. It also means extending concern beyond specific abilities to general well-being in order to encourage the growth of competent and curious people who are keen to continue questioning, experimenting and learning for the whole of their lives. Good teaching comes from an understanding of the developmental processes and social influences through which most children, young people and adults pass, as well as the best conditions in which they can thrive.

Unfortunately, there is not enough practical information emerging from educational psychological research about the development of children's talents. To some extent, much educational advice in this area has been adapted from mainstream psychology, but if knowledge is to be most useful, it has to be generated from dedicated research. Specific answers are not only needed by the teachers, but also by psychologists, about methods of teaching. One reason for the lack of research data is the social inhibitions generated by a concern with 'élitism'. To many it does not seem acceptable to devote time and money to the study of talent, when other groups appear to have greater need because of their intellectual, physical or emotional disadvantage.

Research in learning shows that in the education of highly intelligent schoolchildren the major priority is to help both teachers and pupils understand and improve the way they use their minds in the acquisition both of knowledge and of learning skills. To do this, teaching procedures should be designed to promote curiosity and problem-solving attitudes: these do not occur naturally in all children, however high their potential. There are many reasons, such as lack of self-confidence, poor living conditions, poor teaching or cultural dictates that can inhibit children from being curious and asking questions. What is more, the information given to pupils, as they sit in rows in the classroom, is not usually even ordered in the best manner for it to be absorbed and applied. The change in teaching–learning style has to move from direct instruction to interaction. Learning is an active rather than a passive process. From the very first lessons, knowledge can be taught so that it can be used in an adaptable way, to include realistic problems which are meaningful to the pupils. Without that flexibility in teaching, pupils can be denied the vital ability to transfer and adapt their thinking techniques to other circumstances, and so their ability to progress to a high level of expertise is limited.

The fulfilment of talent depends on the recognition of their potential and of the conditions needed for its development, by parents, teachers and employers. Most importantly, recognizing the needs of the talented is evidence of concern for all children's individual differences, encouraging the eventual emergence of a higher proportion of a more lively-minded and creative population.

Part 1

The Origins of Talent

Chapter 1

Review of Current Thinking on the Development of Talent

Joan Freeman

Towards the end of the nineteenth century, the rigid social order in the Western world began to relax; this allowed much greater personal freedom and the flowering of excellence (Berlin, 1991). The resulting surge of brilliance changed the known world of science and the arts with world figures such as Freud, Mahler, Darwin, Einstein and Curie. The more recent effects of this continuing encouragement of individual fulfilment is the growing awareness of the potential of talented individuals; that they have the same rights as any others to function at their best. There are, though, always forces working against this independence. Spearman, for example, who devised the concept of fixed general intelligence (g) could not accept that children might develop excellence beyond that measurement. He wrote: 'If once, then, a child of 11 years or so has had his relative amount of g measured in a really accurate manner, the hope of teachers and parents that he will ever rise to a much higher standing as a late bloomer would seem to be illusory' (Spearman, 1927, p. 367). More recently, Herrnstein and Murray (1994) have provided evidence, albeit of a highly controversial nature, that not only are abilities fixed, but that these are associated with race. Certainly, when one individual sets out to measure another, there is always some value implied in the measurement, and the likelihood is that the measurer comes out best.

Concern with promoting the upper levels of potential must not only be set in the context of general development, but is often equally applicable to the needs of all. Development is conceptualized as a life-long process that occurs as a result of biological and environmental determinants and their interaction. Yet to reach a standard of achievement which is far above the average calls for the understanding of special problems, material provision, teaching and emotional support. Unfortunately, much of the recognition of these needs, and consequently the provision made for them, depends less on resources than on political and social attitudes. Where resources are particularly limited, the question is often asked whether it is even possible for some to reach a standard of excellence without depriving others. In some countries, such as Sweden and Denmark, it is generally unacceptable to either recognize or provide for exceptional potential, whereas in others, such as China and the former USSR, educational emphasis has been placed on practical provision for the promotion of high ability, largely via specialist schools which have produced many outstanding achievers in sports and mathematics. In the West, fear of élitism has inhibited specialist provision although there has been growth in the development of theories and models, mostly American. Four examples are: the Pentagonal Implicit Theory of Giftedness (Sternberg, 1993), in which individual giftedness has to meet the five criteria of excellence, rarity, productivity, demonstrability and value; the Theory of Coincidence which presents vectors and dimensions of processes involving personal biology and context (Feldman, 1992); the Three-Ring Model (Renzulli, 1977), which presents an interlocking three-circle diagram representing ability, creativity and task commitment by which to identify and provide for the gifted, using the author's special teaching programme; and Simonton's (1990) theory of science learning.

A major difficulty in making provision for the promotion of talent is that it is impossible to make precise definitions by which to identify those who might benefit from it. There are more than 100 definitions of giftedness, most of which refer to children's precocity in psychological constructs, such as intelligence and creativity, or high marks in school subjects, so that social talents or potential business acumen are rarely considered (Hany, 1987). Conventional intelligence tests resulting in an IQ, such as the Stanford-Binet or the Wechsler (on which so many others are validated), are heavily influenced by learned material. To a large extent, they are measures of achievement based on age norms, and those who score much more highly than their age-peers are seen as intellectually gifted. Even so, they are not a sensitive measure of extreme variants of giftedness because of the 'ceiling effect': the upper limit of the tests is too low to differentiate satisfactorily between the top few per cent, nor can they differentiate between learning and thinking processes.

Over the years, intelligent behaviour is affected by the normal processes of ageing, such as thickening of arteries and reduced cardiovascular efficiency, so that reaction time and speed of thinking slow down. But in addition, there may be a more subtle form of psychological disengagement, a lowered motivation to keep up and be involved in the latest progress in one's own subjects or other matters, so that older people appear to be losing their talents. The abilities of talented adults tend to become encapsulated in areas of long-held interest in which they have developed their expertise, and, as experts, their functions are characterized by cognitive processes and responses that are intuitive, automatic, specialized and flexible. It is the fluid aspects of intelligence which tend to decline over time, while crystallized intelligence remains steady. When elderly academics and 'blue-collar' workers were compared with young PhD students and trade apprentices, the hypothesis that high ability is associated with a slower rate of cognitive decline was not supported (Christensen and Henderson, 1991). The authors, however, recognize that most other researchers find otherwise, i.e. that education and intellectual level *do* retard the loss of intellectual processes. To whatever extent they are talented, older people are likely to be hampered in conventional tests of intelligence which are not, after all, reflections of full mental activity in everyday life. Even an extremely high IQ is not enough to predict worldly success, while many people with modest IQs are extremely successful.

IQ scores are very good predictors of school-type achievement – for which they were designed – but research is indicating that intelligence, however defined and measured, is only part of the complex dynamic of exceptionally high-level performance, which include opportunity and motivation. A comparison of intellectual ability and personality types in 500 12-year-olds found that although both were linked with attitudes to school and educational aspirations, these factors were independent of each other: i.e. ability could not predict personality and vice versa (Marjoriebanks, 1992). Even extremely advanced children do not make paradigm changes to knowledge or style within a domain in their early years; Mozart's first major work, for example, was composed 12 years into his intensively pressured musical career (Hayes, 1981). Alternatively, many who became outstanding in later life were not prodigies. In his investigation into great people of this century, such as Freud, Einstein and Martha Graham, Gardner (1993) found that by the age of 20 only Picasso's work had been so outstanding that his world stature could have been predicted.

STUDIES OF THE GIFTED AND TALENTED

Although much has been written about the gifted since Plato and his advice to provide suitably for the 'children of gold', serious scientific study did not begin until the work of Galton (1869; Kail and Pelegrino, 1985). From an investigation of 180 mathematics graduates at Cambridge, Galton concluded that men are not born equal in ability, even though the subject's homes or the amount and quality of their study were unknown. Although research methodology has improved considerably since then, the quality of work in this area still varies widely, and the subject attracts many self-styled 'experts'. There are also many specific research problems, including biased samples, such as children selected for gifted schools, and usually a lack of any comparison groups. Nor do we know what proportion of 'false positives' come from identification, because the children are rarely followed up.

Many studies have taken a retrospective view of outstanding adults (e.g. Goertzel et al., 1978; Wallace and Gruber, 1989; Radford, 1990). However, there are recognized flaws in this method, not least that eminent men have heavily outnumbered eminent women, especially in science (Cox, 1926). In a retrospective look at 120 variously talented young people who had reached 'world-class levels' of accomplishment, Bloom (1985) distinguished several important factors in the promotion of high-level achievement, such as parental encouragement combined with discipline and good teaching. But we do not know the effect of similar parenting behaviour on other children, even in the same families, because no such comparisons were made. However, without some parental pressure (and sometimes great sacrifice), children of high potential may fail to put in the thousands of hours of work that are essential to develop their talent to a level of recognizable gifted achievement (Ericsson et al., 1993; Elshout, 1995). In a study of 291 famous men, Post (1994) describes their powerful drive to create, their 'exceptional industry, meticulousness, and perseverance', often with a preference to work alone: qualities frequently recognized as exceptional even in childhood. Studies are also often small scale. Six American boy 'prodigies' were followed up for 10 years, but did not continue their advantage into adulthood (Feldman, 1986). Nevertheless, a complex theory of giftedness emerged from the study, including the idea of 'trace elements' – a combination of unrecognized chance events which are essential for gifted performance – also suggested in a historical study of outstanding individuals such as Darwin and Piaget (Wallace and Gruber, 1989). An investigation of three Australian 'profoundly gifted children' (IQ greater than 200!) described them as exhibiting symptoms such as school refusal and being without any friends because they had 'nothing in common except the accident of chronological age', not only cognitively but also affectively (Gross, 1992, 114).

Longitudinal studies

The best-known longitudinal study, which reflects the methodological problems of its time, is that of Terman (1925–29), which is still continuing 70 years later. He examined a sample of IQ 140+ children, mostly children of university staff in California, but failed to recognize that they had experienced superior physical and educational nourishment. He concluded that 'geniuses' were highly above-average in every way, including height and leadership qualities. The most recent findings from this continuing study of the same sample are that optimal alterable conditions of childhood, which would add considerably to adult success, can be traced, and that heredity and the first 10 years of life are the most powerful influences (Walberg et al., 1993). However, the subjects were not noticeably more successful in adulthood than if they had been randomly selected from the same social and economic backgrounds, regardless of their IQ scores (Ceci, 1990). The Munich Longitudinal Study of Giftedness (Perleth and Heller, 1994) began in 1985. It has a sample of 26,000 children in six cohorts, identified on a wide variety of cognitive, personality and achievement factors, although personal interactions with the children have only recently been introduced. The team has devised 30 identification scales, which disclosed a significant number of underachievers, who were more likely than the others to be anxious, easily distracted, with lower self-esteem. In a review of 14 longitudinal studies, in spite of the great variety in design and subject attrition in many, Arnold and Subotnik (1994) point to several important factors in the conditions for the manifestation of talent. They suggest an 'inextricable link' between identification and timing: different cohorts collected at different ages touch on different developmental points, and accuracy in predicting achievement increases with the age of the subjects. Looking at the lives of geniuses, Howe (1995) suggests that different talents emerge at different times in the life-span. Accordingly, for the greatest reliability, information should be collected at different points in an individual's life, most reliably with domain-specific tests. The child's own interests appear to be an excellent and often neglected indicator of adult attainment (see Heller, 1988), though school performance was found to explain 'very little of the variation in adult career outcomes'. In a four-year investigation of talented teenagers (Csikszentmihalyi et al., 1993), learning to invest in difficult tasks was found to be very dependent on social support: the stronger the support the more developed the skills. Schools were much less effective than parents because of their curriculum requirements and failure to engage the interests of the students.

Gender has emerged as the single most salient variable across many studies: talented females respond differently to both measures of abilities and educational experiences, and often underestimate their abilities in interviews (Eccles, 1985; Reis and Callahan, 1989). Conflicts may have to be faced by gifted females between issues of achievement and those of social acceptance and 'femininity' (Luthar et al., 1992). Taking a long-term view on the influence of gender stereotypes and talented children's self perceptions and performance in mathematics, Jacobs and Weisz (1994) found that parents held somewhat fixed gender expectations, and that these had more influence on a child's developing self-concept than their previous performances, which served to inhibit girls' ambitions. Stapf (1990) has found that bright young girls, although not as frequently identified as boys, are much like able boys in their intellectual interests and behaviour, but resemble other girls in their social-emotional reactions, a point also noted by Csikszentmihalyi et al. (1993). Intellectually gifted girls have been seen to be more depressed than equally able boys, possibly due to the conflicts surrounding female success (Luthar et al., 1992). However, mentoring and counselling to improve self-esteem have been found to be effective in promoting a more realistic acceptance by girls of their abilities (Arnold and Subotnik, 1994).

A 14-year follow-up study of gifted and non-gifted control children (aged 5 to 14) across Britain was unique in its in-depth interviews with all the subjects in their homes, as well as with their families and teachers (Freeman, 1991a). The children were also given a wide variety of tests and their environmental circumstances were rated. A major aim was to find out why some were seen as gifted, while others – of identical measured ability – were not. Those who had been labelled 'gifted' (whether they actually were so or not) had statistically significantly more behaviour problems than those of equal ability who were not so labelled. However, the possession of an IQ between 140 and 170 was not found to be related to emotional problems, which were instead associated with other difficulties in the child's life. The level of the children's achievements was associated with access to adequate learning material and tuition, as well as with parental involvement and example. Ten years later, using the same methodology, the young people from unhappy homes remained more disturbed, and the children's gifts (manifest or not) were sometimes blamed for this. Pressure to achieve was sometimes imposed on youngsters who were not gifted, though the high achievers often exerted considerable pressure on themselves. Giftedness did not affect the majority in their social relationships, and in fact, the brightest appeared to be exceptionally empathetic. Although overall the brightest usually did best in school and university, life circumstances sometimes had a very harmful effect on individual achievement.

THE PROMOTION OF TALENT

Nature or nurture?

Clearly, excellence does not emerge independently. Firmly in the environmental camp, Howe (1990) writes that 'in the right circumstances almost anyone can . . . acquire exceptional skills' (p.62). In an overview of research concerned with the effects of the school environment, Sylva (1994) concluded that schools do change children's perceptions about themselves, with notable effects on their achievements, both in school and later life, and that the earlier the child starts in formal education the more pronounced the later benefits are likely to be. This effect may be seen, for instance, in the amount and quality of homework that a child does (Timar and Kirp, 1988).

Children who are assigned homework regularly, complete it, and have it marked will perform better at school than those who do none. However, schools appear to have less effect on the fulfilment of high-level potential than on other children of normal potential (Subotnik et al. 1993).

In contrast, the genetic viewpoint is promoted by Thompson and Plomin (1993). Drawing on the Minnesota studies of separated identical and non-identical twins, they concluded that there is 'considerable genetic influence' on general cognitive ability, though they describe it as probabilistic rather then determining – there being no simple gene inheritance for giftedness. Such studies have concluded that about 70 per cent of the variance of the IQ is accounted for by genes (the strongest correlation found for any characteristic), as are about 50 per cent of personality differences, and about 40 per cent of differences in personal interests. Bouchard et al. (1990) have argued that specific talent may be an emergenic trait, one which depends on a particular configuration of genes so finely balanced that any small difference will result in distinct changes of behaviour. Numerous studies indicate that constant stimulation of the brain and its responses can durably change its detailed structure and function, whether directed generally or to a specific part, e.g. visual techniques for helping dyslexics (Renner and Rosenzweig, 1987; Bakker, 1990). The sleep rhythms of intellectually gifted children appear to be different from the average; they have more REM (rapid eye movement) sleep (Grubar, 1985; Dujardin et al., 1990).

Investigating mathematically precocious youth, Benbow and Lubinski (1993) found that although gifted girls do significantly better than boys in mental arithmetic and general mathematics at school, they much less frequently take it to a higher level. Although recognizing the effects of cultural expectations, they concluded that there is a genetic mathematical bias in favour of boys. In Britain, however, girls are now scoring more highly than boys at all levels of school mathematics, but do not go on to study the subject at university in the same proportions.

In Western thought, the concept of intelligence is strangely mixed, being seen as both the inherited raw material to be developed as well as the product of that development in the form of 'intelligent' behaviour, such as capacity for learning. School success is taken as the 'self-evident' criterion of validity – a measurement for which the tests were designed. In Japan and other Eastern nations, though, success is largely attributed to effort (Amano, 1992). This may explain why, although scores on American intelligence tests have risen by about 3.4 points per decade since 1932 (Lynn and Pagliari, 1994), possibly due to improved nutrition, the achievements of Asian Americans are much higher than others of apparently equal potential. Flynn (1991) suggests that it is the culture of hard work which enables many Asians with lower IQs to be more successful than others of greater measured ability.

However, a new approach to intelligence is emerging, both in terms of a more detailed ability profile, such as in the British Ability Scales (Elliot et al., 1984), and Gardner's (1985) more flexible model of distinct and independent intelligences, which may account for exceptionally high achievement in distinct areas. Savants ('idiot savants') may be the purest form of this specialism. The view of intelligence which currently seems to have the widest acceptance is more general and refers to its dynamic elements – that it is an individual way of organizing and using knowledge in an adaptive and goal-directed way, which is heavily dependent on the social and educational environment (Sternberg, 1985; Collier, 1994). Consequently, children in poor environments are handicapped in the development of their learning and coping skills (Freeman, 1992a).

Language

Advanced language is probably the primary indicator of intellectual and possibly other forms of talent; it has an enduring quality, and underpins many other later competencies, including mathematics (Winch, 1990). This begins with non-verbal communication; infants are able to manipulate language correctly, both in its comprehension and its production, earlier than had previously been thought (Tizard, 1985; Papousek et al., 1992; Trevarthen, 1992). The early lives of gifted adults in Fowler's (1990) study were marked by an exceptional amount of verbal stimulation, both spoken and written, even though some came from homes of low socio-economic status. In intellectually advanced children, this is followed by practice in reflecting upon and controlling oral and written language using metalinguistic skills, such as in the enjoyment of challenging discussion — an exercise which is different from simple verbal communication (Gombert, 1992).

In his cultural-historical approach, Vygotsky regarded speech as the most important mediator of developmental change: children use words as 'ready made' parcels of culture or tools of thought (Kozulin, 1990; Wertsch, 1990). He suggested that cognitive meta-activities do not develop spontaneously in children, but must be actively mediated by adults or even close friends who help each other to understand the world. Feuerstein, who has made many of these ideas practical for deprived children (instrumental enrichment), has extended his ideas to gifted underachievers (Feuerstein and Tannenbaum, 1993).

Non-verbal efforts to speak have been identified in babies as indicators of later verbal ability, as have other specific domains, including physical control which predicts gymnastic talent (Lewis and Louis, 1991). The greatest overall intellectual stability appears to be at both extremes of the IQ range, which suggests that extreme intellectual development is qualitatively different from the average. The sample children were traced from the age of three months to around three years, but unfortunately the continuing strength of the predictions is unsure. In addition to language, speed of reaction and memory in babies appear to be indicators of later measurements of intellectual ability (Slater et al., 1989; Colombo, 1993). Indeed, the parents of the exceptionally high IQ children in the follow-up study by Freeman (1991a), compared with children of more average IQ, reported distinct early signs of exceptional concentration, memory and talking. Infancy appears to be the key time when family influences nurture potential giftedness; as children get older, there is in general a widening gap in average intelligence scores between those from differently supportive homes (Mascie-Taylor, 1989).

Self-regulation in learning

High achievers have been found to use self-regulatory learning strategies more often and more effectively than lower achievers, and are better able to transfer them to novel tasks, to such an extent that measures of autonomous learning could even indicate talent (Risemberg and Zimmerman, 1992; Shore and Kanevsky, 1993). There appears to be a qualitative difference in the way the intellectually highly able think, compared with more average-ability or older pupils, for whom external regulation by the teacher often compensates for lack of internal regulation (Paris and Byrne, 1989; Span, 1995). Research with young children has also found an extra quality of playfulness among the gifted learners (Kanevsky, 1992).

The degree to which talent can be strengthened and mobilized depends on the acquisition of the meta-activities needed for autonomy in learning. This not only involves the metacognitive 'overview' and direction of one's own thought processes, but also a mixture of attitudes, such as curiosity, persistence and confidence, as well as the use of strategies, such as planning, monitoring and evaluation. Applied research into how children learn science brought Adey (1991) to the conclusion that 'the children's ability to think about the nature of their own thinking was a critical contributor to their success' (p.28). Differences in problem-solving strategies between high and average school performers were investigated by Shore et al. (1992), who audio-taped and analysed the young pupils' thinking-aloud comments. They concluded that the performance of the more successful learners was closer to that of experts, in that they made more reference to prior knowledge, rather then only to information presented in the problems. Highly achieving, intellectually gifted young adolescents were compared with older adolescents of the same cognitive maturity, and also with two groups of the same age, one of average ability and the other of athletic talent (Luthar et al., 1992). On multiple indices of psychological adjustment and cognitive maturity, the gifted youngsters were found to have similar cognitive skills to the older adolescents, but differed from both groups of age-peers. However, others have concluded that the learning procedures of the highly able are distinct in style, rather than simply being more mature (Kanevsky, 1992).

Knowledge is vital to outstanding performance: individuals who know a great deal about a specific domain will achieve at a higher level than those who do not (Elshout, 1995). But it must be flexibly organized both for fast error-free processing, and slower deliberate processing based on deep understanding (De Corte, 1995). Research with people in creative work (e.g. with scientists; Simonton, 1990) seems to show that above a certain high level, personal characteristics such as independence contribute more to reaching the highest levels of expertise than intellectual factors, due to the great demands of effort and time needed for learning and practice (Chi et al., 1988; Wallace and Gruber, 1989). Creativity in all forms can be seen as expertise combined with a high level of motivation (Weisberg, 1992).

Learning is not just a matter of cognitive processing; it is affected by emotions of both the individual and significant others. Positive emotions facilitate learning, not least in pro-social learning (Williams et al., 1988; Harris, 1989; Urban, 1990; Messer, 1993). Fear, though, can inhibit the development of curiosity, which is a strong force in high-level achievement. Curiosity motivates problem-solving behaviour (Lehwald, 1990). Four-year-olds with high self-concept were not only more intelligent and socially responsible, but better able to plan ahead – a vital part of creative thinking (Mischel et al., 1989). In Boekaerts' (1991) review of affect in the learning of very high IQ and highly achieving children, she concluded that they are not only curious, but often have a strong desire to control their environment, improve their learning efficiency, and increase their own learning resources. For them, too much teacher intervention can inhibit development of the self-regulation of learning, so they become too dependent on the teacher, risking some loss of autonomy and motivation to discover.

EMOTIONAL VULNERABILITIES OF THE TALENTED

There is no reliable evidence that exceptionally high ability in itself is associated with emotional problems. In fact, high achievers of all ages are normally found to be emotionally stronger than others, with higher productivity, higher motivation and drive, and lower levels of anxiety (Olszewski-Kubilius et al., 1988) and even more friends (Czeschlik and Rost, 1995). It is possible that access to a variety of more mature coping strategies enables them to be better emotionally adjusted, possibly helped by a history of frequent success (Zigler and Glick, 1986). Yet paradoxically, the highly able do have particular vulnerabilities. In their exceptionality and sensitivity, they sometimes construct extremely complex, inhibiting psychological barriers, at times encouraged by others who believe that they are too clever to have normal relationships with ordinary people (Freeman, 1991a). Indeed, it has been claimed that the 'special stresses' of gifted adolescents can make them vulnerable to depression and at risk of suicide (Yewchuk and Jobagy, 1991).

As with any individual, emotional problems usually inhibit success and social relationships – the only exceptions to this appear to be poets and artists. In fact, Eysenck (1995) presents a relationship between creative genius and psychopathology, a condition twice as prevalent in men as women on his EPI scale. Schizophrenia too, he says, is related to a high level of creativity in the widening of attention, but whereas the schizophrenic cannot co-ordinate the extra information, the creative person uses it productively.

As children, the talented may be under extra pressure from parents and teachers to be continually successful, so that their time to find out about life at their own pace and in their own ways can be drastically reduced, a problem specifically mentioned in a follow-up of 1964–1968 Presidential Scholars in America (Kaufman, 1992). Although the ex-scholars continued to do well, they often described how as adults they still relied on old academic skills to provide them with an identity. In school there may be stress from the unrelenting pressure of teachers, who expect a high level of absorption and reproduction of information, leaving the gifted feeling strangely intellectually unexercised. It depends how pressure is applied, though. Nathan Milstein, the distinguished pianist, was not noticeably talented as a boy, hated his lessons, but was forced by his mother to practise for long hours, with little thought for his emotional well-being – which nevertheless appears to have developed normally (Milstein and Volkov, 1991). But there are indications that others under a pressured 'hot-house' regime, such as William Sidis (Wallace, 1986) and Jacqueline du Pré (Easton, 1989), were emotionally damaged by it as children and into adulthood.

All long-term studies on the development of exceptional talent have shown the cumulative effects of the interaction of family attitudes with the child (e.g. Bloom, 1985; Heller, 1991; Freeman, 1991a). Problems can arise because a child's gifts produce reactions in others which may be too difficult for the child to adjust to. Thus, in a family where the child is considerably more advanced than siblings, the parents may become confused so that they act inconsistently, and perhaps produce an exaggerated rivalry. Or a child may be brighter than the parents, who may offer too much reverence to their exceptional youngster, feeling that normal structuring of good parenting is inappropriate for such a 'genius'. Abilities may develop at different and extreme rates, which can bring difficulties of developmental coordination and balance (Terassier, 1985), or parents may also raise their all-round expectations, even though the child is only talented in a specific area. Since none can perform at a high level all the time, fear of failure and feelings of failure and of disappointing the parents will inevitably occur, with possible poor emotional consequences for life. The parents of highly able children can themselves have resulting emotional problems, either feeling inadequate, or trying to gain social advantage from living vicariously through their child. Problems that already exist in the family can be intensified when there is an unusual child present (see Freeman, 1993).

The gifted suffer particularly from stereotyping and its expectations, though the distorting myths vary considerably with the society, ranging from emotional impediment to all-round perfection with inevitable human failure. Post (1994), however, found his 291 world-famous men, with few exceptions, to be sociable and 'admirable human beings... Genius as a misunderstood giant is one of the many false stereotypes in this field.' (p.31); he did find, though, that the artists, rather than the scientists, were somewhat likely to have emotional problems. There is often an assumed moral dimension implied in the concept of giftedness, such as the superiority implicit in the American programmes for 'gifted leaders', although the alternative view also exists, that they are morally weaker than other children and will become delinquent unless 'stretched' at school.

EDUCATION TO ACTUALIZE HIGH-LEVEL POTENTIAL

As a method for developing the very highest levels of expertise, current school education appears to be of decidedly limited value: teachers do not always recognize and encourage the skills of their exceptionally bright pupils, often lacking confidence and accuracy in identifying them (Denton and Postlethwaite, 1985; Hany, 1993). Teacher identification of and attitudes towards the gifted can vary from an unwillingness to recognize them (Ojanen and Freeman, 1994) to all-round overestimation (Carr and Kurtz-Costes, 1994). A recent report of the British Schools' Inspectorate concluded that 'only a minority of schools have regarded the development of policies for very able pupils as a high priority' (DES, 1992). However, where the highly able were given special attention, the effects often spread and raised the teachers' expectations for all pupils, sometimes even resulting in an improvement in the school's overall examination results.

Adult outcomes of the effect of specially designed childhood education is not promising. In fact, by the ages of 40 to 50, none of a sample of 210 New York children selected for the Hunter School for the Gifted by their high-IQ scores (mean IQ 157) and provided with a broad and rich education, had reached eminence (Subotnik et al., 1993). The authors concluded that 'educating for eminence is not a feasible goal' (p.115). The American approach to educating the gifted is typified by a concern for their identification – usually by an IQ score – for entry to a variety of 'gifted programs', although this procedure will miss those who are functioning below their potential, such as the disadvantaged (see Wallace and Adams, 1993). Programmes for the gifted have been widely investigated, and found to be variable in educational value, although they do consistently provide opportunities for interaction with equally able and motivated peers, as well as improving home-school relations (Cox et al., 1985). The long-term benefits of early programmes for the gifted are particularly doubtful; in spite of an initial higher measured achievement, the advantage disappears over three years (White, 1992).

Specific educational concerns

Because of their speed and style of learning, experiences of school for highly able pupils are often different from those of other children. In an attempt to make friends in a mixed-ability class, for example, such youngsters may try to hide the evidence of their intellectual exceptionality so as to be like the others. Yet it is virtually impossible to behave in a gifted (especially creative) way without distinguishing oneself from one's school-mates, and constantly functioning at an unnaturally low level can result in stress. Where expectations are not high, underachievement by the potentially talented is easily hidden in an average school performance (Butler-Por, 1993). There are many possible reasons, such as emotional problems, poor provision of learning materials, or a mismatch of thinking styles between teacher and pupil, such as when a visual thinker (like Leonardo da Vinci or Michael Faraday) is taught in a normal linear manner (West, 1991). However, one can distinguish between underachievers and non-producers, even though their actual achievements may be the same (Deslisle, 1992). Underachievers are likely to be emotionally distressed, with a poor self-concept and in need of help, whereas non-producers are psychologically healthy, but nonconforming and confident of their capabilities. In order to produce their best, the gifted may also need specialist counselling and vocational guidance (see Milgram, 1991; Deslisle, 1992).

Boredom is sometimes a problem for the talented, such as a child with a curious mind in a normal classroom (Feldhusen and Kroll, 1991; Freeman, 1992b). It can become a demoralizing and maladaptive habit, especially when developed early, with consequent lowering of motivation for learning. To relieve this unpleasant experience, youngsters may escape into daydreams or deliberately provoke disturbance. They often develop their own strategies for coping with boredom, such as the 'Three Times Problem' (Freeman, 1991a). In this manoeuvre, to avoid the boredom of listening to teacher's repetitions (usually three in number), they develop a technique of intermittently mentally switching-off, then switching on again for the next new point; this involves considerable mental skill in several domains. However, until this technique is running smoothly, they may miss parts of the lessons, so that teachers may underestimate their abilities. As with all habits, this one tends to persist, so that even as adults the talented may not listen carefully to what other people say, appearing to be distracted by higher thoughts.

Throughout their lives, those who have a heightened perception of what could be done can set themselves expectations which are difficult to execute. In their youth they are more likely to be selected for specialist education, such as at a music school or a highly academic school, which brings its own stresses of intense competition and long hours of work. Or they may be accelerated to a higher class within the school by a year or more, which often enhances the normal emotional problems of growing up. Particularly for boys, apparently late physical development encourages the 'little professor' image as being hopeless at everything which is not school learning. The success of acceleration in school is very dependent on the context in which it is done, e.g. the flexibility of the system, how many others in a school are accelerated, the child's level of maturation, and the emotional support received (see Southern and Jones, 1991). In adulthood, the talented often have to work extremely hard in a highly competitive world to accomplish their exceptional performance, with consequent stress (Wallace and Gruber, 1989).

If, as the evidence indicates, the intellectually gifted think and learn differently from others, then it is important for their development to teach them appropriately, with guidance in the development of personal characteristics such as curiosity, persistence and confidence, and general strategies including planning, monitoring and evaluation. In line with Vygotsky, Wertsch (1990) suggests that for young children, guided dialogue with adults becomes internalized as learning techniques, so that there is a shift from regulation by others to self-regulation, influenced by the social context. Child-initiated learning, including high-quality peer interaction, has been found to encourage a sense of self-efficacy, especially in deprived bright children, compared with teacher-initiated learning, which aims more specifically at a product (Ari and Rich, 1992).

Like any other individuals, the talented need consistent challenge. For children in normal schools, this is possible in a variety of forms for speedy learning, and when given the opportunity, at a deeper level. Each method is useful in different ways; for example, enrichment rounds out the basic lessons, part-time withdrawal, selection into different classes by ability, compacted learning, acceleration through the curriculum by promotion to a class above their age-group, or extra-curricular activities. Within a single classroom, teachers may divide the pupils into flexible ability groups, which can interact at different levels. Sometimes, though, the only route for enrichment of highly able children's education is what can be provided by parents (Freeman, 1991b); consequently, parents' self-help groups have grown in many countries, which at best also include a counselling service (Wagner, 1995).

Yet given the opportunity and with some guidance, the talented (and motivated) should be able to select themselves to work at any subject at a more advanced or deeper level. The writer has termed this 'The Sports Approach'. In the same way that those who are talented and motivated can select themselves for extra tuition and practice in sports, they could opt for extra French or chemistry. This would mean, of course, that such facilities must be available to all, in the way that sport is, rather than only to those preselected by tests, experts or money. Above all, what is needed is a policy for the continuing education of the talented (see Freeman, 1995).

CONCLUSIONS

Now, towards the end of the twentieth century, about 17 per cent of the population of the developed world is over 60 years old, and by 2000 it will be more than 20 per cent. It is no less true for the adult than for the child that talent requires the opportunity to flourish, which includes materials to learn with as well as teaching and encouragement to practice. From both investigations and biographical studies, it is clear that schools, the primary educational base, appear to be ineffective for the development of talent in terms other than of school-type learning, whether in initiating interest or promoting aptitudes. In fact, parents appear to be far more effective than teachers in promoting talent: in its detection, provision of materials, emotional support and encouragement for the thousands of hours of learning and practice needed to develop talent to a level of recognizable excellence. Indeed, the assumption that a high IQ is essential for outstanding achievement is giving way to recognition of the vital role of support and example, knowledge acquisition, and personal attributes such as motivation, self-discipline, curiosity, and a drive for autonomy – all this being present at the right developmental time. Hence, it is suggested that rather than continuing to search for the definition and identification of the talented, it would be more productive to look at the dynamic interaction between individuals and their opportunites, to take a long-term developmental approach to talented – especially creative – behaviour.

Increased research based on both reliable scientific methodology and case studies is essential in this complex area, not only to discover the antecedents and progress of talent within the context of general development, but to indicate measures for its nurturance. This means taking a longer look at the life-span progress of talent. This includes biological maturation and age-determined socialization events, involving the family, and progression through the educational, work and retirement stages of life. It should also include cross-cultural and social comparisons to test the concepts of universality, experimental interventions in and out of places of education, and investigation into high-level learning and thinking, so that further evidence can be made available to support the recognition, care and actualization of talent.

NOTE

This chapter is based on the invited annotation for the *Journal of Child Psychology and Psychiatry*, 'Recent Studies of Giftedness in Children', May 1995, Vol. 4.

REFERENCES

Adey, P. (1991) 'Pulling yourself up by your own thinking', *European Journal for High Ability*, **2**, 28–34.
Amano, I. (1992) 'The bright and dark sides of Japanese education', *Royal Society of Arts Journal*, **140**, 119–28.
Ari, B.A. and Rich, Y. (1992) 'Meeting the educational needs of all students in the heterogeneous class', in P.S. Klein and A.J. Tannenbaum (eds), *To Be Young and Gifted*. Norwood, NJ: Ablex.
Arnold, K.D. and Subotnik, R.F. (1994) 'Lessons from contemporary longitudinal studies', in R.F. Subotnik and K.D. Arnold (eds), *Beyond Terman: Contemporary Longitudinal Studies of Giftedness and Talent*. Norwood, NJ: Ablex.
Bakker, D.J. (1990) *Neuropsychological Treatment of Dyslexia*. Oxford: Oxford University Press.
Benbow, C.P. and Lubinski, D. (1993) 'Psychological profiles of the mathematically talented:

some sex differences and evidence supporting their biological basis', in Ciba Foundation Symposium, *The Origins and Development of High Ability*. Chichester: Wiley.
Berlin, I. (1991) 'The crooked timber of humanity', in H. Hardy (ed.), *Chapters in the History of Ideas*. New York: Knopf.
Bloom, B.S. (1985) *Developing Talent in Young People*. New York: Ballantine Books.
Boekaerts, M. (1991) 'The affective learning process and giftedness', *European Journal for High Ability*, **2**, 146–60.
Bouchard, T.J. Jr, Lykken, D.T., McGue, M., Segal, N.L. and Tellegen, A. (1990) 'Sources of human psychological differences: the Minnesota study of twins reared apart', *Science*, **250**, 2223–8.
Butler-Por, N. (1993) 'Underachieving gifted students', in K.A. Heller, F.J. Mönks and A.H. Passow (eds), *International Handbook of Research and Development of Giftedness and Talent*. Oxford: Pergamon Press.
Carr, M. and Kurtz-Costes, B.E. (1994) 'Is being smart everything? The influence of student achievement on teachers' perceptions', *British Journal of Educational Psychology*, **64**, 263–76.
Ceci, S.J. (1990) *On Intelligence . . . More or Less*. Englewood Cliffs, NJ: Prentice Hall.
Chi, M.T.H., Glaser, R. and Farr, M.J. (1988) *The Nature of Expertise*. Hillsdale, NJ: Lawrence Erlbaum.
Christensen, H. and Henderson, A.S. (1991) 'Is age kinder to the initially more able? A study of eminent scientists and academics', *Psychological Medicine*, **21**, 935–46.
Collier, G. (1994) *Social Origins of Mental Ability*. Chichester: Wiley.
Colombo, J. (1993) *Infant Cognition: Predicting Later Intellectual Functioning*. London: Sage.
Cox, C.M. (1926) *The Early Mental Traits of Three Hundred Geniuses*. Vol. 2, *Genetic Studies of Genius*. Stanford: Stanford University Press.
Cox, J., Daniel, N. and Boston, B.A. (1985) *Educating Able Learners: Programs and Promising Practices*. Austin: University of Texas Press.
Csikszentmihalyi, M., Rathunde, K. and Whalen, S. (1993) *Talented Teenagers: The Roots of Success and Failure*. Cambridge: Cambridge University Press.
Czeschlik, T. and Rost, D.H. (1995) 'Sociometric types and children's intelligence', **13**, 177–89.
De Corte, E. (1995) 'Acquiring high-level learning skills: a perspective from instructional psychology'. Chapter 5, this volume.
Denton, F.CJ. and Postlethwaite, K. (1985) *Able Children*. Windsor: NFER/Nelson.
DES (Department of Education and Science) (1992) *The Education of Very Able Children in Maintained Schools. A Review by HMI*. London: HMSO.
Deslisle, J.R. (1992) *Guiding the Social and Emotional Development of Gifted Youth*. London: Longman.
Dujardin, K. Guerrien, A. and Leconte, P. (1990) 'Sleep, brain activation and cognition', *Physiology and Behaviour*, **47**, 1271–8.
Easton, C. (1989) *Jacqueline du Pré*. London: Hodder and Stoughton.
Eccles, J.S. (1985) 'Why doesn't Jane run? Sex differences in educational and occupational patterns', in F.D. Horowitz and M. O'Brien (eds), *The Gifted and Talented: Developmental Perspectives*. Washington, DC: American Psychological Association, pp. 253–95.
Elliot, C.D., Murray, D.J. and Pearson, L.S. (1984) *British Ability Scales*. Slough: NFER Nelson.
Elshout, J. (1995) 'Talent: the ability to become an expert'. Chapter 7, this volume.
Ericsson, K.A., Krampe, R.Th. and Heizmann, S. (1993) 'Can we create gifted people?', in Ciba Foundation Symposium, *The Origins and Development of High Ability*. Chichester: Wiley.
Eysenck, H.J. (1995) *Genius: The Natural History of Creativity*. Cambridge: Cambridge University Press.
Feldhusen, J.F. and Kroll, M.D. (1991) 'Boredom or challenge for the academically talented in school', *Gifted Education International*, **7**, 80–1.
Feldman, D.H. (1992) 'The theory of coincidence: how giftedness develops in extreme and less extreme cases', in F.J. Mönks and W. Peters (eds), *Talent for the Future*. Assen: Van Gorcum.
Feldman, D.H. with Goldsmith, L.T. (1986) *Nature's Gambit: Child Prodigies and the Development of Human Potential*. New York: Basic Books.
Feuerstein, R. and Tannenbaum, A.J. (1993) 'Mediating the learning experience of gifted

underachievers', in B. Wallace and H.B. Adams (eds), *Worldwide Perspectives on the Gifted Disadvantaged*. Bicester: AB Academic Publishers.
Flynn, J.R. (1991) *Asian Americans: Achievement Beyond IQ*. London: Erlbaum.
Fowler, W.F. (1990) *Talking from Infancy: How to Nurture and Cultivate Early Language Development*. Cambridge, MA: Brookline Books.
Freeman, J. (1983) 'Environment and high IQ: a consideration of fluid and crystallised intelligence', *Personality and Individual Differences*, **4**, 307–13.
Freeman, J. (1991a) *Gifted Children Growing Up*. London: Cassell.
Freeman, J. (1991b) *Bright as a Button*. London: Optima.
Freeman, J. (1992a) *Quality Education: The Development of Competence*. Geneva: UNESCO.
Freeman, J. (1992b) 'Boredom, high ability and underachievement', in V. Varma (ed.), *How and Why Children Fail*. London: Jessica Kingsley.
Freeman, J. (1993) 'Parents and families in nurturing giftedness and talent', in K.A. Heller, F.J. Mönks and A.H. Passow (eds), *International Handbook of Research and Development of Giftedness and Talent*. Oxford: Pergamon Press.
Freeman, J. (1995) 'Towards a policy for actualizing talent'. Chapter 13, this volume.
Galton, F. (1869) *Hereditary Genius*. London: Macmillan.
Gardner, H. (1985) *Frames of Mind: The Theory of Multiple Intelligences*. New York: Basic Books.
Gardner, H. (1993) *Creating Minds*. New York: Basic Books.
Goertzel, M.G., Goertzel, V. and Goertzel, T.G. (1978) *300 Eminent Personalities*. San Francisco: Jossey-Bass.
Gombert, J.E. (1992) *Metalinguistic Development*. Hemel Hempstead: Harvester Wheatsheaf.
Gross, M.U.M. (1992) 'The early development of three profoundly gifted children of IQ > 200', in P.S. Klein and A.J. Tannenbaum (eds), *To Be Young and Gifted*. Norwood, NJ: Ablex.
Grubar, J.-C. (1985) 'Sleep and mental efficiency', in J. Freeman (ed.), *The Psychology of Gifted Children: Perspectives on Development and Education*. Wiley: Chichester.
Hany, E.A. (1987) 'Models and Strategies in the Identification of Gifted Students'. Unpublished PhD. Thesis, University of Munich.
Hany, E.A. (1993) 'How teachers identify gifted students: feature processing or concept based classification', *European Journal for High Ability*, **4**, 196–211.
Harris, P.L. (1989) *Children and Emotion: The Development of Psychological Understanding*. Oxford: Blackwell.
Hayes, J.R. (1981) *The Complete Problem Solver*. Philadelphia: The Franklin Institute Press.
Heller, K.A. (1988) The First International Conference on Leisure Time Activities and Non-academic Accomplishments of Gifted Students. *Conference Report*. Munich: Institute of Educational Psychology.
Heller, K.A. (1991) 'The nature and development of giftedness: a longitudinal study', *European Journal for High Ability*, **2**, 174–8.
Herrnstein, R.J. and Murray, C. (1994) *The Bell Curve*. New York: Free Press.
Howe, M.J.A. (1990) *The Origins of Exceptional Abilities*. Oxford: Blackwell.
Howe, M.J.A. (1995) 'What can we learn from the lives of geniuses?' Chapter 3, this volume.
Jacobs, J.E. and Weisz, V. (1994) 'Gender stereotypes: implications for gifted education', *Roeper Review*, **16**, 152–5.
Kail, R. and Pelegrino, J.W. (1985) *Human Intelligence: Perspectives and Prospects*. New York: Freeman.
Kanevsky, L. (1992) 'The learning game', in P.S. Klein and A.J. Tannenbaum (eds), *To Be Young and Gifted*. Norwood, NJ: Ablex.
Kaufman, F.A. (1992) 'What educators can learn from gifted adults', in F.J. Mönks and W. Peters (eds), *Talent for the Future*. Assen: Van Gorcum.
Kozulin, A. (1990) *Vygotsky's Psychology*. Hemel Hempstead: Harvester Wheatsheaf.
Lehwald, G. (1990) 'Curiosity and exploratory behaviour in ability development', *European Journal for High Ability*, **1**, 204–10.
Lewis, M. and Louis, B. (1991) 'Young gifted children', in G.A. Colangelo and G.A. Davis (eds), *Handbook of Gifted Education*. Boston: Allyn and Bacon.
Luthar, S.S., Zigler, E. and Goldstein, D. (1992) 'Psychosocial adjustment among intellectually

gifted adolescents: the role of cognitive-developmental and experiential factors', *Journal of Child Psychology and Psychiatry*, **33**, 361–73.
Lykken, D.T., McGue, M., Tellegan, A. and Bouchard, T.J. (1992) 'Emergensis: genetic traits that may not run in families', *American Psychologist*, **47**, 1565–77.
Lynn, R. and Pagliari, C. (1994) 'The intelligence of American children is still rising', *Journal of Biosocial Science*, **26**, 65–7.
Marjoriebanks, T. (1992) 'Ability and personality correlates of children's abilities and aspirations', *Psychological Reports*, **17**, 847–50.
Mascie-Taylor, C.G.N. (1989) 'Biological and social aspects of development', in N. Entwistle (ed.), *Handbook of Educational Ideas and Practices*. London: Routledge.
Messer, D.J. (1993) 'Mastery, attention, IQ, and parent-infant social interaction', in D.J. Messer (ed.), *Mastery Motivation in Early Childhood: Development Measures and Social Processes*. London: Routledge.
Milgram, R.M. (ed.) (1991) *Counselling Gifted and Talented Children*. Norwood, NJ: Ablex.
Milstein, N. and Volkov, S. (1991) *From Russia to the West*. London: Barrie and Jenkins.
Mischel, W., Shoda, Y. and Rodriguez, M. (1989) 'Delay of gratification in children', *Science*, **244**, 933–8.
Ojanen, S. and Freeman, J. (1994) *The Attitudes and Experiences of Headteachers, Class-teachers, and Highly Able Pupils Towards the Education of the Highly Able in Finland and Britain*. Savonlinna: University of Joensuu.
Olszewski-Kubilius, P.M., Kulieke, M. and Krasney, N. (1988) 'Personality dimensions of gifted adolescents: a review of the empirical literature', *Gifted Child Quarterly*, **2**, 347–52.
Papousek, H., Jurgens, U. and Papousek, M. (eds) (1992) *Non-verbal Vocal Communication: Comparative and Developmental Aspects*. New York: Wiley.
Paris, S.G. and Byrne, J.P. (1989) 'The constructivist approach to self-regulation and learning in the classroom', in B.J. Zimmerman and D.H. Schunk (eds), *Self-regulated Learning and Academic Achievement: Theory, Research and Practice*. New York: Academic Press.
Perleth, C. and Heller, K.A. (1994) 'The Munich longitudinal study of giftedness', in R.F. Subotnik and K.D. Arnold (eds), *Beyond Terman: Contemporary Longitudinal Studies of Giftedness and Talent*. Norwood, NJ: Ablex.
Post, F. (1994) 'Creativity and psychopathology. A study of 291 world-famous men', *British Journal of Psychiatry*, **165**, 22–34.
Radford, J. (1990) *Child Prodigies and Exceptional Early Achievers*. Hemel Hempstead: Harvester Wheatsheaf.
Reis, S.M. and Callahan, C.M. (1989) 'Gifted females: they've come a long way – or have they?' *Journal for the Education of the Gifted*, **12**, 99–117.
Renner, M.J. and Rosenzweig, M.R. (1987) *Enriched and Impoverished Environments: Effects on Brain and Behaviour*. New York: Springer.
Renzulli, J.S. (1977) *The Enrichment Triad Model: A Guide for Developing Defensible Programs for the Gifted and Talented*. Wethersfield, CT: Creative Learning Press.
Risemberg, R. and Zimmerman, B.J. (1992) 'Self-regulated learning in gifted students', *Roeper Review*, **15**, 98–100.
Shore, B.M. and Kanevsky, L.S. (1993) 'Thinking processes: being and becoming gifted', in K.A. Heller, F.J. Mönks and A.H. Passow (eds), *International Handbook of Research and Development of Giftedness and Talent*. Oxford: Pergamon Press.
Shore, B.M., Coleman, E.B. and Moss, E. (1992) 'Cognitive psychology and the use of protocols in the understanding of giftedness and high-level thinking', in F. J. Mönks and W. Peters (eds), *Talent for the Future*. Assen: Van Gorcum.
Simonton, D.K. (1990) *Scientific Genius: A Psychology of Science*. Cambridge: Cambridge University Press.
Slater, A.M., Cooper, R., Rose, D. and Morison, V. (1989) 'Prediction of cognitive performance from infancy to early childhood', *Human Development*, **32**, 137–47.
Southern, W.T. and Jones, E.D. (eds) (1991) *The Academic Acceleration of Gifted Children*. New York: Teachers College Press.
Span, P. (1995) 'Self-regulated learning by talented children'. Chapter 6, this volume.
Spearman, C. (1927) *The Abilities of Man*. New York: Macmillan.

Stapf, A. (1990) 'Hochbegabte Mädchen: Entwicklung, Identifikation und Beratung, insbesondere im Vorschualter [Highly able girls: development, identification and counselling, especially at pre-school age]', in W. Wieczerkowski and T.M. Prado (eds), *Hochbegabte Mädchen*. Bad Honnef: K.H. Bock.

Sternberg, R.J. (1985) *Beyond IQ: A Triarchic Theory of Human Intelligence*. Cambridge: Cambridge University Press.

Sternberg, R.J. (1993) 'Procedures for identifying intellectual potential in the gifted: a perspective on alternative "metaphors of mind"', in K.A. Heller, F.J. Mönks and A.H. Passow (eds), *International Handbook of Research and Development of Giftedness and Talent*. Oxford: Pergamon Press.

Subotnik, R., Kassan, L., Summers, E. and Wasser, A. (1993) *Genius Revisited: High IQ Children Grow Up*. Norwood, NJ: Ablex.

Sylva, K. (1994) 'School influences on children's development', *Journal of Child Psychology and Psychiatry*, 35, 135–70.

Terman, L.M. (1925–1929) *Genetic Studies of Genius Vols. 1–4*, Stanford, CA: Stanford University Press.

Terassier, J.-C. (1985) 'Dysynchrony: uneven development', in J. Freeman (ed.), *The Psychology of Gifted Children*. Chichester: Wiley.

Thompson, L.A. and Plomin, R. (1993) 'Genetic influences on cognitive ability', in K.A. Heller, F.J. Mönks and A.H. Passow (eds), *International Handbook of Research and Development of Giftedness and Talent*. Oxford: Pergamon Press.

Timar, T.B. and Kirp, D.L. (1988) *Managing Educational Excellence* (Stanford Series on Education and Public Policy). Brighton: Falmer.

Tizard, B. (1985) 'Social relationships between adults and young children, and their impact on intellectual functioning', in R.A. Hinde, A.-N. Perret-Clermont and J. Stevenson-Hinde (eds), *Social Relationships and Cognitive Development*. Oxford: Clarendon Press.

Trevarthen, C. (1992) 'An infant's motives for speaking and thinking in the culture', in A.H. Wold (ed.), *The Dialogical Alternative*. Oslo: Scandinavian University Press.

Urban, K.K. (1990) 'Social behaviour of gifted pre-school children', *European Journal for High Ability*, 1, 172–8.

Wagner, H. (1995) 'Complementary approaches to talent development'. Chapter 11, this volume.

Walberg, H.J., Zhang, G., Haller, E.P., Sares, T.A., Stariha, W.E., Wallace, T. and Zeiser, S.F. (1993) 'Early educative influences on later outcomes: the Terman data revisited', in K.A. Heller, F.J. Mönks and A.H. Passow (eds), *International Handbook of Research and Development of Giftedness and Talent*. Oxford: Pergamon Press.

Wallace, A. (1986) *The Prodigy: A Biography of William James Sidis, the World's Greatest Child Prodigy*. London: Macmillan.

Wallace, B. and Adams, H.B. (eds) (1993) *Worldwide Perspectives on the Gifted Disadvantaged*. Bicester: AB Academic Publishers.

Wallace, D.B. and Gruber, H.E. (1989) *Creative People at Work*. Oxford: Oxford University Press.

Weisberg, R.W. (1992) *Creativity: Beyond the Myth of Genius*. New York: Freeman.

Wertsch, J.D. (1990) *Voices of the Mind: A Sociocultural Approach to Mediated Action*. Hemel Hempstead: Harvester Wheatsheaf.

West, T. (1991) *In the Mind's Eye*. Buffalo, NY: Prometheus.

White, K.R. (1992) 'The relation between socio-economic status and academic achievement', *Psychological Bulletin*, 91, 461–81.

Williams, J.M., Watts, F.N., Macleod, C. and Mathews, A. (1988) *Cognitive Psychology and Emotional Disorders*. Chichester: Wiley.

Winch, C.W. (1990) *Language, Ability and Educational Achievement*. London: Routledge.

Yewchuck, C. and Jobagy, S. (1991) 'Gifted adolescents: at risk for suicide', *European Journal for High Ability*, 2, 73–85.

Zigler, E. and Glick, M. (1986) *A Developmental Approach to Adult Psychopathology*. New York: Wiley.

Chapter 2

Where Talent Begins

Joan Freeman

Every baby's situation is different – in genetic make-up, the effect of experiences, and the mediating role of those who look after them, so that discovering exactly how these different kinds of influences are received by each baby is impossible. What is more, there is sufficient evidence to show that the unborn baby is subject to environmental influences (Rosenblith, 1992): for example, it could not be assumed that an hour-old baby who is slow-moving has a genetic tendency to act in that way, because this behaviour may be the result of drugs, disease or simply exhaustion. But the effects of drugs on new-born responses are confused because each drug acts differently at different times, and differently on mothers and babies. Strong analgesic drugs can interfere with both the mother's and the baby's responses, and so may have longer-term consequences on their emotional bonding; however, tranquillizers have been found to have a beneficial effect on mother–baby bonding, through reduction of anxiety (Rosenblith, 1992). There are also different kinds of 'social' birth experiences. It has been claimed that kinder styles of birthing, such as that of Leboyer (1975) in France, with low lights and gentle handling, result in livelier babies who develop faster. However, no study has been made of the outcomes of these methods using adequate control groups; the mothers and fathers who chose the method were self-selected, with all the bias that this implies. Moreover, the children most likely to succeed and score most highly on intelligence tests – first-borns – have much more difficult births that later-borns – their mother's labours last about half as long again, with greater likelihood of birth complications, and the babies' birth-weights are lower.

Once the baby is in the world, every sense modality becomes operative. Newborns can distinguish tastes, smells and tactile experiences, discriminate pitch and loudness, and locate sounds. Their eye movements are partly organized, they can track a moving object, and distinguish colours, often seek out visual stimuli, and they particularly favour sharp contrasts. Refinement of these early efforts is swift, so that by five months, the brightest can even distinguish between strangers in photographs. There are distinct practical outcomes from this very early responsiveness. Many learning processes – conditioning, extinction, shaping, modelling – are used to some degree even by the second month of life (Rosenblith, 1992). There has been speculation about the inheritance of such new-born capacities, such as Jung's Collective Unconsciousness, an inherited memory over generations (Jung, 1916), or Chomsky's (1968) hypothesis that babies inherit a Universal Grammar, a plan common to all languages. Pinker (1994) describes language as an instinct.

The idea of critical periods, or prime developmental times, has been promoted by many, such as Maria Montessori (Montessori, 1964). They certainly exist for pre-birth physical development, as was clear from the thalidomide tragedy: the type of disfigurement identified the point of development at which the drug was taken. But are such precise stages likely to happen in cognitive and emotional growth? Tinbergen showed that among ducks an infant's attachment to its mother had to be made at a critical time or it might be too late to promote bonding, as indeed did Harlow with his baby monkeys (Harlow and Harlow, 1966). Freud maintained that the ability to love had to be formed in infancy (quoted in Clark, 1980). But research into their possible existence in humans can only be done with deprived babies, such as those in old-style orphanages, and it is difficult to separate the effects of long-term deprivation from those of adverse experiences at precise times. Obviously, one cannot ask parents to deprive their children of possible learning experiences, so that it is necessary to use large population studies. A large British study of a cohort of children (National Child Development Study, Butler and Golding, 1986) born between 3 and 9 March 1958 showed that at 5 years of age, those from socially disadvantaged backgrounds differed, not only in being physically smaller and having more medical problems, but also in having more difficult behaviour, lower intelligence and poor educational attainment. It is known that, within certain limits, there can be recovery from mental deprivation when the conditions for intellectual growth improve, but millions of economically and culturally impoverished children must carry their very early educational disadvantages as handicaps for the rest of their lives (see Freeman, 1992).

The rate of all growth in infancy is more rapid than at any time during the rest of life. In contradiction to previously held beliefs, new evidence shows that within the second half of the second year, the following range of mental skills are developed enough to be seen in action. None are discrete; each affects the growth of the others (White, 1985; Rosenblith, 1992).

Mental skills appearing at age 18 to 24 months

- Representation in language and thought
- A mature level of object permanence
- Ability to solve problems through mental combinations
- Ability to categorize two classes at the same time
- Between 2/3 to 3/4 of all the language ever used in ordinary conversation, including a receptive vocabulary of about a thousand words and all the primary grammatical elements
- Many lifelong attitudes towards learning
- A full array of social skills
- A basic awareness of the self – for good or ill

Research methods

The early, naturalistic way of investigating babies' intellectual abilities was by observation, as used by Piaget in the 1930s watching his own three children, and using simple experiments. However, observers do not always recognize their own biases, or agree as to what happened – i.e. exactly what the infants have responded to, which makes it difficult to qualify results. But as techniques have improved, many previously unseen changes, such as heart-rate reactions, began to be measured, and by the 1950s, slow-motion film and video was beginning to identify many fine-motor responses. The detailed experimental work which followed brought its own research problems, because it meant that babies were often measured in a regulated environment, which was different from that at home. Such work is always valuable for the measurement of reflexes or focal distances, but generalization from there to overall cognitive development is not always useful. On the other hand, it is clearly impossible to expect a balanced and large enough sample of parents to alter their everyday care of their baby for scientific purposes. Current methods are attempting to combine both home observations and laboratory situations, e.g. filming the interaction of mothers and babies at home and in the laboratory. This wider view, together with much more sophisticated measurement technology, has provided a considerable volume of information about very early development. It has shown that the previously defined limits of babies' abilities were too restricted. Three major techniques are used:

Preference – in which more than one stimulus are presented together, to see which ones the baby prefers (turns to) under different conditions.

Habituation – a measure of how long a baby attends to a stimulus, which tests the ability to discriminate. For example, when the baby is looking at one kind of stimulus and another is presented, if it cannot perceive the difference between the two, it will not switch its attention to the second one.

Discrimination learning – a form of operant conditioning in which babies are trained to respond or not respond to different stimuli; the objective is to see how much they can generalize from their learning.

VERY EARLY COGNITIVE DEVELOPMENT

Potential talent is already present in newborns, and for those with supportive homes it will continue to grow. Colombo (1993), who has contributed to and surveyed research in the prediction of childhood intellectual processing from infant measurement, concludes:

> The fact that individual differences in some aspect(s) of information processing survive the tumultuous period of early infancy (during which there are constant reorganisations in affective, social, and motoric domains) suggests the existence of a robust, independent, and perseverative core of cognitive ability that is present quite early in the human life span...This thread of mental function can be assessed from the first year of life through school age.
>
> (p.126)

Such continuity appears to be attributable to two fundamental constructs – processing and memory. However, the double-edge to this powerful predictive sword is that such early labelling, especially of deficit, can affect others' attitudes and so bias care-giving. Also, as Colombo says, 'The utility of these measures in identifying the "gifted" end of the intellectual spectrum is yet to be empirically evaluated' (p.126).

Unfortunately, current general intelligence tests for infants do not give reliably stable scores from the time of birth to early childhood. There are several probable reasons. The tests themselves may not be sufficiently sophisticated for the task. The cognitive system – the capacity to process information – is not fully developed at birth, and so environmental influences will change it during those first few months of life. Perhaps reliability is lost because the wrong things are being measured and confused. The two major tests, the Bayley and the Gesell, are dominated by sensori-motor rather than cognitive measures, and are possibly too heavily influenced by the baby's social responsiveness.

There are statistical problems. Two major life-events can significantly lower the intelligence scores of infants, and so affect the reliability of tests. The first is some specific stress on the infant, such as the absence or loss of a care-giver, but individual strength of reaction to specific stress varies: those of particularly high intelligence seem to be better at withstanding such shocks (Arnold, 1990). The second is well known – continual deprivation: without the stimulation and means to learn, early infant promise will not be developed (Lewis and Louis, 1991).

But later IQ scores can be predicted to a large extent by focused tests of attention, memory, and mastery motivation (the effort the baby makes to succeed at the task) (Lewis and Brooks-Gunn, 1981). Lewis and his colleagues (Lewis and Louis, 1991) have moved from attempting to produce measures of general infant intelligence to predicting this from babies' skills in specific areas: early motor development, for example, may predict subsequent physical aptitude. They have found distinct but related paths of development which are stable over the first three years of life. The strongest path, which can be traced from three months, is verbal, but there are also spatial and non-verbal paths. They find the greatest overall stability of development at the extremes of both gifted and low-IQ children, and suggest that intellectual development for the gifted is somewhat different from the average. Each growing attribute is associated with more efficient information-processing, and is indeed part of the same cognitive process. The basis of metacognition begins here, with the inter-relatedness of these very early attributes which Lehwald (1990) terms the quest for knowledge – curiosity, preference, attention and motivation – the roots of future high ability. It begins, he says, with the emergence of the mental processes that control the way knowledge is used, and this seems to be very early indeed. But it is only when little children are able to plan ahead in a controlled way – to defer gratification – that they can acquire much more knowledge and use it in a highly able way.

Communication can be regarded as the cradle of intelligence, and clear evidence of a built-in ability to interact with others at birth has been demonstrated many times. Butterworth and Grover (1989) showed how newborns can turn towards a sound; from two months, a baby can follow a pointing finger, then soon after that look to where someone else is looking. This apparently insignificant information provides considerable counter-evidence to the Piagetian acceptance of the baby's total egocentricity, since even tiny babies can alter their own viewpoint to that of someone else. Children under three years old, who were assessed as having a high quality of both verbal and non-verbal communication with their mothers from birth, showed more advanced intellectual progress than children who had not been given that amount and quality of input (Tulkin, 1977). They played with toys for longer times, were less distractible, more easily soothed, had better perceptual discrimination and – eventually – higher IQ scores. From the beginning, imitation serves as a bonding procedure as well as a learning base, usually from the first day. The reciprocal, non-verbal, imitative communication which mothers and babies enjoy begins then and continues throughout infancy, even though babies may only begin to produce words at the age of about a year. Such a conversation can be started by either one. For example, mother looks at baby and baby catches her eye; then she leans forward and says 'Who's a lovely baby then?'. He purses his lips and coos. She copies. He does it again. And so on, until interest wanes. By this means, the style of the mother–baby relationship may well have been initiated and set within the first two weeks.

Cognitive attributes

Mastery motivation. Working on mastery motivation in infants, Messer (1993) writes that 'motivation and cognition are inextricably bound together' (p.8). Whether motivation is present at birth or internalized later, having been affected by environmental experiences, it is likely to change over the short term due to successes and failures, and over the longer term as these become internalized to some extent as self-concept. Mastery motivation is more than the capacity to persevere, as was once thought, but is the result of a variety of processes: 'attentional, social, contingent, cognitive, and so on' (*ibid.*, p. 14), all of which affect later competence and talent. Work in England with babies under one year old found that it is not so much the baby's actual results on a task which may provide the guide to future ability, but the enthusiasm with which an infant approaches the task (Messer, 1993). It seems that infants who are attracted by novelty are likely to acquire and process more information, which will further assist their intellectual development.

Attention. Babies of 3 to 14 weeks were allowed to choose how much attention they paid to a visual stimulus – i.e. the experimenter did not decide when the baby had had enough – the babies decided by crying and fussing (Slater et al., 1989). They also looked for much longer times at the stimulus than the researchers had originally believed possible, times over two minutes being common. Indeed, Kagan et al. (1979) followed up 4-month-old infants for 10 years, finding that their very early measures of attentiveness were related to later IQ and reading ability. However, they also found them to be more closely related with parental occupation, and concluded that social influences had a predominant effect on eventual IQ scores. By the age of 3 to 4 months, measures of how long the baby's attention stays on the stimulus (habituation) already account for about a quarter of the variance in later IQ scores. The different kinds of input, though, such as visual or auditory, do produce somewhat different results (Bornstein and Sigman, 1986; Rose et al., 1986).

Memory. Newborns are capable of holding events in their memory for a few minutes. They can move their heads in response to stimuli which they have experienced before, and must therefore be remembering them – the start of a recognizable knowledge base. Newborns are thus able to retrieve information reviewed via their sense receptors, and are thus laying the foundations for more complicated processing. By 2 to 4 months, they can remember new learning for days or even weeks, and this measurable time is an indication of cognitive development (Lewis and Michalson, 1985). All babies have to organize their mental experiences in memory, in order to cope with them, but it may be that brighter, more attentive infants have to manage an exceptional amount of incoming information. They would then need an appropriately more complex or advanced system of mental organization than their baby age-peers, in order to reach the highest levels of thought and performance of which they are capable. Scarr and McCartney (1983) suggest that this depends on the maturation of the central nervous system, suggesting that as it develops, previously irrelevant aspects of the environment become relevant, so that learning occurs and cognition develops further. A swifter than average neural maturation would then be expected to produce precocity in learning.

Advancement. Even in infants, advanced cognitive development can be thought of in terms of their level of problem-solving skills; their expertise depends both on the knowledge they have acquired and on the sophistication of the way they have organized it to find what they need quickly and easily. But most of all, it is the quality of their mental representations of the problem which help them (Chi, 1981). Later, as children, the talented will develop a wider view of problem-solving, in which they can use the principles of connecting the specific to the general, and in Elshout's terms (1995), go through the developmental curve from novice to expert more rapidly. In fact, the parents of the exceptionally able children in the writer's follow-up study, compared with those of average-ability children, reported very early signs of exceptional concentration, memory, and talking (Freeman, 1991a). Advanced language is probably the first thing to look for in assessing potentially high ability; it has an enduring quality and underpins many other later competencies, including mathematics. In a summary of research on very early verbal ability and its outcomes, Fowler (1990) concluded that an advanced level of language is very dependent on adult stimulation and practice, such as being read to and talked with from birth. Looking at the early lives of recognized gifted adults, he found that they had enjoyed an enormous amount of verbal stimulation, both spoken and written. Radford (1990), too, in his survey of exceptional early achievers, found that although some appeared to come from homes of low socio-economic status, further investigation showed that they all came from lively, stimulating ones.

Social influences on cognition

For several decades it was thought that structural demographic factors, such as social class, income level and parents' education, were responsible for the differences in children's achievements. For example, during the British National Child Development Study, no less than 29 variables emerged as having an effect on IQ, varying from maternal smoking to financial status (Mascie-Taylor, 1989). Although there is much contention about whether vitamin supplements really do increase overall IQ in non-deprived communities, there is some indication that they might increase the non-verbal intelligence of children with deficient diets (Benton, 1991). But the focus is now on processes, such as expectations, example, values and general educational awareness. Support for this has come from a British longitudinal study on children tested at 7, 11, and 15 years, which concluded that educational disadvantage was 'cumulative, and most strongly influenced by early home environment, notably of literacy knowledge and interest, but also by home stability in the school years' (Cox, 1990).

Cognitive development can be seen as taking two possible directions, outwards and inwards. Piaget, for example, saw it as moving outwards from the infant, who used its experience of acting on the physical world to reach conclusions and thought processes. Only afterwards were these discoveries public and sharable. But for others, such as Vygotsky, with his 'socio-historical' approach to cognitive development, it was the other way round: the infant takes 'ready made' tools of thought inwards from the public domain. These were described by his student, A.R. Luria:

> Children develop language – a ready-made product of sociohistorical development – and use it to analyze, generalize, and encode experience. They name things, denoting them with expressions established earlier in human history, and thus assign them to certain categories and acquire knowledge. Language mediates human perception, resulting in extremely complex operations: the analysis and synthesis of incoming information, the perceptual ordering of the world, and the encoding of impressions into systems ... and thus serves as a basis for highly complex creative processes.
> (quoted by Pickering and Skinner, 1991, p. 184)

Words are symbols which stand for an accepted meaning; they are what every human baby learns as part of its cultural birthright. Wertsch of Clark University (1991), calls it 'ventriloquating' through the voices of others. This 'grabbing' from one's culture to symbolize growing awareness is the pivotal event in the evolution of human consciousness – the transition from sentience (awareness) to symbols (Pickering and Skinner, 1991).

The distinction between the inwards and outwards points of view was seen in practice when Bryant's pioneering experimental work in Oxford in the early 1970s recognized little children as social beings. By working with them in normal surroundings, he altered the then generally accepted Piagetian stages, as well as many psychologists' perception of the development of infant cognition. He showed, for example, how young children judge by codes, using relative positions, shapes and sizes in a context. He concluded that it was not immature perception which made them give the wrong answers, but failure to understand the experimenter's words. Thus, rather than perceptual reasoning, as Piaget had assumed, it was rather the child's symbolic (i.e. language) knowledge that was being tested (Bryant, 1974). In fact, much supporting evidence has accumulated since then to show that infants' awareness is indeed greater than they are able to express in words (Gombert, 1992). By two months, communication with other language users – language experience – already affects a baby's ability to discriminate language-like sounds, implying that they have learned something of the structure of language (Atkinson and Braddick,

1989; Harris, 1989). In a Canadian study, the language of 2-year-old boys was found to be the best measure of their cognitive ability at 9 (Lytton et al., 1990).

Emotional influences

Babies' emotions play a vital role in both their personal and interpersonal development from birth. Where once emotions were seen as merely disruptive, they are now recognized as part of the processes of individual adaptation in building cognitive responses from experience (Williams et al., 1988). In an overview of research in this area, Collins and Gunnar (1990) concluded that by seven to nine months, all the basic emotions can be detected, and that individual differences in the expression of anger and fear continue to be remarkably stable, at least through childhood.

Probably the major emotional influence on the development of high potential is self-esteem, though there is also the danger that some insecure bright children can take far too much of their self-esteem from the success itself (Freeman, 1991a). But good feelings about oneself bring the ability to control one's own behaviour and expectations. The ability to control the need for instant reward was investigated by Mischel et al. (1989) with 4-year-olds. They found that although the ability to delay gratification increased with age, as might be expected, it also correlated positively with intelligence and greater social responsibility, a delay vital in the production of high-level achievement.

In many, if not most cultures mothers provide babies' introduction to their culture by mediating experiences of the outside world. It is this mediating facility which Feuerstein has recognized and applied with success, not only to children with learning problems, but to the gifted (Feuerstein and Tannenbaum, 1993). Even newborns respond selectively to social stimuli, and babies are highly sensitive to the kind of care they receive. By two weeks, a baby will respond to the mother's characteristics, such as voice and smell, and by six weeks, will become distressed if the social contacts between them are even slightly disturbed. Between three and six months, a baby starts to discriminate between the emotional expressions on people's faces, and from three to nine months, will search for clues from other faces.

The mother's emotions play a role in this mediation, which can significantly affect the intellectual growth of the baby. Even infants of ten weeks can discriminate her state of happiness, sadness or anger. Her happiness encourages them to explore, joy giving joy; whereas her distress causes them to withdraw, sadness producing sadness or anger. The implications are profound: if an infant is unresponsive, this may be a sign of autism, often mistaken for deafness, or it may be a more subtle warning of poor cognitive learning. A negative emotional atmosphere inhibits cognitive development, but positive emotions have a facilitating effect, not least in pro-social learning, such as helping, sharing, empathizing and showing physical affection for the benefit of others (Abroms, 1985; Williams et al., 1988; Harris, 1989).

In Britain, about ten per cent of mothers suffer from non-psychotic post-natal depression. A depressed mother is relatively unresponsive to her baby's attempts to elicit attention, and consequently the baby also loses interest and becomes discontented. Such mothers are found to be less helpful in their children's play, and their children more negative towards their mothers. Recent follow-up studies have found that the children's emotional and cognitive development were often adversely affected in later childhood by their mother's depression at birth, even when this remitted within a few months (Cogill et al., 1986). However, social support can substantially improve the impact of such stressful experiences on mothers, and this is associated with more secure attachment to children. Mothers with small children in the upper floors of tower blocks are more likely to be depressed: they should not be there. In cultures which do not permit women to develop their intellects, to the extent of forbidding reading, the development of the children's intellects must also be affected. Research in areas of high illiteracy, where one group of mothers was taught to read and a control group was not, found that women with even a little education produced healthier and cognitively brighter children (Hundeide, 1991).

Any condition that causes stress to infants increases their need for their mothers, and decreases their urge to explore. What is more, when toddlers experience successive anxiety-arousing experiences, the effect is cumulative. On the other hand, fortunate three-and-a-half-year-olds, who had been classified in infancy as securely attached, were found to initiate and participate more in nursery activities, and were sought out by other children. Their teachers rated them as more curious, eager to learn, self-directed, and forceful (Waters et al., 1979). A firm early attachment relationship is probably a positive force in the development of high-level creative thought, although there is not yet enough evidence to draw long-term conclusions about this.

More sensitive parents seem to structure social interaction, to keep babies at an optimal level for taking-in and processing information. From the beginning, they are more aware when the baby's attention begins to drop, and change their behaviour to keep its interest, by a change of voice or holding a toy in a different light. Thus, the lucky babies are not only given sensitive and appropriate input, but are encouraged to reach optimal mental state to deal with it. Infants cared for in this way are more likely to persist with their own explorations, especially as the tasks become more complex; indeed, tutoring families to foster feelings of mastery has been found to improve performance on learning tasks (Messer, 1993).

In fact, demanding infants probably trigger special family attention and resources, and if these are of an appropriate nature, they can stimulate the infant's intellectual development. But this option is not open to all babies. Interaction is the key. It is only in families where the parents are good communicators that the baby's demands are likely to be beneficially effective. This implies a decidedly active role for the baby, but one which positively involves the parents too (Maziade et al., 1987). It is open to question whether demanding babies are those with the potential for high ability, and whether parents should stimulate passive babies into demanding more for their intellectual health.

Pro-social skills are more often shown by gifted pre-schoolers than by average children (Abroms, 1985). Such children are also much better able to make use of adults as resources, and to play more imaginatively (White, 1985). This fits very well with Bandura's (1989) views on the effects of self-efficacy, although he has not applied them specifically to infants. He says that those who have a sense of effectiveness, aim higher, persist at the task and actually reach higher achievements. If the infant believes, through experience, that it has some control over its life, then the route is open to future giftedness. It seems that motivation, persistence and task orientation count towards achievement as much in early development as they do throughout the life-span.

CONCLUSIONS

Focusing on very early development implies a strong concern with prediction, which usually works best when it is based on present performance, so that the clearest sign of future talent in an infant is advanced behaviour. It is easier to be a gifted child than a gifted adult, when advancement no longer counts. But the most advanced children can become 'merely' competent successful adults, as happened with most of Terman's 'genii', and also with many of the children in the writer's own long-term follow-up study (Freeman, 1991a). It is not so much 'burn-out' as the others catching up.

But information does exist about the kinds of early preparation which helps high level potential to flower, notably a stimulating home environment with lively-minded, concerned mentors, parents and teachers. These influences are particularly important for infants of high potential who are able to extract relatively more benefit from their surroundings (Freeman, 1983). The evidence presented here shows that the experiences which occur in the brief period of infancy are vital for the development of talent. Yet children's development is continuously affected by ongoing events and circumstances operating on an active individual, which makes it virtually impossible to isolate the effectiveness of each dimension of influence. There are babies who show great promise in reaching for objects, imitating with precision, and getting the idea of the permanence of objects. But still one cannot say with reliability how their intellects will develop, nor can one calculate the extent to which social interaction contributes to an infant's cognitive development. Yet, although we cannot identify with certainty babies who will grow up to give consistently superior performances on any measure, or in any field of endeavour, enough is already known to significantly increase the proportion of talented children in the world. If this were to be done on a large enough scale, it might even change the shape of the normal curve of intelligence, by extending the height of the curve at the high-ability end. It is clear how vital the first two years are, and there is no lack of evidence that the style parents use in bringing up their children is highly effective in the child's eventual intellectual development and outlook.

Attitudes to learning start in infancy, coming from the association of learning with pleasure, and from good feelings about oneself while doing it: early curiosity and enthusiasm are associated with later gifts. No child can make progress in any sphere of development without the means to do so, yet inadequate physical and mental provision are not only the result of physical poverty: it includes ignorance of what to do. High-level performance unquestionably requires great amounts of practice. Infants need plenty of practice to get their verbalizing and sensori-motor skills running smoothly, so that the best infant toys are those which provide visual, auditory and tactile stimulation; they should provide physical characteristics to be explored, problems to be solved, and the possibility of classifying aspects or objects. The classic form-board, in which rods have to be fitted into holes, is an excellent example. Much of a child's intellectual future can be enhanced by stimulation and interaction with language – not just in passing, but systematically. Taken as part of wider cognitive development, this interaction should include encouragement to see how to get to the goal (the means-end routes) and the acquisition of knowledge. It should start from birth, and continue well beyond the child's mastery of the basics. Children who emerge from infancy with exceptional verbal skills, reading well by the ages of 3 to 5, are fitted for exploring broader horizons on their own. Early verbal mastery is not only the precursor of eventual excellence, but is associated with the necessary curiosity and drive for the child to reach the heights. However, the following qualifications need to be recognized:

- Stimulation must be of the right kind to encourage learning. If it is not meaningful to the baby, it can be merely confusing. Loud clashing noises and screaming can actually be detrimental to smooth development, but soft, continuous background music seems to be without effect.
- A variety of activities and experiences is important, particularly through parents who are responsive to their child in play and conversation. Children's verbal abilities are clearly related to family verbal interaction.
- Learning materials should be generously provided.
- Example is more effective than expectation.
- Love should be given unconditionally.

It seems as though the future talented adult is to be found in the infant who pays attention, is attracted by novelty, enjoys a challenge, makes a concerted effort to succeed at a task, and is advanced in delaying gratification. It will have the best chance if born to a happy, lively family of secure socio-economic status, enjoying good emotional and psychological nourishment with plenty of play opportunities and verbal interaction. Such infants have good feelings about themselves, and so are happy babies with the courage to investigate. Certainly, that describes the earliest lives of most children who are identified as talented. But where does the spark of originality come from, the emotional strength that produces great works and ideas? Less definable signs might be the absolute faith parents place in their children. In a statement about himself, which can certainly be extended to others, Freud said:

> If a man has been his mother's undisputed darling, he retains throughout life the triumphant feeling, the confidence in success, which not seldom brings actual success along with it.
>
> (quoted by Clark, 1980)

REFERENCES

Abroms, K.I. (1985) 'Social giftedness and its relationship with intellectual giftedness', in J. Freeman (ed.), *The Psychology of Gifted Children*. Chichester: Wiley.

Arnold, L.E. (1990) *Childhood Stress*. Chichester: Wiley.

Atkinson, J. and Braddick, O. (1989) 'Development of basic visual functions', in A. Slater and G. Bremner (eds), *Infant Development*. Hillsdale, NJ: Erlbaum.

Bandura, A. (1989) 'Perceived self-efficacy in the exercise of personal agency', *Psychologist*, **2**, 411–24.

Benton, D. (1991) 'Vitamins and IQ', *British Medical Journal*, **302**, 1020–1.

Bornstein, M.H. and Sigman, M.D. (1986) 'Continuity in mental development from infancy', *Child Development*, **57**, 251–74.
Bryant, P. (1974) *Perception and Understanding in Young Children*. London: Methuen.
Butler, N.R. and Golding, J. (1986) *From Birth to Five: A Study of the Health and Behaviour of Britain's Five Year Olds*. Oxford: Pergamon Press.
Butterworth, G.E. and Grover, L. (1989) 'Joint visual attention, manual pointing and pre-verbal communication in human infancy', in M. Jeannerod (ed.), *Attention and Performance*, vol. 13. New York: Erlbaum.
Ceci, S.J. (1990) *On Intelligence . . . More or Less*. Englewood Cliffs, NJ: Prentice Hall.
Chi, M.T.H. (1981) 'Knowledge development and memory performance', in J.P. Das and N. O'Conner (eds), *Intelligence and Learning*. New York: Plenum Press.
Chomsky, N. (1968) *Language and Mind*. New York: Harcourt Brace Jovanovich.
Clark, R.W. (1980) *Freud: The Man and the Cause*. London: Jonathan Cape/Weidenfeld and Nicolson.
Cogill, S., Caplan, H., Alexandra, H., Robson, K. and Kumar, R. (1986) 'Impact of post-natal depression on cognitive development in young children', *British Medical Journal*, **292**, 1165–7.
Collins, W.A. and Gunnar, M.R. (1990) 'Social and personality development', *Annual Review of Psychology*, **41**, 387–419.
Colombo, J. (1993) *Infant Cognition: Predicting Later Intellectual Functioning*. London: Sage.
Cox, T. (1990) 'Educational disadvantage: the bearing of the early home background on children's academic attainment and school progress', in A.S. Honig (ed.), *Early Parenting and Later Child Development*. New York: Gordon and Breach.
Elshout, J. (1995) 'Talent: the ability to become an expert', Chapter 7, this volume.
Feuerstein, R. and Tannenbaum, A.J. (1993) 'Mediating the learning experiences of gifted underachievers', in B. Wallace and H.B. Adams (eds), *Worldwide Perspectives on the Gifted Disadvantaged*. Bicester: AB Academic Publishers.
Fowler, W.F. (1990) *Talking from Infancy: How to Nurture and Cultivate Early Language Development*. Cambridge, MA: Brookline Books.
Freeman, J. (1983) 'Environment and high IQ: a consideration of fluid and crystallised intelligence', *Personality and Individual Differences*, **4**, 307–13.
Freeman, J. (1991a) *Gifted Children Growing Up*. London: Cassell.
Freeman, J. (1991b) *Bright as a Button*. London: Optima.
Freeman, J. (1992) *Quality Education: The Development of Competence*. Geneva: UNESCO.
Gombert, J.E. (1992) *Metalinguistic Development*. Hemel Hempstead: Harvester Wheatsheaf.
Harlow, H.F. and Harlow, M.K. (1966) 'Learning to love', *American Scientist*, **54**, 1–29.
Harris, P.L. (1989) *Children and Emotion: The Development of Psychological Understanding*. Oxford: Blackwell.
Howe, M.J.A. (1990) *The Origins of Exceptional Abilities*. Oxford: Blackwell.
Hundeide, K. (1991) *Helping Disadvantaged Children*. London: Jessica Kingsley/Søreidgrende, Norway: Sigma Forlag.
Jung, C.G. (1916) *Analytical Psychology*. New York: Moffat.
Kagan, J., Lapidus, D.R. and Moore, M. (1979) 'Infant antecedents of cognitive functioning: a longitudinal study', in S. Chess and A. Thomas (eds), *Annual Progress in Child Psychiatry and Child Development*. New York: Bruner Mazel.
Leboyer, F. (1975) *Birth Without Violence*. New York: Knopf.
Lehwald, G. (1990) 'Curiosity and exploratory behaviour in ability development', *European Journal for High Ability*, **1**, 204–10.
Lewis, M. and Brooks-Gunn, J. (1981) 'Visual attention at three months as a predictor of cognitive functioning at two years of age', *Intelligence*, **5** (2), 131–40.
Lewis, M. and Louis, B. (1991) 'Young gifted children', in G.A. Colangelo and G.A. Davis (eds), *Handbook of Gifted Education*. Boston: Allyn and Bacon.
Lewis, M. and Michalson, L. (1985) 'The gifted infant', in J. Freeman (ed.), *The Psychology of Gifted Children*. Chichester: Wiley.
Lytton, H., Watts, D. and Dunn, B. (1990) 'Early mother–son relations and son's cognitive

and social functioning at age 9: a twin longitudinal study', in A.S. Honig (ed.), *Early Parenting and Later Child Development*. New York: Gordon and Breach.
Mascie-Taylor, G.C.N. (1989) 'Biosocial correlates of IQ', in C.J. Turner and H.B. Miles (eds), *The Biology of Human Intelligence*. Driffield: Nafferton Books.
Maziade, M., Cote, R., Boutin, P., Bernier, H. and Theivierge, J. (1987) 'Temperamental and intellectual development: a longitudinal study from infancy to four years', *American Journal of Psychiatry*, **144** (2), 144–50.
Messer, D.J. (1993) 'Mastery motivation; an introduction to theories and issues', in D.J. Messer, *Mastery Motivation in Early Childhood*. London: Routledge.
Mischel, W., Shoda, Y. and Rodriguez, M. (1989) 'Delay of gratification in children', *Science*, **244**, 933–8.
Montessori, M. (1964) *The Montessori Method*. New York: Schocken.
Pickering, J. and Skinner, M. (1991) *From Sentience to Symbols: Readings on Consciousness*. Hemel Hempstead: Harvester Wheatsheaf.
Pinker, S. (1994) *The Language Instinct*. Harmondsworth: Penguin.
Radford, J. (1990) *Child Prodigies and Exceptional Early Achievers*. Hemel Hempstead: Harvester Wheatsheaf.
Rose, D.H., Slater, A.M. and Perry, H. (1986) 'Predictions of childhood intelligence from habituation in early infancy', *Intelligence*, **10**, 251–63.
Rosenblith, J.F (1992) *In the Beginning: Development from Conception to Age Two*. London: Sage.
Scarr, S. and McCartney, K. (1983) 'How people make their own environments: a theory of genotype ⟶ environment effects', *Child Development*, **54**, 424–35.
Slater, A.M., Cooper, R., Rose, D. and Morison, V. (1989) 'Prediction of cognitive performance from infancy to early childhood', *Human Development*, **32**, 137–47.
Tulkin, S.R. (1977) 'Social class differences in maternal and infant behaviour', in P.H. Leiderman, S.R. Tulkin and A. Rosenfield (eds), *Culture and Infancy*. New York: Academic Press.
Waters, E., Wippman, J. and Stroufe, L.A. (1979) 'Attachment, positive effect and competence in the peer group: Two studies in construct validation', *Child Development*, **50**, 821–9.
Wertsch, J.D. (1991) *Voices of the Mind*. Hemel Hempstead: Harvester Wheatsheaf.
White, B. (1985) 'Competence and giftedness', in J. Freeman (ed.), *The Psychology of Gifted Children*. Chichester: Wiley.
Williams, J.M., Watts, F.N., Macleod, C. and Mathews, A. (1988) *Cognitive Psychology and Emotional Disorders*. Chichester: Wiley.

Chapter 3

What Can We Learn from the Lives of Geniuses?
Michael Howe

One way to extend our practical knowledge of how to help young people and adults to make the best of their lives and maximize their chances of being competent and self-fulfilled individuals is to examine the lives of those people who have been most conspicuously successful. In this chapter the author looks at a number of individuals whose creative achievements have made a lasting contribution, in some cases affecting millions of people. Then some modern research will be described which further investigates the influence of some of the factors that are seen to be important in the lives of geniuses.

The word 'genius' is customarily used as a label for those people whose contributions are the most extraordinarily impressive, and there is no doubt that it is an extremely useful term. However, we need to be aware that, strictly speaking, 'genius' is not a description of a person, and there is no objective measure of attributes that makes it possible to decide, once and for all, if a person is a genius or not. The word is more of an accolade, an acknowledgement of a person's achievements. Because of that, decisions about who to include in a list of geniuses are inevitably to some extent subjective. Although there are a few individuals who almost everyone, at least in the Western world, would agree were geniuses (such as Shakespeare, Mozart, and perhaps a couple of hundred others) there is a much larger number of creative individuals who would be regarded as being geniuses by some people but not by others. In most cases, there is no objective way of answering the question 'Was X a genius or not?'

Not surprisingly, most geniuses have some attributes in common, beyond being capable of producing creative achievements. Almost all geniuses are very highly motivated and work hard and for long hours at the activity that most interests them (although they would not think of work as being an activity that is contrasted with leisure or play). Most geniuses are very single-minded, with a clear sense of direction. Many appear indifferent to activities that are unrelated to the ones that interest them most keenly, and there are numerous anecdotes of geniuses forgetting to eat, or neglecting guests, or putting odd clothes on, especially at times when they are most consumed by their main endeavours. The majority of geniuses are markedly self-confident, and while there are some exceptions (for instance James Watt, the engineer whose inventions led to great improvements in the efficiency of steam engines) in these few cases there has usually been someone in the background to provide constant support and encouragement.

Up to a point this knowledge of characteristics of geniuses is useful when we are trying to understand how to help promising individuals who are clearly not geniuses to achieve more. But while it is interesting to know that geniuses are diligent, highly self-motivated, confident, with a strong sense of direction, and so on, the really important question of where these attributes come from remains largely unanswered. Are they inherited? If they are not, how is it that one person's experience of life makes him or her more highly motivated to work for success than another person? If we knew more about what makes some people unusual in these respects, we would be well on the way to having a practical understanding of how best to help young people extend themselves.

The ways in which geniuses tend to be similar to one another are outnumbered by the ways in which they are different. They greatly differ in the age at which they start to create major achievements. Charles Dickens exploded onto the English literary scene with *The Pickwick Papers*, an instant *succés d'estime*, as well as a best-seller, when he was only 24. At that age, George Stephenson, the great inventor who made steam-powered rail travel a practical possibility, was still an unknown colliery mechanic, employed as a brakesman on the stationary engines used to pull coal wagons on ropes or chains up short hills. It was a skilled job, but hardly a prestigious one, and at that time there was not the slightest hint that Stephenson would ever come to be regarded as a genius.

Geniuses also differ enormously in the wealth and prosperity of their family backgrounds. George Stephenson grew up in considerable poverty. His father worked as a poorly paid mine labourer. His parents brought up their six children in one room of a small cottage, and because there was never sufficient money to send any of the children to school, George Stephenson did not begin to learn to read and write until he was 18, and finally able to spare a few pennies for lessons. In sharp contrast to Stephenson, Charles Darwin came from a wealthy family, and it was easy for his father to afford to send him to school and two different universities, and pay the costs of the travel that contributed to his education, as well as making it possible for Charles to go on the voyage of the *Beagle*. The kind of life and education Darwin experienced in his first 25 years would have been unthinkable without his father's money.

Geniuses differ, too, in the extent to which they show promise when they are still children. Until Charles Darwin was about 17, he never displayed any kind of ability or talent that was at all remarkable, or gave any sign of having abilities that were exceptional in a child. But others, such as Mozart, John Ruskin and John Stuart Mill were clearly exceptional children as well as exceptional adults. Although by no means all geniuses were regarded as prodigies when they were children, it can certainly help to get a good early start.

As well as differing in their degree of wealth, the family backgrounds of creative achievers also vary considerably in other ways. For instance, they differ in the extent to which they were relatively stable or relatively chaotic. The families of individuals such as Balzac, Dickens and George Bernard Shaw were not at all stable: parental affection was changeable and uncertain, as were the families' finances. It is interesting that all three of these individuals were writers of fiction: it seems that some of the qualities that contribute to a person becoming a writer of fiction thrive on an early life that is more colourful than predictable. Amongst scientists, however, a more dependable home background appears to be necessary: Zuckerman (1977) discovered that the early lives of Nobel prizewinners in the sciences were characterized by stability and relative harmony, but that these qualities were often absent in the childhoods of those individuals who have won Nobel Prizes for literature.

Also, whilst all highly creative individuals are intelligent in the broadest sense, they are intelligent in very different ways. The absurd but still-common practice of regarding intelligence as forming a single dimension has encouraged the assumption that through the application of IQ tests a person's intelligence can be indicated by a single score. If we gave IQ tests to a variety of geniuses, the chances are that some individuals, such as Einstein and John Stuart Mill, would gain extremely high scores, whereas others, such as Mozart and George Stephenson, would have much lower scores, with others, such as Darwin, somewhere in between. A possible inference from this would be that not all geniuses are highly intelligent. A more sensible deduction would be that the single dimension of intelligence assessed in IQ tests fails to do justice to the range and variety of people's intelligence. If we decided who to designate as geniuses on the bases of their IQ scores, many widely acknowledged geniuses would be excluded, and the vast majority of the newly included individuals would be nonentities who had never produced any creative or scholarly achievements at all.

The dangers of relying too heavily on IQ scores are evident in the well-known study initiated at the beginning of the present century by Louis Terman (1925–1929). He organized the testing of large numbers of California schoolchildren, and used their intelligence test scores as a basis for making predictions about their lifetime successes. The predictions Terman arrived at have turned out to be no more accurate than those he could have made on the basis of knowledge of the children's social backgrounds alone, without doing any testing. Moreover, although some of the individuals in his study went on to do well, none of them distinguished themselves as outstandingly creative in later life, whereas two of the children he rejected because their IQs were too low went on to win Nobel Prizes (Ceci, 1990). The moral is clear: if you want to know which children are likely to succeed, don't put all your eggs into the IQ test basket. It is very unlikely that we will ever discover a test that can be administered in childhood that will reliably predict eventual adult achievement.

ONE EARLY LIFE: GEORGE BIDDER

Reflecting the enormous variety of ways in which creative people are exceptional, the routes by which they progress through their lives are similarly varied. But in every case there is some kind of route to be traced: abilities do not just appear from out of the blue. By tracing an exceptional individual's route through life, and thereby obtaining a good description of that individual's early progress, we may come close to being able to explain why that individual became an unusually capable adult. As an interesting example of the rather inspiring progress of one outstanding individual, consider the case of George Bidder, who became a highly distinguished engineer although perhaps not an eminent enough one to be regarded as a genius.

George Parker Bidder was born in rural Devonshire, in England, in 1806 (by coincidence, within one month of the birth of John Stuart Mill, perhaps the best known of the relatively small number of child prodigies who eventually became eminent adults). With Brunel and the Stephensons, Bidder was one of the great engineers of an age in which engineering was transforming life in Britain. As well as building many railways, George Bidder created the Victoria Docks in London. He also made ships, bridges, aqueducts and viaducts.

Bidder was the third son of a stonemason. By the age of 6, with the help of an older brother, he became interested in mental arithmetic. His own account gives a flavour of how other people's responses to his first small accomplishments encouraged him to go further. He recalled,

> There resided, in a house opposite my father's, an aged blacksmith, a kind old man . . . on winter evenings I was allowed to perch myself on his forge hearth, listening to his stories. On one of these occasions, somebody by chance mentioned a sum; I gave the answer correctly. This occasioned some little astonishment; they then asked me other questions, which I answered with equal facility. They then went on to ask me up to two places of figures . . . I gave the answers correctly, as was verified by the old gentleman's nephew, who began chalking it up to see if I was right . . . this increased my fame still more, and what was better, it eventually caused halfpence to flow into my pocket; which, I need not say, had the effect of attaching me still more to the science of arithmetic, and thus by degrees I got on.
>
> (Clark, 1983, pp. 3–4)

After a few tastes of success like this there was no stopping young George. Soon his father started displaying the child at local fairs. By the time George Bidder was nine he was being exhibited up and down the country. He became known throughout England as 'The Calculating Boy'. This was about 50 years after Mozart had been dragged round Europe by his father.

A handbill describes Bidder's recent feats in order to drum up attendance at a demonstration of his talents: it mentions his success in front of a previous audience, which included George III's wife, Queen Charlotte, as well as dukes, earls, the Lord Mayor of London and other notables. According to the handbill, the Queen asked Bidder, who is described as 'Master G. Bidder, a native of Devonshire', how many days it would take a snail, creeping at the rate of eight feet per day, to travel the 838 miles from the Land's End in Cornwall to Farret's Head in the north of Scotland. He quickly gave the correct answer: it would take 553,000 days plus another 80 (Howe, 1990, pp. 127–31).

These exhibitions given by the young George Bidder were quite numerous, a fact which family tradition attributed to the greed of his father, who seems to have made a fair amount of money from them. At the age of 12 Bidder even entered into a kind of 'calculating match' against another child prodigy, an American boy named Zerah Colburn. According to the pamphlet printed in Exeter, the American had given up after nine minutes on a question which Bidder had correctly answered in just two minutes. The pamphlet tells us, 'Many other questions were proposed to the American boy, all of which he refused answering; while young Bidder readily replied to all' (Howe, 1990, pp. 127–31).

Bidder was fortunate because his feats of mental calculating brought him to the attention of people who were willing to pay for him to receive a better education than would otherwise have been available. It was not uncommon in those days for wealthy individuals to provide the cost of educating a promising youngster. John Stuart Mill's father, James Mill, had benefited from a similar arrangement, enabling him to go to Edinburgh University. As it happened, Bidder too went to Edinburgh, starting at the age of 14, which was then fairly usual. He flourished there.

To cut a very long story short, George Bidder had seen the green light and never looked back. As well as being able and reliable he was fortunate in having influential friends, notably Robert Stephenson (the son of George Stephenson), whom he met at Edinburgh when they were both students. Bidder also had the enormous energy which seems to have characterized so many early Victorians. Just reading about his daily routine is exhausting. For instance, at the age of 18, we find him working for a fortnight, constantly on the move, and spending his last night in a stable, then having one day in London to clear up his business, and leaving at nine in the same evening for Exeter, where he arrives at half past ten the next morning and goes straight on to more work, still always on the move until Christmas, when back with his family, he passes his time making merry until three in the morning.

It would be nice to think that Bidder's life is typical of child prodigies. Sadly it is not. Stories like that are all too rare, and the family backgrounds of child prodigies usually turn out to have been prosperous if not privileged. Nevertheless, Bidder's life *does* illustrate the fact that when we look as closely as we can at an individual's childhood in its entirety, we can discern a route which takes the person from the earliest years until maturity. That is true of any life. But with exceptional people's lives we always find, that one thing leads to another; creative achievements are the culmination of years of preparation, characterized by plenty of hard work and practice. Some children get an especially early start, and other things being equal, this increases an individual's chances of high achievement in adulthood. In some areas of expertise the period of preparation required to gain essential skills is so long that someone who by their mid-teens has not already made a serious beginning may have left things to late.

When we have only a few brief glimpses at an outstanding individual's life, it often does seem that there are sudden leaps and inexplicable new developments, with new accomplishments appearing out of the blue. But when we are able to take a closer and more detailed look, and can follow the precise route and direction it takes over the formative years, we gain a different perspective. The leaps and the gaps tend to disappear. The impression that stays with us is one of relatively steady progress. Exceptional people climb higher than the rest of us do, though they may climb faster and more efficiently. But they do climb all the same, just like everyone else. No-one miraculously arrives at the peak of their accomplishments.

PRACTICE AND PREPARATION

Practice and preparation are always essential. It is often believed that while we ordinary mortals have to slog away at practising for hour after hour in order to improve our skills, for a few lucky individuals who are innately talented, such hard work is not necessary. Among musicians, for instance, even as brilliant a person as Mozart only began to produce his greatest music after many years of rigorous training. Furthermore, as Hayes (1981) discovered after studying the output of 76 well-known composers, all composers take a long period of preparation to reach the peak of their powers, with apparently no exceptions.

Hayes found that 73 of the 76 composers did not create any of their major works prior to the tenth year of their composing career, the three exceptions being Shostakovich and Paganini, each of whom produced a major work after nine years, and Erik Satie, who composed *Trois Gymnopédies* in his ninth year as a composer. In order to decide whether or not a musical composition can be considered to be a major work, Hayes looked in current catalogues of recordings to see which items were available in several versions. The reason for insisting on several different recordings being available, rather than just one, was to leave out musical works that might have been made available just as disk-fillers or for their novelty value.

Just as composers require a great deal of preparation, performing musicians have to have very considerable amounts of practice. A number of studies have looked at the relationships between performing standards and the amount of instrumental practising musicians do. The results of this research show that for all performing musicians high levels of skill depend upon large quantities of daily practice. In one investigation the number of hours of formal practice done by German student violinists in their early twenties was estimated. By the age of 21 the very best students in the performance class of a conservatoire had practised for about 10,000 hours. Some other violinists, who were less accomplished and who were training to be violin teachers rather than professional performers, had devoted only about half of that time to practising (Ericsson *et al.*, 1993). There were no cases of players reaching very high performance standards without frequently and regularly practising over a substantial number of years. Further studies of the backgrounds of successful performers found them to have done substantially more practice than less capable young musicians; the least capable players had done the least practice of all.

The research findings demonstrate that formal practising is a principal cause of musical achievement. Although it would be absurd to claim that practice is the only cause of success as a musician, the findings make it impossible to deny that the sheer amount of formal practising is very important indeed, and more so than is widely appreciated. It is undoubtedly the best single predictor of a player's level of accomplishment.

Lengthy practice and preparation, sometimes over periods of many years, appear to be equally necessary in other fields of accomplishment (Elshout, 1995). In chess, for instance, at least ten years of sustained preparation are essential in order for a player to reach international levels. For eminence in mathematics, the sciences, tennis, athletics, and a number of other sports, similar amounts of time also seem to be required. As in music, the view that there are some fortunate individuals who are able to reach the highest levels without having to undertake the lengthy practising that ordinary people must do is not generally supported by empirical evidence.

Factors like hard and sustained work, practice, motivation, enjoyment of what one is doing, sufficient intelligence, self-confidence, perseverance, having the right temperament, and attentiveness, are all vital if a person is to become capable of major human achievements. But, are they *enough*; is it also essential for a person to have particular innate gifts? It is important to avoid insisting they must be present unless we have direct evidence that they are. When people observe a young person who is unusually able and successful, it is tempting to assume that the person must possess an innate gift, if only because we can't think of alternative ways to account for a person's remarkable abilities, because 'everyone knows' that this is the explanation, or because it appears to be 'self-evident'. But if we are serious about understanding the real causes of high abilities, it is essential to insist on firm evidence, to be as scientific and rigorous as possible, and to avoid making assumptions or starting with preconceptions that cannot properly be justified. It is not at all easy to think clearly about the causes of high abilities. One reason why we find it so difficult is that most of us go through life with all kinds of 'commonsense psychology' assumptions which may be incorrect. We may strongly resist the suggestion that our commonsense psychology beliefs may be wrong, because they are often deep-rooted, firmly established elements of the way in which we think about certain topics. In everyday life it does not matter too much if our commonsense assumptions about psychological matters are inaccurate or oversimplified. They are usually harmless enough even if they are not strictly correct. But in order to extend our understanding it is sometimes helpful to re-examine and reconsider some of our everyday commonsense.

FAMILY BACKGROUND

It was said earlier that the majority of very high achievers, perhaps especially in the sciences, have enjoyed stable family backgrounds. Why does that help? Some findings obtained by a research team headed by Mihalyi Csikszentmihalyi shed some light on that question (Csikszentmihalyi and Csikszentmihalyi, 1993). He worked with able adolescents, investigating why some of them were considerably more successful than others in various areas of competence. The obvious answer to this question is that some of them spend much more time than others studying, or rehearsing, and generally concentrating on the learning activities that lead to competence. So far as it goes, that answer is entirely correct, as is clearly shown by the research already described. But why is it that some adolescents are more able and willing to spend time on these studying, learning and practising activities?

One of the first things Csikszentmihalyi and his colleagues noticed was that, on the whole, adolescents do not like practising and studying. They do not like doing effortful things on their own, especially when these require concentrated solitary effort. They prefer to spend their time in other ways, hanging around with their friends, watching television and doing all the things that adolescents usually enjoy. Studying is about their least favoured activity. So we have a problem. For a young person to do well, you have to study or practise. But those are disliked activities. Can anything be done about it? Can we find a way to help adolescents enjoy learning more?

Csikszentmihalyi's approach was to identify those adolescents who don't mind studying and find out how they differ from those who do. He has a very neat technique that makes it possible to measure how people are experiencing what they are doing at any time. He gets adolescents to carry with them a small beeper. Ten times every day, on randomly timed occasions, the beeper sounds. The participants have previously been given a little booklet, with a number of short questions to answer. Every time the beeper sounds, the adolescents get out their booklet and write down various items of information about their activity at the time; for example, what they are doing, where they are, whether they are alone or in company. One of the questions asks whether the person is enjoying whatever it is that he/she is doing. Another question asks how alert the person feels at the time.

The adolescents were divided into four groups on the basis of information about their family backgrounds. These were rated as potentially more or less stimulating, based on the extent to which parents provided opportunities to learn and had high educational expectations. Families were also rated as more or less supportive. This dimension referred to the amount of support and structure available. For instance, a family in which there were clear rules and clearly allotted tasks, where individuals could depend upon one another, was rated as being supportive. A family in which structured support was unavailable or unreliable tended to be one in which young people spent a lot of their energy complaining, negotiating and saying things like 'it's not fair', or 'it's not my turn'.

Family backgrounds could be of four types: neither stimulating nor supportive, supportive but not stimulating, stimulating but not supportive, or both supportive and stimulating. Did this have an influence on how the adolescents responded to these questions about how they were experiencing studying? When Csikszentmihalyi observed how the adolescents felt about other kinds of activities such as talking to friends or watching television, he found that on the questions of their enjoyment of the activities and their attentiveness to them, family background did not make any difference. But when the participants were asked to report how they were experiencing the activity of studying, three of the groups reported very negative responses – they did not enjoy solitary study and their level of alertness was very low. But one group was very different. That was the group whose family backgrounds were both supportive and stimulating. Adolescents from these family backgrounds, but not the others, were quite positive about studying. They enjoyed it more than the others did, and while they were engaged in study on their own they reported being much more attentive and alert than the others.

It is clear that those young people who are functioning in a way that is likely to help them succeed are experiencing studying activities very differently from others, and this is closely related to family background. Some young people, those from family backgrounds that are not just stimulating, and not just supportive, but both of those, have learned to get on with the job of studying; this will yield them rich benefits. That is not to deny that young people who are not so fortunate in their backgrounds may well catch up, but they do seem to be at a temporary disadvantage.

CONCLUSIONS

From studying the lives of geniuses we learn that they do not gain their special abilities by magic. The capabilities of an unusually able person are gradually acquired over many years. Modern research provides insights into some of the influences that make that possible. First, lengthy practice and preparation are necessary, if not sufficient, ingredients of major accomplishments and creative achievements. Secondly, such practice and preparation is most likely to be undertaken by young people whose home backgrounds are stimulating, structured and supportive.

REFERENCES

Ceci, S.J. (1990) *On Intelligence ... More or Less: A Bio-ecological Theory of Intellectual Development*. Englewood Cliffs, NJ: Prentice Hall.

Clark, E.F. (1983) *George Parker Bidder: The Calculating Boy*. Bedford: KSL Publications.

Csikszentmihalyi, M. and Csikszentmihalyi, I.S. (1993) 'Family influences on the development of giftedness', in G.R. Bock and K. Ackrill (eds), *The Origins and Development of High Ability*. Ciba Foundation Symposium 178. Chichester: Wiley.

Elshout, J. (1995) 'Talent: the ability to become an expert', Chapter 7, this volume.

Ericsson, K.A., Tesch-Romer, C. and Krampe, R.T. (1993) 'The role of deliberate practice in the acquisition of expert performance', *Psychological Review*, **100**, 363–406.

Hayes, J.R. (1981) *The Complete Problem Solver*. Philadelphia: The Franklin Institute Press.

Howe, M.J.A. (1990) *The Origins of Exceptional Abilities*. Oxford: Blackwell.

Terman, L.M. (1925–1929) *Genetic Studies of Genius*. Vols. 1–5. Stanford: Stanford University Press.

Zuckerman, H. (1977) *Scientific Elite: Nobel Laureates in the United States*. New York: The Free Press.

Chapter 4

Psychosocial Dimensions of Talent: Some Major Issues

Ulrike Stedtnitz

The early literature on talent and affect dealt almost exclusively with the pathological aspects of exceptionally high ability, as in John Nisbet's *The Insanity of Genius*, which appeared in 1891. Although the work of Terman and his colleagues at Stanford University in the 1920s and 1930s marked a general departure from this perspective, it took some time for understanding of the psychosocial components of high ability to move from speculation to empirical investigation. Even in the 1960s and 1970s, the literature was still permeated by vague myths and generalizations, often based on only a few unrepresentative cases. However, contemporary research in child development is increasingly emphasizing the importance of psychosocial factors in fostering talent, particularly the intimate relationship between cognitive and affective development as a vital aspect of the development of infants and very young children. In fact, a positive trend appears to have been gaining momentum over the past few years, with the move away from concern with problems and pathological manifestations, and towards an exploration of the conditions which promote growth, how these can be created or nurtured, and how individuality can best be promoted. This can be compared to the influential rise of developments in counselling and psychotherapy initiated by Abraham Maslow and Carl Rogers.

Cognitive and developmental psychologists have increasingly turned to studying the relationship between affect and cognition. Investigations (Mönks and Lehwald, 1991) on curiosity, exploration, and ability in small children have substantiated what sensitive educators have suspected for a long time – that all learning is first and foremost social and emotional, and that the nature of the relationship between parent and child, and between learner and teacher, makes the crucial difference. Indeed, there is evidence from cognitive psychology that affect may have direct effects on information processing, notably in selection and recall, and it has been shown to provide a significant input for social cognition in influencing decision-making and problem-solving (Hoffman, 1986).

Unfortunately too many investigations into social-emotional development are plagued by serious methodological problems. For example, suitable control groups are often lacking, and samples are too small; and although high ability is most frequently defined using IQ scores, comparisons with other data using the IQ are difficult because different instruments are used to assess it, or because IQ cut-off points vary. The frequent use of univariate rather than multivariate statistics has led to findings which seem to be significant, but may not actually be so. Czeschlik and Rost (1988) have pointed out that questionnaires and interviews have usually been used to assess behavioural dimensions, which would have been better measured with behavioural observations, which could significantly increase the validity of the findings. This is probably why the 'assessment centre method' (simulations of social situations) is now widely used in business selection procedures. More longitudinal and case studies are needed, the latter being particularly appropriate for the assessment of affective aspects of very high ability (e.g. Feldman, 1986; Wallace and Gruber, 1989; Wallace, 1986; Freeman, 1991; Gardner, 1993).

Although there have been few investigations of high-ability adults, especially of those with poor accomplishments, more extensive data exist on those who reach eminence. There are valuable biographical researches into the childhood environments of eminent or outstandingly creative adults in a variety of professions, such as historians, artists and scientists. Walberg *et al.* (1981), identified traits by statistical analysis on contemporary ratings of biographical data – of men only – which included cognitive, affective and physical traits, as well as family, educational, social and cultural conditions. As a group, poets, novelists and dramatists were found to be more 'concentrated and neurotic', while showing less 'openness and receptivity to varied cultures and ideas', and being 'less optimistic'. Religious leaders were found to be more 'sensitive and ethical', but less 'versatile and impatient', etc. (see Radford, 1990).

ISSUES IN PERSONALITY DIMENSIONS OF TALENTED INDIVIDUALS

There are several aspects of personality in the talented which surface in the literature with notable frequency, of which the effects are still uncertain and the theories as yet unclear.

Motivation

Motivational factors, even more than a generally advantageous mix of personality traits, are as important to human accomplishment as intellectual ones (Howe, 1987). The existing body of research on intrinsic motivation seems to be particularly relevant for high ability. Deci and Ryan (1985), for example, analysed over 200 studies on motivation, and formulated an empirically based theory of human motivation which accounted for both positive and detrimental influences on self-determination, relevant personality factors, and other variables. They say that no matter how competent individuals feel, they would not be intrinsically motivated when under pressure. Csikszentmihalyi *et al.* (1993), working with talented teenagers, used the conception of 'flow', a trance-like state which happens to people functioning at high levels (whether playing chess, climbing rocks or undertaking surgical operations). He concluded that a talent will be developed if it produces 'optimal experiences' – 'flow' in their talent area. Intrinsic motivation and flow do seem to have a common core, which is the involvement of the individual in the activity.

Other, more frequently studied mediators to motivation are the predominantly affective 'self-concept' and – increasingly of late – the mostly cognitive self-efficacy construct (Bandura and Schunk, 1981). In an investigation of university students' perceived self-efficacy Vrugt (1994) found that positive feelings about their own skills clearly enhanced their course scores, and in an upward spiral: 'these feelings in turn were influenced by perceived self-efficacy' (p.471). But a number of researchers have pointed out some serious problems with research on self-concept, which has often been used as a global construct, i.e. without differentiating between its physical, social and academic aspects (Byrne, 1984; Marsh and Shavelson, 1985). In research on self-concept and talent, although varying criteria for the identification of self-concept were often used, important moderating variables such as gender, classroom setting, and socio-economic status were ignored, while control groups, such as test-manual norm groups, were either inadequate or missing. However, recent well-controlled work which differentiated academic and other aspects of self-concept, found that special classes for the gifted reduced the former, while leaving all other forms of self-concept untouched (Marsh *et al.*, 1995). Because of these problems, the results of many studies are practically impossible to evaluate or compare. Rather, it might be more precise and useful to investigate self-efficacy as a mediating factor between high-level achievement and social behaviour: an 'efficacy expectation' referring to the conviction that one's behaviour will produce a desired outcome.

Stress

Stress is considered to result from such factors as overcommitment and high expectations (internal or external). Following the classic work of Selye (1956), a plethora of both research reports and self-help books for stress victims have appeared, in parallel with many investigations on stress as it afflicts individuals in various occupations. The phenomenon of 'burn-out' has been related to high professional success (Freudenberger, 1980), but in fact, there are few empirical data on this phenomenon in highly achieving adults. On the contrary, in her clinical study of over 40 'workaholics', Machlowitz (1980) found that the stereotype of the unhappy and distressed adult 'workaholic' does not seem to be supported: as a group, they were generally content with their lives. Nor are there adequate data on the relationship between stress and advanced achievement in children. After looking at a sample of adolescents, Karnes and Oehler-Stinnett (1986) found that those who were recognized as 'gifted' did not differ significantly from the normal population in their perception of stressors. In particular, they neither perceived the label 'gifted' as stressful nor saw events related to achievement (such as social status and career aspirations) in that way.

Perfectionism

Even though both clinical experience (Hollender, 1965) and biographies suggest the reality of this problem in many cases, there is little scientific evidence to support the belief that the highly able are more likely to be perfectionists in comparison with average-ability control groups. Possibly related to perfectionism is procrastination – the stress-producing habit of putting work off until the last minute – in case the product is less than perfect. Again, although every counsellor has seen clients with this problem, very few empirical data support the view that it occurs more frequently in people with high abilities, as opposed to the normal population. Another such 'mystery variable' is the 'heightened emotional sensitivity' often ascribed to highly able individuals, although it is much written about in counselling books for the gifted.

Emotional disorders

A highly intelligent subgroup of young psychiatric patients was compared with a control group of normal intelligence by Detzner and Schmidt (1986): they found half as many conduct disorders, but significantly more cases of anorexia nervosa. Both a large number of recent investigations and comprehensive reviews of the literature have firmly dispelled the notion that as children the gifted suffer from psychosocial adjustment problems to a higher degree than the normal population (Olszewski-Kubilius *et al.*, 1988; Czeschlik and Rost, 1988; Freeman, 1991; Sayler and Brookshire, 1993; Goh and Feldhusen, 1994).

Even fewer investigations have been carried out on the mental states of highly able adults, an exception being those from the on-going Terman study (Grossberg and Cornell, 1988). A typical finding is: 'When differences are found between gifted students and chronological peers, they tend to favour the gifted. Specifically, there are lower levels of anxiety, fewer indications of psychological problems, generally higher scores on multidimensional personality instruments such as the California Personality Inventory (CPI)' (Olszewski-Kubilius *et al.*, 1988). These researchers discovered many similarities between male and female personality profiles among the highly able, and found most deviations from the normal population on motivational and achievement variables. Czeschlik and Rost (1988) concluded that 'moderately gifted' primary age children (IQ below 150, but above 120) were usually socially well integrated, well accepted and popular with their peers, and only seldom socially isolated. Positive social integration was also found by Urban (1990) in his Hanover pre-school programme for children of high-ability. Using the Child Behaviour Checklist, Galluci (1988) found a normal incidence of psychopathology in a sample of 83 adolescents with IQs greater than 135, some even above 150.

But why should highly able individuals show such positive social adjustment? Is this a function of their intelligence, or rather an outcome of the same favourable child-rearing techniques which optimized the development of their high abilities in the first place?

SPECIAL POPULATIONS

Gender

Unfortunately, in almost all research on gender, the categories of 'girl' and 'boy' are used as though they were fixed and unquestionable. In addition, most psychological research is done on males (even male rats) because they are seen as neutral and unaffected by sex. Thus the male image is often taken as the norm, and female behaviour is seen as deviant. Although this makes calculating the statistics easier, it also means that the more subtle, overlapping and complex characteristics, as well as the similarities between masculinity and femininity, are relatively ignored. It is possible that there are indeed minute tendencies in genetic make-up between the sexes, which are exaggerated by social pressures to distinguish gender-roles. But emerging research on highly talented teenagers finds that talented boys and girls are more likely to reject gender categories than youngsters of average ability, especially the girls; a feature referred to by the researchers as 'androgynous traits' (Csikszentmihalyi et al., 1993). From clinical experience, Stapf (1990) postulates that bright young girls are much like able boys in their intellectual interests and behaviour, but resemble other girls in their social-emotional reactions.

Talented girls suffer a number of disadvantages. For example, there is a considerable lack of successful female role models to follow. Even in primary schools in Europe, there are relatively few female heads. In fact, a general dominance of men is to be found in senior school posts and the educational establishment in most of the world. Science teaching is particularly noted for categorization of the sexes. As pupils get older, their likelihood of being taught science by a woman tails off. Added to that, most science teachers expect girls to produce conscientious neat work, but not to understand what they are writing about, whereas boys can be seen as having a good grasp of science, but produce untidy work (Spear, 1989). In a longitudinal study of hundreds of highly able German pupils, Heller (1991) found that teachers more frequently judged boys as superior in intelligence, though girls were seen as better at music. Girls were less successful in measurement and practical-technical abilities, but better at speed of information-processing and verbal creativity. They were also somewhat better than the boys in schoolwork – except in mathematics and physics. Out of school, girls had more musical-artistic interests, and less often had scientific ones. Heller writes: 'Obviously girls are not as well able as boys to turn achievements in scientific-technical areas into social recognition' (p. 186).

Girls tend not to get identified as talented as often or as early as boys, while highly able women receive relatively little attention (see Walker et al., 1992). For example, although a study was made of the 'sources of life satisfactions of the Terman gifted men', no such data are available on the female cohort (Sears, 1977). There are some interesting psychosocial data from case studies, however, such as those on the often tragic lives of the sisters of 'famous men' (Pusch, 1985), or of Mileva Einstein, the first wife of Albert Einstein (Trbuhovic-Gjuric, 1985), as well as figures such as Zelda Fitzgerald and Dorothy Wordsworth.

There have been some major changes in Britain, with the introduction of the national curriculum. Girls and boys now study the same subjects and there is not only a formal but a practical commitment to equal opportunities at all levels of education. In 1992, for the first time, more women than men entered university. If bright girls are doing better at school than boys, at least up to the age of about 16, what is the problem? The answer is that although they may pass examinations better than boys up to their mid-teens, they still far too often 'underachieve' in post-school life, doing much less well than their school achievement indicates they should. It is important to know why this is so, in order to do something about it (for further discussion on this subject see Freeman, 1995).

Underachievers

Another well-known subgroup are highly able but underachieving individuals. Whilst there is relatively much information on youngsters (Colangelo *et al.*, 1993; Butler-Por, 1993), we know less about adults who are not realizing their potential abilities. In this connection, the prevailing cultural definitions of 'underachievement' and 'achievement' respectively, seem to be important, whilst personal satisfaction must be an additional key variable since some 'underachieving' individuals do not seem to suffer from the implications of being an 'underachiever'.

Other sub-groups that have only been minimally investigated include prodigies or extremely able individuals (Feldman, 1986; Radford, 1990), the learning disabled (Baum and Owen, 1988), the physically disabled (Whitmore and Maker, 1985), and culturally diverse individuals. An investigation of highly able migrant labourers' children, many of whom go unrecognized and face an extremely difficult psychosocial situation, would seem to be particularly relevant in present-day Europe, though such work has not yet been done.

HIGHLY ABLE INDIVIDUALS WITHIN THE FAMILY, SCHOOL AND SOCIO-CULTURAL SETTING

Issues of development

Research on developmental questions related to high ability has mainly focused on two major issues: whether there is a gap between affective and cognitive development in the highly able, and whether there are particular crisis periods for psychosocial adjustment. Neither issue has been sufficiently investigated in the case of adults.

There is a widespread assumption that psychosocial maturity in gifted children and adolescents lags behind cognitive development (Terassier, 1985), although this is far from proven. It militates against, for example, early admission to school and educational acceleration, because of the potential harm to a child's social and emotional development (Southern *et al.*, 1993). Some American reviews (Alexander and Skinner, 1980; Pollins, 1983; Proctor *et al.*, 1986; Cohen *et al.*, 1994) have concluded that no harm has been documented by such action, even for markedly accelerated students at the college level who had entered at age 14 or younger: most reported an excellent social life, with intense and regular social contacts (Janos *et al.*, 1988). However, Freeman (1991) in a unique counselling style follow-up investigation, found that acceleration could be decidedly harmful, not only emotionally but also academically.

Are there critical periods or times when psychosocial adjustment in the highly able might be particularly affected? The 'midlife crisis' has not been investigated in relation to high ability, except in the work of Bamberger (1982) on musical prodigies, and the situation in top-level sports could well be similar (Rowley, 1995). The last year of kindergarten and the first years of school might be a difficult time for potentially talented children, who may be bored by learning material that they know already, but who have not yet acquired the social skills to establish meaningful relationships with age-mates who have quite different interests and might not 'speak their language'. Further investigations of the psychosocial implications of this situation are most desirable. Another possible time of potential crisis is adolescence: peer pressure then increases, causing girls in particular to deny their abilities. Kerr *et al.* (1988) found that gifted adolescents saw their abilities as positive for both their personal growth and academic performance, but negative for their social relations.

Labelling

Labelling refers to the description of a child as 'gifted' or talented. One of the most comprehensive investigations on labelling by parents was carried out by Freeman (1991) in Britain. This study was remarkable because the 210 gifted and non-gifted children, their teachers and parents were studied in depth in their own environments, using interviews, tests and observations. The label of 'gifted' was associated with emotional problems, but this was not true for others with identical IQ or other achievement scores. The label of 'gifted' was also found to be associated with home difficulties. However, an American study of 600 primary and high school pupils in schools provided evidence that the label tended to be positively perceived (Hershey and Oliver, 1988). The important role of the professional in explaining exceptionally high ability to parents and teachers has also been pointed out: sensitive handling of this matter can help prevent isolation of the child, and can promote shared advocacy with other educational groups (Sapon-Shevin, 1987).

At all levels of age and ability, it is almost impossible to take account of the wide variety of individual styles in a group of learners, especially of a school class. Practical experience shows that much has already been gained if educators develop some awareness that different learning styles exist at all.

NEGLECTED AND PROBLEM AREAS OF TALENT DEVELOPMENT

There are some areas of the development of talent that might be particularly relevant to practitioners such as counsellors and educators, which have not yet been sufficiently explored. Some key issues are now addressed, where additional research data could lead to the improved provision of such services. Two major types of questions can be distinguished here: firstly, those related to psychosocial aspects of the development of talent over the life-span, and secondly, diagnostic and therapeutic questions.

Psychosocial aspects

With the exception of specific case studies, there have been far too few investigations with a life-span perspective concerned with psychosocial aspects. Even such popular research topics as self-concept have been mainly investigated in school-age children and young adolescents, which is strange, considering that for some time now, a life-time perspective has been common in psychology and sociology (Honzik, 1984; Baltes, 1987).

We know almost nothing about the course of talent in middle-aged or elderly individuals. Are old people who are still realizing superior abilities happier than those who are not? Can abilities be developed for the first time late in life? With the exception of Heller (1988), not much attention has been paid to the development of leisure-time activities in highly able individuals over the life-span and the relationship of this to psychosocial adjustment. These are questions that could become more salient as the widespread trend continues towards an 'ageing society' and increasing part-time employment for both sexes.

Another interesting question relates to seemingly or actually less creative or productive phases during the course of a lifetime. What characterizes such phases? Some gifted people have many careers over a lifetime: what do such multitalented people have in common, and what prompts them to change direction, sometimes in dramatically new directions? What implications does this have for counselling highly able young people? Additionally, too little information exists on the development of talent in different domain-specific areas. How do highly verbal individuals differ psycho-socially from those whose major strength lies in mathematical thinking? What about those whose major area of strength is spatial abilities? Could their abilities be coordinated with Gardner's (1983) theories of seven intelligences – linguistic, musical, logical-mathematical, spatial, bodily-kinaesthetic, and personal (knowledge of the self and others)? Dauber and Benbow (1990) found psychosocial differences between verbally and mathematically gifted adolescents, but do such differences persist as these adolescents turn into adults?

For talent development over the life-span, the possibly crucial effects of mentorship might have been underestimated. A mentor is another person, usually older, who takes a special personal interest in the intellectual, emotional or professional development of an able individual. The biographical study by Walberg *et al.* (1981) on the traits and environmental conditions of 221 eminent men shows that 60 per cent of them had early exposure to other eminent persons, and 78 per cent were encouraged by someone other than their parents or teachers. For gifted sub-populations, such as women, suitable mentors might be even more crucial than for gifted boys and men, because appropriate role-models are much more difficult for them to find – there are just not enough around, although this is changing. Mentors could be sought out and used more systematically in relation to the provision of education and counselling for the talented. For example, mentoring and counselling to improve self-esteem were found to be effective in promoting a more realistic acceptance by girls of their abilities (Arnold and Subotnik, 1994), and it helps in educational achievement (Daloz, 1986). But what kinds of mentors are suitable for whom? What is their influence in highly able individuals, on psychosocial adjustment, or on career choices?

Social intelligence – the sensitive perceptions of others and the resulting intelligent behaviour – has been postulated as a bona fide area of 'giftedness' for some time now, but there have been few deliberate efforts to develop it in children and adolescents, in spite of the fact that we know much about the development of prosocial behaviour from developmental psychology and related disciplines. It is currently more of an issue for sales people and managers, where communication training and coaching are now commonplace.

In his theory of multiple intelligences, Gardner (1983) recognized that the 'personal intelligences' – knowledge of self and others – are an important part of the 'seven intelligences', because: '. . . these forms of knowledge are of tremendous importance in many, if not all, societies in the world – forms that have, however, tended to be ignored or minimised by nearly all students of cognition' (p. 241). Passow (1988) and Tannenbaum (1993) make the point that the sensitization of highly able young people to moral and ethical issues, to prosocial behaviour and to the major problems facing society today must be an integral part of education for the highly able. We need to shift our current emphasis from merely the psychosocial 'adjustment' of highly able individuals to increasingly recognizing and developing emotional and social sensitivity as abilities in their own right.

Correspondingly, a much more precise concept is needed of 'social-emotional maturity', particularly as it applies to highly able individuals. Abroms (1985) postulated four areas to make up social giftedness: social cognition, prosocial or constructive social behaviour, moral reasoning or awareness, and leadership. Urban (1990) has pointed out that the difference between social cognition and social behaviour has often been disregarded in investigations, and can only be picked up by behavioural observations. While social cognition is often positively related to IQ, prosocial behaviour results from active involvement in a variety of social situations, and benefits from adult guidance. This also applies to leadership abilities, which are a complex interaction of high levels of social cognition, prosocial behaviour and (ideally) also moral reasoning (Sisk, 1988).

To help people develop high-level prosocial behaviour, the activities of both educational and work-setting must be conducive to this effort, but often they are not. In Kohn's (1986) compilation of arguments for cooperative behaviour, especially in business, he makes a strong case against constant competition. He argues that it poisons our relationships and diminishes our self-respect, because it makes us dependent on external evaluation. It also leads to lower productivity, because it diminishes our sense of personal control. Aggression and anxiety are further undesirable personal outcomes of constant competition.

Diagnostic and counselling issues

Innovative diagnostic measures – tests, interview and observation guidelines, or parents' and teachers' questionnaires – are needed to assess non-pathological aspects of psychosocial functioning. We need an increased emphasis on affective strengths, rather than on maladaption, but very few such measures are currently available, although the California Psychological Inventory can also be used to assess psychosocial strengths. There are hardly any suitable instruments to assess social cognition and prosocial behaviour in children and adolescents, while the commonly used norms of diagnostic measures to assess psychosocial adjustment may well be inadequate for the highly able. Silver and Clampit (1990), for example, found a completely different interpretation of verbal-performance discrepancies for highly able as opposed to normal children on the WISC-R, as did Wilkinson (1993). Similarly, social-emotional issues as a function of marked strengths and weaknesses in individual ability profiles, as on the WISC-R, have not been sufficiently investigated in the highly able. Clinical experience seems to indicate, for example, that a relatively low score for 'coding' combined with a high Verbal Performance score, seems to lead very often to a host of scholastic and adjustment problems in schoolchildren.

The goals and objectives of guidance and counselling for the talented have been reviewed by several authors (e.g. Landrum, 1987; Milgram, 1991; Deslisle, 1992), so that concrete and useful information on how to work with highly able individuals on psychosocial issues is begining to be available. However, practitioners still need more clinical evidence, case studies, transcripts of therapeutic sessions and evaluations of outcome to know which therapeutic and counselling approaches would work best with highly intelligent children and adults. So far, both empirical and clinical evidence is very limited, even in accounts of counselling work with the gifted (Feger and Prado, 1985). A step was made in the right direction with a collection of articles on providing psychotherapy for creative individuals of all ages (Borduin and Mann, 1987). Strip *et al.* (1991) described a model of providing highly able adolescents with basic intervention techniques to counsel their peers, dealing with the need for immediate intervention in emotional crises.

Specific recommendations as to what type of counselling might be useful are also needed. For example, Cornell (1990) finding that less popular gifted children tended to be characterized by a lower social self-concept, lower academic self-esteem, and less prestigious paternal occupations, suggested that for them assessment and counselling should focus on the social self-concept and perhaps also social skills, but not on general personality or academic ability. This kind of differentiated approach, as opposed to the indiscriminate prescription of 'play therapy' for children, seems likely to be a useful one. There are some appealing practical suggestions for teaching and counselling, mostly derived from North American experience, which would need validation in other cultural settings before they could be put into action (e.g. Butler, 1984; Milgram, 1991).

Boekaerts (1991) has presented a useful framework for analysing affective learning processes that has important implications for both teaching and counselling highly able individuals. She describes how the creation of an optimal internal learning environment is characterized by self-regulation, as opposed to teacher regulation, and that this plays an integral role in the learning of the highly able – closely linked with self-efficacy (see also De Corte, 1995 and Span, 1995). Pupils with high self-efficacy believe that they have the skills to regulate their learning processes, which are increased with intrinsic motivation. Consequently, rather than focusing on an optimal teaching environment, counselling for highly able underachievers might be better focused on the acquisition of such self-regulatory skills and the promotion of a sense of self-efficacy. Boekaerts, in fact, points out that it might even be detrimental for highly able learners to have extra teacher support and guidance, because this can interfere with their personal learning strategies and self-regulatory skills.

On the adult level, an innovative approach is 'management coaching' – a kind of counselling with often highly able adults in a top management setting, to enable them to deal with the various stressors that such a position entails. This interesting field might be difficult to investigate, however.

OUTLOOK

What could be part of an adequate perspective for the role of psychosocial factors in the actualization of abilities over the life-span? From what we know so far, it seems that this would have to be a dynamic and process-oriented view, accounting for the interrelationship of the individual and his/her environment over time. Psychosocial development depends as much on the social context as on the individual's perceptions of various influences on the self. Increasingly, we seem to be realizing that a positive and growth-oriented outlook might carry us further than an overemphasis on maladjustment and pathology. This might result in the greater development of assessment measures that are more situational and less orientated towards personality traits. Interesting parallels to this situation can be found in contemporary strategic human resource management, as practised in corporate settings: there, too, it has been recognized that the needs of individuals and their working environments are constantly changing. Therefore, Boerlijst and Meijboom (1989), amongst others, recommend an ongoing process of mutual fine-tuning, which includes career analysis, career development policy, career planning, counselling and mentoring.

REFERENCES

Abroms, K.I. (1985) 'Social giftedness and its relationship with intellectual giftedness', in J. Freeman (ed.), *The Psychology of Gifted Children*. Chichester: Wiley.

Alexander, P. and Skinner, M. (1980) 'The effects of early entrance on subsequent social and emotional development: a follow-up study', *Journal for the Education of the Gifted*, 3, 147–92.

Arnold, K.D. and Subotnik, R.F. (1994) 'Lessons from contemporary longitudinal studies', in R.F. Subotnik and K.D. Arnold (eds), *Beyond Terman: Contemporary Longitudinal Studies of Giftedness and Talent*. Norwood, NJ: Ablex.

Baltes, P.B. (1987) 'Theoretical propositions of life-span developmental psychology: on the dynamics between growth and decline', *Developmental Psychology*, 133 (5), 611–26.

Bamberger, J. (1982) 'Growing-up prodigies: the midlife crisis', in D.H. Feldman (ed.), *Developmental Approaches to Giftedness*. San Francisco: Jossey-Bass.

Bandura, A. and Schunk, D.H. (1981) 'Cultivating competence, self-efficacy, and intrinsic interest through proximal self-motivation', *Journal of Personality and Social Psychology*, 41, 536–98.

Baum, S. and Owen S.V. (1988) 'High ability/learning disabled students: how are they different?', *Gifted Child Quarterly*, 32, 321–6.

Boekaerts, M. (1991) 'The effective learning process and giftedness', *European Journal for High Ability*, 2, 146–60.

Boerlijst, G. and Meijboom, G. (1989) 'Matching the individual and the organization', in P. Herriot (ed.), *Assessment and Selection in Organizations*. Chichester: Wiley.

Bourduin, C.M. and Mann, B.J. (1987) 'On keeping out of the briar patch: a family-ecological systems approach to treating the behaviour problems of creative adolescents', *Psychotherapy Patient*, 4, 75–90.

Butler, K.A. (1984) *Learning and Teaching Style in Theory and Practice*. Maynard, MA: Gabriel Systems Inc.

Butler-Por, N. (1993) 'Underachieving gifted students', in K.A. Heller, F.J. Mönks and A.H. Passow (eds), *International Handbook of Research and Development of Giftedness and Talent*. Oxford: Pergamon Press.

Byrne, B.M. (1984) 'Investigating measures of self-concept', *Measurement and Evaluation in Guidance*, 16, 115–26.

Cohen, R., Duncan, M. and Cohen, S.L. (1994) 'Classroom peer relations of children participating in a pull-out enrichment program', *Gifted Child Quarterly*, 38, 33–7.

Colangelo, N., Kerr, B., Kristensen, P. and Maxey, J. (1993) 'A comparison of gifted underachievers and gifted high achievers', *Gifted Child Quarterly*, 37, 155–60.

Cornell, D.G. (1990) 'High ability students who are unpopular with their peers', *Gifted Child Quarterly*, 34, 155–60.

Csikszentmihalyi, M., Rathunde, K. and Whalen, S. (1993) *Talented Teenagers. The Roots of Success and Failure*. Cambridge: Cambridge University Press.
Czeschlik, T. and Rost, D.H. (1988) 'Hochbegabte und ihre Peers [The gifted and their peers]', *Zeitschrift für Pädagogische Psychologie*, 21, 1–23.
Daloz, L.A. (1986) *Effective Teaching Mentoring*. San Francisco: Jossey-Bass.
Dauber, S.L. and Benbow, C.P. (1990) 'Aspects of personality and peer relations of extremely talented adolescents', *Gifted Child Quarterly*, 34, 10–14.
Deci, E.L. and Ryan, R.M. (1985) *Intrinsic Motivation and Self-determination in Human Behaviour*. New York: Plenum.
De Corte, E. (1995) 'Acquiring high-level learning skills: a perspective from instructional psychology'. Chapter 5, this volume.
Deslisle, J.R. (1992) *Guiding the Social and Emotional Development of Gifted Youth*. London: Longman.
Detzner, M. and Schmidt, M.H. (1986) 'Are highly gifted children and adolescents especially susceptible to anorexia nervosa?', in K.A. Heller and J.F. Feldhusen (eds), *Identifying and Nurturing the Gifted*. Toronto: Huber.
Feger, B. and Prado, T. (1985) 'The first information and counselling centre for the gifted in West Germany', in K.A. Heller and J.F. Feldhusen (eds), *Identifying and Nurturing the Gifted*. Toronto: Huber.
Feldman, D.H. (1986) *Nature's Gambit: Child Prodigies and the Development of Human Potential*. New York: Basic Books.
Freeman, J. (1991) *Gifted Children Growing Up*. London: Cassell.
Freeman, J. (1995) *Highly Able Girls and Boys*. Northampton: NACE Publications.
Freudenberger, H.J. (1980) *Burn Out: How to Beat the High Cost of Success*. Toronto: Bantam Books.
Galluci, N.T. (1988) 'Emotional adjustment of gifted children', *Gifted Child Quarterly*, 32, 273–6.
Gardner, H. (1983) *Frames of Mind: The Theory of Multiple Intelligences*. New York: Basic Books.
Gardner, H. (1993) *Creating Minds: An Anatomy of Creativity Seen through the Lives of Freud, Einstein, Picasso, Stravinsky, Eliot, Graham, and Gandhi*. New York: Basic Books.
Goh, B.E. and Feldhusen, J.F. (1994) 'A cross-cultural study of leadership, social maturity and creative potential in adolescents', *European Journal for High Ability*, 5, 39–48.
Grossberg, I.N. and Cornell, D.G. (1988) 'Relationship between personality adjustment and high intelligence: Terman versus Hollingworth', *Exceptional Children*, 55, 266–72.
Heller, K.A. (1988) *Conference Report. The First International Conference on Leisure Time Activities and Non-academic Accomplishments of Gifted Students*. Munich: Institute of Educational Psychology.
Heller, K.A. (1991) 'The nature and development of giftedness: a longitudinal study', *European Journal for High Ability*, 2, 174–8.
Hershey, M. and Oliver, E. (1988) 'The effects of the label gifted for students identified for special programs', *Roeper Review*, 11, 33–4.
Hoffman, M.L. (1986) 'Affect, cognition and motivation', in R.M. Sorrentino and E.T. Higgins (eds), *Handbook of Motivation and Cognition: Foundations of Social Behaviour*. Chichester: Wiley.
Hollender, M.H. (1965) 'Perfectionism', *Comprehensive Psychiatry*, 6 (2), 94–103.
Honzik, M.P. (1984) 'Life-span development', *Annual Review of Psychology*, 35, 309–31.
Howe, M.J.A. (1987) 'Motivation, cognition, and individual achievements', in E. de Corte, H. Lodewijks, R. Parmentier and P. Span (eds), *Learning and Instruction*. Chichester: Wiley.
Janos, P.M. and Robinson, N.M. (1985) 'Psychosocial development in intellectually gifted children', in F.D. Horowitz and M. O'Brien (eds), *The Gifted and Talented: Developmental Perspectives*. Washington, DC: American Psychological Association.
Janos, P.M., Robinson, N.M., Carter, C., Chapel, A. *et al.* (1988) 'A cross-sectional developmental study of the social relations of students who enter college early', *Gifted Child Quarterly*, 32, 210–15.

Karnes, F.A. and Oehler-Stinnett, J.J. (1986) 'Life events as stressors with gifted adolescents', *Psychology in the Schools*, **23**, 406–14.
Kerr, B., Colangelo, N. and Gaeth, J. (1988) 'Gifted adolescents' attitudes towards their giftedness', *Gifted Child Quarterly*, **32**, 245–7.
Kohn, A. (1986) *No Contest. The Case Against Competition*. Boston: Houghton Mifflin.
Landrum, M.S. (1987) 'Guidelines for implementing a guidance/counselling programme for gifted and talented students', *Roeper Review*, **10**, 103–7.
Machlowitz, M. (1980) *Workaholics: Living with Them, Working with Them*. New York: New American Library.
Marsh, H.W. and Shavelson, R.J. (1985) 'Self-concept: its multi-faced, hierarchical structure', *Educational Psychologist*, **20**, 107–23.
Marsh, H.W., Chessor, D., Craven, R. and Roche, L. (1995) 'The effects of gifted and talented programs on academic self-concept: the big fish strikes again', *American Educational Research Journal*, **2**, 285–319.
Milgram, R.M. (ed.) (1991) *Counselling Gifted and Talented Children*. Norwood, NJ: Ablex.
Mönks, F.J. and Lehwald, G. (1991) *Neugier, Erkundung und Begabung bei Kleinkindern. [Curiosity, Exploration and Ability in Young Children]*. Munich: Ernst Reinhardt Verlag.
Olszewski-Kubilius, P.O., Kulieke, M.J. and Krasney, N. (1988) 'Personality dimensions of gifted adolescents: A review of the empirical literature', *Gifted Child Quarterly*, **32**, 347–52.
Passow, A.H. (1988) 'Educating gifted persons who are caring and concerned', *Roeper Review*, **11**, 13–15.
Pollins, L.D. (1983) 'The effects of acceleration on the social and emotional development of gifted students', in C.P. Benbow and J.C. Stanley (eds), *Academic Precocity: Aspects of Its Development*. Baltimore: Johns Hopkins University Press.
Proctor, T.B., Black, K.N. and Feldhusen, J.F. (1986) 'Early admission of selected children to elementary school: a review of the research literature', *Journal of Educational Research*, **80**, 70–6.
Pusch, L.F. (1985) (ed.) *Schwestern berühmter Männer [Sisters of Famous Men]*. Frankfurt: Insel Verlag.
Radford, J. (1990) *Child Prodigies and Exceptional Early Achievers*. Hemel Hempstead: Harvester Wheatsheaf.
Rowley, S. (1995) 'Identification and development of talent in young athletes'. Chapter 10, this volume.
Sapon-Shevin, M. (1987) 'Explaining giftedness to parents: why it matters what professionals say', *Roeper Review*, **9**, 80–4.
Sayler, M.F. and Brookshire, W.K. (1993) 'Social, emotional and behavioural adjustment of accelerated students, students in gifted classes, and regular students in eighth grade', *Gifted Child Quarterly*, **37**, 150–4.
Sears, R.R. (1977) 'Sources of life satisfactions of the Terman gifted men', *American Psychologist*, **32**, 119–28.
Selye, H. (1956) *The Stress of Life*. New York: McGraw-Hill.
Silver, S.J. and Clampit, M.K. (1990) 'WISC-R profiles of high ability children: interpretation of verbal-performance discrepancies', *Gifted Child Quarterly*, **34**, 76–9.
Sisk, D.A. (1988) 'A case for leadership development to meet the need for excellence in teachers and youth', *Roeper Review*, **11**, 43–6.
Southern, W.T., Jones, E.D. and Stanley, J.C. (1993) 'Acceleration and enrichment: the content and development of program options', in K.A. Heller, F.J. Mönks and A.H. Passow (eds), *International Handbook of Research and Development of Giftedness and Talent*. Oxford: Pergamon Press.
Span, P. (1995) 'Self-regulated learning by talented children'. Chapter 6, this volume.
Spear, M.G. (1989) 'Written work of boys and girls', *British Educational Research Journal*, **15**, 271–7.
Stapf, A. (1990) 'Hochbegabte Mädchen: Entwicklung, Identifikation und Beratung, insbesondere im Vorschualter [Highly able girls: development, identification and counselling, especially at pre-school age]', in W. Wieczerkowski and T.M. Prado (eds), *Hochbegabte Mädchen*. Bad Honnef: K. H. Bock.

Strip, C., Swassing, R. and Kidder, R. (1991) 'Counselling female adolescents: a first step in emotional crises intervention', *Roeper Review*, **13**, 124–8.
Tannenbaum, A.J. (1993) 'History of giftedness and "gifted education" in world perspective', in K.A. Heller, F.J. Mönks and A.H. Passow (eds), *International Handbook of Research and Development of Giftedness and Talent*. Oxford: Pergamon Press.
Terassier, J.-C. (1985) 'Dysynchrony: uneven development', in J. Freeman (ed.), *The Psychology of Gifted Children*. Chichester: Wiley.
Trbuhovic-Gjuric, D. (1985) *Im Schatten Albert Einsteins. Das tragische Leben der Mileva Einstein-Maric [The Tragic Life of Mileva Einstein-Maric]*. Bern: Paul Haupt Verlag.
Urban, K.K. (1990) 'Social behaviour of gifted pre-school children', *European Journal for High Ability*, **1**, 172–8.
Vrugt, A. (1994) 'Perceived self-efficacy, social comparison, effective reactions and academic performance', *British Journal of Educational Psychology*, **64**, 465–72.
Walberg, H.J. et al. (1981) 'Childhood traits and environmental conditions of highly eminent adults', *Gifted Child Quarterly*, **25**, 103–7.
Walker, B.A., Reiss, S.M. and Leonard, J.S. (1992) 'A developmental investigation of the lives of gifted women', *Gifted Child Quarterly*, **36**, 201–6.
Wallace, A. (1986) *The Prodigy: A Biography of William James Sidis, the World's Greatest Child Prodigy*. London, Macmillan.
Wallace, D.B. and Gruber, H.E. (1989) *Creative People at Work*. Oxford: Oxford University Press.
Whitmore, J.R. and Maker, C.J. (1985) *Intellectual Giftedness in Disabled Persons*. Rockville, MD: Aspen.
Wilkinson, S.C. (1993) 'WISC-R profiles of children with superior intellectual ability', *Gifted Child Quarterly*, **37**, 84–91.

Part 2

The Processes of High-level Learning

Chapter 5

Acquiring High-level Learning Skills: A Perspective from Instructional Psychology

Erik De Corte

Unfortunately, there is a lack of coordination between studies of high ability and mainstream psychological and educational research. Cropley (1993a, p. 4) puts it explicitly: '... the area of giftedness suffers from patchiness of research or absence of appropriate investigations; frequently empirical work consists mainly of descriptions of programs accompanied by ringing phrases'. Fortunately, though, help is at hand from research in instructional psychology, which for several decades has made considerable progress, notably in the areas of cognition, learning, and development (Glaser and Bassock, 1989). It offers a route for bringing the somewhat marginal study of high ability into the wider psychological context, providing insights in both theory and method (Jackson, 1993), as well as a knowledge base for the design and evaluation of powerful teaching–learning environments – a two-way exchange which benefits instructional psychology itself.

This chapter discusses the relevance of recent findings in instructional psychology to actualizing talent, and to educational practice for the highly able. It will also describe a theory of learning, focusing on the processes which facilitate the acquisition of expert performance (De Corte, 1990).

TALENT AND A THEORY OF EXPERTISE

For about 20 years, a substantial amount of research in cognitive psychology has been devoted to the analysis of expertise in a variety of fields, mainly by comparing the performances of experts with those of novices. This has enabled the major characteristics of expert performance to be distinguished, as summarized here by Glaser and Chi (1988, pp. xvii–xx):

- Experts excel mainly in their own domain.
- Experts perceive large meaningful patterns in their domain.
- Experts are fast: they are faster than novices at performing the skills of their domain, and they quickly solve problems with little error.

- Experts have both superior short-term and long-term memory in their domain.
- Experts see and represent a problem in their domain at a deeper (more principled) level than novices: novices tend to represent a problem at a more superficial level.
- Experts spend a great deal of time analysing a problem qualitatively.
- Experts have strong self-monitoring skills.

This list of cognitive processes involved in exceptional performance (see, e.g. Okagaki and Sternberg, 1988), is part of the two-way exchange of information referred to above, in that the study of giftedness has already contributed to mainstream cognitive psychology in furthering the understanding of metacognitive skills. On the basis of an excellent review of work in that area, Cheng (1993) concluded that metacognition is an important component of giftedness (see also Kanevsky, 1995; Span, 1995). This importance was seen, for example, in two investigations using a variant of expert-novice studies. Overtoom-Corsmit et al. (1990) analysed mathematical problem-solving processes in elementary school pupils, and Elshout et al. (1993, and see Elshout, 1995) investigated the performance of youngsters analysing physics problems. Both drew the same conclusions, that the gifted groups invested more time and effort than the average-ability pupils in an important self-regulatory activity – orienting themselves to the problems.

The analysis of expertise is an important means of understanding the determinants of exceptional performance, particularly in identifying the characteristics of high-level cognitive activity. It has undermined the traditional view of innate general intellectual abilities as the major part of outstanding achievement, although the impact of such abilities cannot be completely denied. Instead, there is now convincing evidence that expertise is strongly promoted by the combination of high-level cognitive skills with a large domain-specific knowledge base, both acquired as a result of long intensive training and practice (Ericsson and Charness, 1994; Schneider, 1993). The vital place of knowledge has been demonstrated in a wide variety of subject areas, including musical composition and painting. Hayes (1985), for instance, carried out an extensive biographical study of 76 composers and 132 painters, and reported that in both fields the earliest a high level of productivity and creativity could be reached was after a learning period of 6 to 10 years, during which large amounts of knowledge and techniques were acquired (see also Cropley, 1993b).

A better understanding of the nature of expertise is not only important from a theoretical point of view, but also in relation to defining educational objectives. For example, there is broad consensus that becoming competent in mathematics requires the integrated acquisition of the following four categories of aptitudes (for a more detailed discussion see De Corte, 1995; De Corte et al., 1996):

- A well-organized and flexibly accessible domain-specific knowledge base, i.e. the facts, symbols, algorithms, concepts and rules that constitute the contents of mathematics as a subject-matter field.
- Heuristic methods, i.e. search strategies for problem-solving which do not guarantee, but significantly increase the probability of finding the correct solution, because they induce a systematic approach to the task.
- Metacognition, which involves knowledge concerning one's cognitive functioning, on the one hand, and skills relating to the self-regulation of one's cognitive processes on the other.

- Affective components such as beliefs, attitudes and emotions relating to mathematics.

Yet competence in mathematics requires more than the above four points. For example, it has often been observed that even when students possess suitable aptitudes, they may fail to apply them in relevant situations, such as solving an unfamiliar problem – the phenomenon of 'inert knowledge'. They also need to acquire a mathematical disposition (National Council of Teachers of Mathematics, 1989). According to Perkins *et al.* (1993) a disposition not only involves the ability but also the inclination to use it, guided by a sensitivity for appropriate situations and opportunities. In practice, then, it is not enough for would-be mathematicians to acquire mathematical concepts and skills, such as estimation; they also need to develop an inclination to apply them where and when they may be useful. Such a disposition – especially the inclination and sensitivity aspects – cannot be taught directly. It comes from extensive experience with the above four categories in a wide variety of situations.

However, as Boekaerts (1993) pointed out in her model of affective learning process, students can only access a disposition if there are no emotional barriers, i.e. if the demands of a learning task or problem situation do not evoke negative feelings and expectations. If the situation is seen as threatening, students tend to develop a coping rather than a learning intention, so that they are less concerned with learning than about restoring their feeling of well-being. This model is important from both theoretical as well as practical perspectives, and provides a convincing explanation of much underachievement in gifted children and adults (Butler-Por, 1993). From a practical point of view, it implies that learning environments for the gifted should be designed to generate a real learning intention in them, or at least make them aware of the fact that to achieve certain goals, one sometimes has to discard one's feelings of well-being for a while (Boekaerts, 1988).

This dispositional view of mathematics learning certainly represents a legitimate objective for the mathematically talented, i.e. those whose ability reaches or exceeds the 'threshold' value of exceptional performance (Schneider, 1993), although one might question whether acquiring a mathematical disposition is an attainable goal for the majority of the students.

TALENT AND A THEORY OF ACQUISITION

What kind of learning processes should we elicit and maintain in students in order to help them reach their potential level of performance? The study of the processes of learning seems to have been neglected in talent research. Recently, though, research on learning in educational settings has yielded a series of empirically supported characteristics of effective learning processes that are important for the education of potential high achievers. These characteristics are summarized in the following definition, which is then described in more detail with particular regard to the actualization of talent. Learning is a constructive, cumulative, self-regulated, goal-orientated, situated, collaborative and individually different process of knowledge building and meaning construction.

Learning is constructive. This major characteristic is supported by a substantial amount of empirical work (De Corte, 1990; Glaser, 1991; Cobb, 1994), promoting the 'constructionist' view that learners are not passive recipients of information, but actively construct their own knowledge and skills. Some psychologists, though, take an extreme view in this respect, claiming that all knowledge is subjective, a purely idiosyncratic cognitive construction, and in no way reflects objective reality 'out there' (e.g., von Glaserfeld, 1991). Other constructionists (including this author) take a more realistic position, which accepts the possibility of mediating learning through appropriate intervention and guidance. Learning, then, requires cognitive processing from the learner (Shuell, 1992), in mindful and effortful activity (Salomon and Globerson 1987). This conception of active learning contrasts sharply with the implicit view of learning reflected in most current teaching practice – as the transmission and rather passive absorption of knowledge gained and institutionalized by past generations.

Learning is cumulative. This characteristic stresses the important role of formal as well as informal prior knowledge in subsequent learning (Dochy, 1992; Shuell, 1992; Vosniadou, 1992) implied in the constructive nature of learning. Indeed, it is only on the basis of what they already know and can do, that students can actively process new information, and as a consequence derive new meanings and acquire new skills.

Learning is self-regulated. This aspect refers to the metacognitive nature of effective learning, especially the managing and monitoring activities of the student (De Jong, 1992; Shuell, 1992; Simons, 1989; Span, 1995; Vermunt, 1992). More specifically, this involves such activities as orientating oneself to a learning task, taking the necessary steps to learn, regulating one's learning, providing for one's own feedback and performance judgements, keeping oneself concentrated and motivated (Simons, 1989). The more learning becomes self-regulated the more the students assume control and agency over their own learning and as a consequence are less dependent on instructional support for performing these regulatory activities. Taking into account that having strong self-monitoring skills is a major characteristic of exceptional performance, it is obvious that it is of great importance to foster self-regulated learning in gifted children and students who learn differently from others.

Learning is goal-orientated. Although there is always some incidental learning, the presence of a goal, producing explicit awareness and orientation, assists meaningful and effective learning (Bereiter and Scardamalia, 1989; Shuell, 1992). Learning is likely to be most productive when students choose and determine their own objectives, because of its constructive and self-regulated nature. Therefore, it is desirable to stimulate and support goal-setting activities in students. Nonetheless learning can also be successful when objectives are put forward by a teacher, a textbook, a computer program, etc., though on the condition that those objectives are accepted and adopted by the students themselves, so that they generate in them a real learning intention.

Learning is situated. The view that learning and cognition are situated – in the subject and social context – is in contrast to the information-processing approach. In that, learning and thinking are seen as highly individual and purely cognitive processes by which mental representations are constructed, all inside the head. The situated view stresses that learning and cognition are not 'solo' activities, but are distributed over the individual student, any partners in the learning environment, and the resources and tools that are available (Brown et al., 1989; Greeno, 1991; Lave and Wenger, 1991; Resnick, 1994; Salomon, 1993). This implies the need to anchor learning into authentic, real-life social and physical contexts that are representative of the situations in which students will have to use their knowledge and skills afterwards (Brown et al., 1989).

Learning is collaborative. Because the situated learning and cognition perspective stresses the importance of interaction and participation in social and cultural practices, it implies the collaborative nature of effective learning which is reflected in such activities as exchanging ideas, comparing solution strategies, and discussing arguments (Vygotsky, 1978; Brown et al., 1989). It is also of special significance that interaction and cooperation induce and mobilize reflection, and thus foster the development of metacognitive knowledge and skills.

Learning is individually different. The processes and outcomes of learning vary because of individual differences, such as learning potential, prior knowledge, approaches to and conceptions of learning, interest, self-efficacy, self-worth, etc. (Snow and Swanson, 1992; Ackerman et al., 1993; Marton et al., 1993). These differences demand appropriately differentiated instruction for the best results, a matter of particular importance to the education of the talented who need specialist teaching. Marton and Säljö (1984) identified two distinct approaches to learning – deep and surface. Those adopting a deep approach try to understand the intention of the learning material and search for meaningful relations within it: surface learners try to memorize the information. The deep approach achieves better results than the surface approach.

These characteristics of effective learning processes mirror many important features of exceptional performance, discovered in analyses of expertise. Experts, for instance, are very active and goal-directed performers in their domain; they look for meaningful patterns and relations, consider problems at a deep level, and master self-monitoring skills. Powerful learning environments in line with these characteristics are essential to actualize talents, i.e. situations and contexts that can elicit and keep the appropriate learning processes going.

TALENT AND A THEORY OF INTERVENTION

The focus of a theory of intervention is the design of powerful learning environments. Although considerable resources and effort have been invested (at least in the United States) in the development of curricula and programmes for the education of the gifted, they are not usually theory-driven, nor are they based on the outcomes of well-designed research, and there are few evaluation studies of the merits and weaknesses. Rather than being fuelled by well-founded scientific arguments, the field is often dominated by philosophical discussions and sterile controversies, such as the arguments about acceleration or enrichment (Fox and Washington, 1985). In addition, the available programmes are mostly – albeit largely implicitly – in line with the traditional conception of school learning as knowledge and information transmission.

Instead, it is proposed that the design of intervention programmes for the highly able would benefit from the bases of both the dispositional and the constructivist conceptions of effective learning processes. These match the objectives of gifted education, including desirable learning activities. By taking this direction, gifted education could possibly achieve what has been put forward by Cohen and Ambrose (1993), namely taking a leading role in bringing about fundamental changes in regular schooling by creatively transforming the educational system itself.

The remaining part of this chapter first briefly outlines a series of design principles for powerful learning environments that derive from the characteristics of effective learning processes (as above) and which are in line with the dispositional view of skilled learning and thinking. Then, an example of a powerful computer-supported learning environment is discussed. This environment, CSILE (Computer-Supported Intentional Learning Environments) (Scardamalia and Bereiter, 1992) is a good illustration of those design principles, and it seems particularly well suited for use with gifted learners.

Design principles for powerful learning environments

- Learning as an active and constructive process includes intervention to increase knowledge and the building of meaning by teachers, peers and educational media. Powerful learning environments should induce and support constructive, cumulative and goal-orientated acquisition processes in all learners. They are characterized by a balance between discovery learning and personal exploration on the one hand, and systematic instruction and guidance on the other.
- Learning environments should enhance self-regulation of acquisition processes. For this, the external regulation of knowledge and skill acquisition in the form of systematic instruction should be gradually removed, so that students become more and more agents of their own learning.
- The constructive learning processes should be embedded as much a possible in authentic contexts that are rich in resources, tools and learning materials, and which offer ample opportunities for social interaction and collaboration. In order to foster the development of a disposition to productive learning and thinking (especially the inclination and sensitivity aspects), learning environments should provide extensive opportunities for practice with the different categories of knowledge and skills in a large variety of situations.
- To take individual differences into account, learning environments should allow for the flexible adaptation of instruction, especially the balance between self-regulation and external regulation, and that between cognition and emotion, conditional on whether the student is in the learning or in the coping mode.
- Because domain-specific knowledge, heuristic methods, and metacognitive aspects play a complementary role in competent learning and problem solving, powerful learning environments should facilitate the acquisition of general learning and thinking skills that are embedded in the different subject-matter domains of the curriculum.

CSILE: AN EXAMPLE OF A POWERFUL (COMPUTER-SUPPORTED) LEARNING ENVIRONMENT

Computers have been massively introduced into schools since the early 1980s, and in spite of the predictions that this new interactive technology would significantly change the quality and the outcomes of schooling, particularly for the most able, there is considerable evidence that this has not happened. This is mostly because the computer is usually a mere add-on to a traditional classroom setting. To use this technology at its most productive requires that computers are embedded in powerful learning environments. Embedded means that the technology is judiciously integrated into the learning environment, capitalizing on its particular strengths to present, represent and transform information (e.g. simulations of phenomena and processes), and to initiate constructive activities and effective forms of interaction and cooperation (e.g. through exchanging data, information, and problems via a network) (De Corte, 1993).

What is true for education in general is certainly true for the development of talent: exploiting appropriately the potential of the technology requires its embedding in teacher-mediated learning situations that induce active and collaborative processes of knowledge building and meaning construction. CSILE (Scardamalia and Bereiter, 1992) is a good example of a computer-supported learning system that is in line with both the general conception of powerful learning environments and the view of productive educational computing described above. While CSILE has been designed as a computer-based programme for education in general, it looks especially useful for inducing and supporting constructive acquisition processes in talented students.

The background of CSILE

Procedural facilitation of writing CSILE has grown out of work by Scardamalia, Bereiter and their colleagues on the teaching and learning of writing, in which they had observed important differences between the approach to writing by experts and by novices. Children who are novices typically use a so-called 'knowledge-telling' approach: they start writing down immediately what they know about a given topic. On the other hand, competent writers spend much more time and effort in planning and revising their text; as a consequence, they engage in a knowledge-transforming process, involving goal-setting and problem-solving, along with generating text.

Starting from a detailed analysis of the writing activities of experts, Scardamalia *et al.* (1984) developed a procedure aimed at eliciting and promoting students' metacognitive activities during writing. This procedure – procedural facilitation – consists in providing computer support in the format of planning and revision prompts presented as open sentences (such as 'A better argument would be . . .') to guide and orientate text production. This mediating activity stimulates students to exploit and use their own cognitive potential, and is therefore in line with the view that effective learning is a constructive, goal-orientated, and self-regulated process. Scardamalia *et al.* (1984) have found that procedural facilitation has a favourable influence on children's planning and reflectivity during writing, and that it improves the quality of their texts.

Design principles and architecture of CSILE

From their initial work, Scardamalia and Bereiter (1992) have expanded their system into a more general computer-based learning environment, that does not focus on a particular subject-matter domain, but aims at penetrating and affecting the whole curriculum. Technically speaking, CSILE is a networked hypermedia system which allows students to construct their own common database consisting of text and graphical material. All students have access to the database, and they can comment on each others' notes. This basic feature of the system aims at inducing the construction of collaborative knowledge building in the classroom. Seven design principles underlying CSILE are intended to facilitate the development of such a knowledge-building community (see Scardamalia and Bereiter, 1992, for a more detailed discussion).

Objectification: the system should help learners to treat knowledge as an object that can be discussed, criticized, changed, and related to other knowledge.

Progress: constructing knowledge within the system should yield perceptible progress for the learners.

Synthesis: the system should stimulate and facilitate the integration of knowledge as well as higher-order representations.

Consequence: the system should ensure that each learner is informed about the outcomes of their contributions (e.g., use of one's ideas, comments on one's notes).

Contribution: the system should help learners to see how they contribute to the progress of the group's knowledge.

Cross-fertilization: the system should maximize the chances of discovering interesting and useful related information.

Sociality: the system should be embedded in and help to integrate the intellectual and social life of the classroom.

An architecture for CSILE has been developed to support these design principles, and to facilitate the conscious, collaborative construction of shared knowledge in the classroom. The major component of this knowledge-building architecture is the community database, which involves all the knowledge entered in the system in the form of student-generated notes. A main characteristic of the database is its differentiation along two dimensions: knowledge-building environments and thematic spaces. The knowledge-building environments represent and foster different knowledge operations: the *Explanation* environment supports the search for coherent explanations of some facts and the testing of the explanatory power of hypotheses; the *How-it-works* environment guides the identification and elaboration of causal mechanisms; the *Meaning* environment supports the extraction of domain vocabulary from students' notes and the construction of a network of terms in a thematic space. The thematic spaces represent different topics and substantive domains involved in the database, such as fossil fuels, smoking and health, developments in Eastern and Central Europe. Both dimensions – knowledge-building environments and thematic spaces – should be considered as intersecting; for instance, working in the 'smoking and health' space students may want to find out why smoking often causes coughing, and, therefore, move from the undifferentiated *Home* environment to the *How-it-works* environment.

Procedural facilitation constitutes another component of the system, and is selectively used to stimulate learners to come up with more interesting notes than they produce spontaneously (e.g. 'My hypothesis is different from yours. I think . . . .'), and to support students in thinking more effectively about the content of their own notes. CSILE also involves background operations that are automatically executed without the intervention of the learner; one important example is providing students with information about related notes of interest, on the basis of an automatic screening of the entire database.

Some research results

CSILE has already been implemented in a number of schools, and the results are very promising. Working with 10- to 12-year-olds in an early school try-out, Scardamalia *et al.* (1989) observed that: 'Students used the system to elaborate models and hypotheses, to delve into difficult texts, to seek deeper levels of explanation, to elaborate confusions, and generally to engage in processes thought to be beyond their years' (p. 65). A more systematic study with the same age-group (Scardamalia and Bereiter, 1991) showed that children in the CSILE-environment can generate educationally productive or knowledge-building questions, i.e. questions which are valuable to guide further learning on a topic, because their investigation involves the potential to advance their knowledge and understanding substantially. Being able to ask such questions, beyond purely text-based ones, is seen as an indication that children can take responsibility for their own learning. With respect to two topics which differed in terms of the amount of children's prior knowledge – endangered species and fossil fuels – a significant number (46 per cent) of knowledge-building questions were generated (e.g. When an animal is endangered, how does it make a comeback? Does fossil fuel affect the ozone layer?). The same study demonstrated how cooperative knowledge-construction is supported in the CSILE environment. In this respect, CSILE allows for another form of cooperation than face-to-face (small) group work – cooperation through commenting on or using information from notes of other learners. For instance, a student can ask a question relating to a note of another pupil, refer to additional data sources, express a critical comment, etc.

Other data illustrate how students collaboratively elaborate a topic (e.g. fossil fuels) by producing a network of charts showing the different uses of fuels in the kitchen. One example of a result is a chart relating to wrapped food, accompanied by the following comment: 'The wrapping on this bowl of chilli is made of plastic. Plastic comes from petroleum. Plastic causes a lot of pollution. Wax paper is much better for the environment' (Scardamalia and Bereiter, 1991, p. 65).

In a more recent series of investigations, Scardamalia and Bereiter (in press) have shown that students in CSILE-supported classroom settings outperform pupils in control groups on measures relating to in-depth comprehension of difficult texts, explaining difficult concepts (e.g., continental drift) using graphics, and demonstrating in a written report what they have learned about a topic. The investigators also observed more mature views and beliefs about learning in students from a CSILE-supported classroom, especially the beliefs that understanding requires self-directed effort, and that they must assume an active role in order to take control over their own learning and thinking. Similar promising findings have emerged from other technology-orientated projects that also aim at restructuring whole classroom environments, on the basis of the same conception of learning as a constructive and distributed activity (see De Corte et al., 1992).

Such open environments are particularly suited to the gifted, for several reasons. First, they offer opportunities for active, self-initiated and persistent learning and problem-solving, for building meaning and creative production, and for reflection and self-regulation; thus, they match nicely some major characteristics of high performers. But in addition, those environments almost automatically take into account individual differences in abilities and motivation. Indeed, due to the fact that they have no 'ceiling', as compared to classroom situations based on traditional school programmes and curricula, they are flexible and challenging for talented students, and therefore stimulate them to push continually the limits of their performance levels. Powerful learning environments, as defined in this chapter, provide the gifted with opportunities for acceleration as well as for enrichment, and for studying in depth as well as for broadening their knowledge and skills. Although computers may not be a necessary component of productive and challenging instructional settings, there is no doubt that today their integration as tools for (distributed) learning and problem-solving can facilitate the design of powerful learning environments for gifted and talented students.

CONCLUSIONS

Recent research has questioned the traditional view that exceptional performance is highly determined by innate talent and abilities. Indeed, a substantial amount of current empirical work supports the opposite conception – that outstanding performance is acquired as a result of intensive and persistent training, experience and practice under optimal environmental conditions.

In this chapter, it has been shown that over the past few decades research in instructional psychology has built up a substantial knowledge base that can guide the design of optimal environmental conditions for the learning and teaching of the talented. Basing the teaching and learning of the gifted on the view of learning described above could contribute to initiating fundamental innovations in the general school system. But research in instructional psychology would certainly also benefit from a closer relationship with the study of giftedness and of the education of talented children and students. For instance, longitudinal studies are very helpful in unravelling the development of expertise in a particular domain.

Throughout this chapter it has been stressed that creating powerful environments for the elicitation of constructive learning processes involves an alteration in the position and role of the students, who have to become agents of their own acquisition processes. However, it is important to add that powerful learning environments also require fundamental changes in the role of the teacher. Instead of being the only source of information and having full control over the teaching-learning situation, as in the traditional classroom, the teacher becomes a 'privileged' member of the knowledge-building community, who creates an intellectually stimulating classroom climate, models learning and problem-solving activities, asks provoking questions, provides support to students through coaching and structuring, and fosters students' agency over and responsibility for their own learning.

The second focus of this chapter was on the education of talented pupils in school. However, fostering talent should start before children enter compulsory education. Therefore, creating optimal environmental conditions for the acquisition and development of exceptional performance should start as early as possible (see Freeman, 1995). Additionally appropriate support and guidance, in line with the basic ideas of powerful learning environments during early childhood at home and during pre-school education, are of the utmost importance.

NOTE

This chapter is based on the keynote lecture given at the 4th conference of the European Council for High Ability (ECHA) in Nijmegen, the Netherlands, October 1994.

REFERENCES

Ackerman, P.L., Sternberg, R.J. and Glaser, R. (eds) (1989) *Learning and Individual Differences: Advances in Theory and Research.* New York: Freeman.

Bereiter, C. and Scardamalia, M. (1989) 'Intentional learning as a goal of instruction', in L.B. Resnick (ed.), *Knowing, Learning, and Instruction. Essays in Honor of Robert Glaser.* Hillsdale, NJ: Erlbaum.

Boekaerts, M. (1988) 'Motivatie en cognitief functioneren van de leerling [Motivation and cognitive functioning of the pupil]', in G. Kanselaar, J.L. van der Linden and A. Pennings (eds), *Begaafdheid: Onderkenning and beinvloeding [Individual Differences in Giftedness: Identification and Education].* Amersfoort/Leuven: Acco.

Boekaerts, M. (1993) 'Being concerned with well-being and with learning', *Educational Psychologist,* **28**, 149–67.

Brown, J.S., Collins, A. and Duguid, P. (1989) 'Situated cognition and the culture of learning', *Educational Researcher,* **18** (1), 32–42.

Butler-Por, N. (1993) 'Underachieving gifted students', in K.A. Heller, F.J. Mönks and A.H. Passow (eds), *International Handbook of Research and Development of Giftedness and Talent.* Oxford: Pergamon.

Cheng, P. (1993) 'Metacognition and giftedness: the status of the relationship', *Gifted Child Quarterly,* **37**, 105–12.

Cobb, P. (1994) 'Constructivism and learning', in T. Husen and T.N. Postlethwaite (eds), *International Encyclopedia of Education.* (2nd edn). Oxford: Pergamon.

Cohen, L.M. and Ambrose, D.C. (1993) 'Theories and practices for differentiated education for the gifted and talented', in K.A. Heller, F.J. Mönks and A.H. Passow (eds), *International Handbook of Research and Development of Giftedness and Talent.* Oxford: Pergamon.

Cropley, A.J. (1993a) 'Giftedness and school: new issues and challenges. Guest editorial', *International Journal of Educational Research,* **19**, 3–4.

Cropley, A.J. (1993b) 'Giftedness: recent thinking', *International Journal of Educational Research,* **19**, 89–98.

De Corte, E. (1990) 'Acquiring and teaching cognitive skills: a state-of-the-art of theory and research', in P.J.D. Drenth, J.A. Sergeant and R.J. Takens (eds), *European Perspectives in Psychology.* Vol. 1. London: Wiley.

De Corte, E. (1993) 'Psychological aspects of changes in learning supported by informatics', in

D.C. Johnson and B. Samways (eds), *Informatics and Changes in Learning*. Proceedings of the IFIP TC3 WG3.1/3.5 Open Conference, Gmunden, Austria, June 1993. Amsterdam: Elsevier Science.

De Corte, E. (1995) 'Fostering cognitive growth: a perspective from research on mathematics learning and instruction', *Educational Psychologist*, **30**, 37–46.

De Corte, E., Greer, B. and Verschaffel, L. (1996) 'Mathematics teaching and learning', in D.C. Berliner and R.C. Calfee (eds), *Handbook of Educational Psychology*. New York: Macmillan.

De Corte, E., Linn, M.C., Mandl, H. and Verschaffel, L. (eds) (1992) *Computer-based Learning Environments and Problem Solving* (NATO ASI Series F: Computer and Systems Sciences, Vol. 84). Berlin: Springer-Verlag.

De Jong, F.P.C.M. (1992) *Zelfstandig leren. Regulatie van het leerproces en leren reguleren: Een procesbenadering [Independent Learning. Regulation of the Learning Process and Learning to Regulate: A Process Approach]*. Tilburg, The Netherlands: Katholieke Universiteit Brabant.

Dochy, F.J.R.C. (1992) *Assessment of Prior Knowledge as a Determinant for Future Learning*. Utrecht: Lemma.

Elshout, J. (1995) 'Talent: the ability to become an expert', Chapter 7, this volume.

Elshout, J., Veenman, M. and Van Hell, J. (1993) 'Using the computer as a help tool during learning by doing', *Computers and Education*, **21**, 115–22.

Ericsson, K.A and Charness, N. (1994) 'Expert performance: its structure and acquisition', *American Psychologist*, **49**, 725–47.

Fox, L.H. and Washington, J. (1985) 'Programs for the gifted and talented: past, present, and future', in F.D. Horowitz and M. O'Brien (eds), *The Gifted and Talented. Developmental Perspectives*. Washington, DC: American Psychological Association.

Freeman, J. (1995) 'Where talent begins'. Chapter 2, this volume.

Glaser, R. (1991) 'The maturing of the relationship between the science of learning and cognition and educational practice', *Learning and Instruction*, **1**, 129–44.

Glaser, R. and Bassock, M. (1989) 'Learning theory and the study of instruction', *Annual Review of Psychology*, **40**, 631–66.

Glaser, R. and Chi, M.T.H. (1988) 'Overview', in M.T.H. Chi, R. Glaser and M.J. Farr (eds), *The Nature of Expertise*. Hillsdale, NJ: Erlbaum.

Glaserfeld, E. von (ed.) (1991) *Radical Constructivism in Mathematics Education*. Dordrecht: Kluwer.

Greeno, J.G. (1991) 'Number sense as situated knowing in a conceptual domain', *Journal for Research in Mathematics Education*, **22**, 170–218.

Hayes, J.R. (1985) 'Three problems in teaching general skills', in S.F. Chipman, J.W. Segal and R. Glaser (eds), *Thinking and Learning Skills. Vol. 2: Research and Open Questions*. Hillsdale, NJ: Erlbaum.

Jackson, N.E. (1993) 'Moving into the mainstream? Reflections on the study of giftedness', *Gifted Child Quarterly*, **37**, 46–50.

Kanevsky, L. (1995) 'Group and individual differences in gifted students' learning potentials', *Roeper Review*, **17**, 157–63.

Lave, J. and Wenger, E. (1991) *Situated Learning. Legitimate Peripheral Participation*. Cambridge: Cambridge University Press.

Marton, F., Dall'Alba, G. and Beaty, E. (1993) 'Conceptions of learning', *International Journal of Educational Research*, **19**, 277–300.

Marton, F. and Säljö, R. (1984) 'Approaches to learning', in F. Marton, D.J. Hounsell and N.J. Entwistle (eds), *The Experience of Learning*. Edinburgh: Scottish Academic Press.

National Council of Teachers of Mathematics (1989) *Curriculum and Evaluation Standards for School Mathematics*. Reston, VA: NCTM.

Okagaki, L. and Sternberg, R.J. (1988) 'Unwrapping giftedness', in G. Kanselaar, J.L. van der Linden and A. Pennings (eds), *Begaafdheid: Onderkenning and beinvloeding [Individual Differences in Giftedness: Identification and Education]*. Amersfoort/Leuven: Acco.

Overtoom-Corsmit, R., Dekker, R. and Span, P. (1990) 'Information processing in intellectually highly gifted children by solving mathematical tasks', *Gifted Education International*, **6**, 143–8.

Perkins, D.N., Jay, E. and Tishman, S. (1993) 'Beyond abilities: a dispositional theory of thinking', *Merrill Palmer Quarterly*, **39**, 1–21.
Resnick, L.B. (1994) 'Situated rationalism: biological and social preparation for learning', in L. Hirschfeld and S. Gelman (eds), *Mapping the Mind: Domain Specificity in Cognition and Culture*. Cambridge: Cambridge University Press.
Salomon, G. (ed.) (1993) *Distributed Cognitions: Psychological and Educational Considerations*. Cambridge: Cambridge University Press.
Salomon, G. and Globerson, T. (1987) 'Skill may not be enough: the role of mindfulness in learning and transfer', *International Journal of Educational Research*, **11**, 623–37.
Scardamalia, M. and Bereiter, C. (1991) 'Higher levels of agency for children in knowledge building: a challenge for the design of new knowledge media', *Journal of the Learning Sciences*, **1**, 37–68.
Scardamalia, M. and Bereiter, C. (1992) 'An architecture for collaborative knowledge building', in E. De Corte, M.C. Linn, H. Mandl and L. Verschaffel (eds), *Computer-based Learning Environments and Problem Solving* (NATO ASI Series F: Computer and Systems Sciences, Vol. 84). Berlin: Springer-Verlag.
Scardamalia, M. and Bereiter, C. (in press) 'Adaptation and understanding: a case for new cultures of schooling', in S. Vosniadou, E. De Corte, H. Mandl and R. Glaser (eds), *International Perspectives on the Design of Computer-supported Learning Environments*. Hillsdale, NJ: Erlbaum.
Scardamalia, M., Bereiter, C., McLean, R.S., Swallow, J. and Woodruff, E. (1989) 'Computer-supported intentional learning environments', *Journal of Educational Computing Research*, **5**, 51–68.
Scardamalia, M., Bereiter, C. and Steinbach, R. (1984) 'Teachability of reflective processes in written composition', *Cognitive Science*, **8**, 173–90.
Schneider, W. (1993) 'Acquiring expertise: determinants of exceptional performance', in K.A. Heller, F.J. Mönks and A.H. Passow (eds), *International Handbook of Research and Development of Giftedness and Talent*. Oxford: Pergamon.
Shuell, T.J. (1992) 'Designing instructional computing systems for meaningful learning', in M. Jones and P.H. Winne (eds), *Adaptive Learning Environments: Foundations and Frontiers*. (NATO ASI Series F: Computer and Systems Sciences, Vol. 85.) Berlin: Springer-Verlag.
Simons, P.R. (1989) 'Learning to learn', in P. Span, E. De Corte and B. van Hout-Wolters (eds), *Onderwijsleerprocessen: Strategieen voor de verwerking van informatie. [Teaching-learning Processes: Strategies for Information Processing]*. Amsterdam/Lisse: Swets and Zeitlinger.
Span, P. (1995) 'Self-regulated learning by talented children'. Chapter 6, this volume.
Vermunt, J.D.H.M. (1992) *Leerstijlen en sturen van leerprocessen in het hoger onderwijs: Naar procesgerichte instructie in zelfstandig denken [Learning Styles and Regulation of Learning Processes in Higher Education: Toward Process-oriented Instruction in Independent Thinking]*. Amsterdam/Lisse: Swets and Zeitlinger.
Vosniadou, S. (1992) 'Knowledge acquisition and conceptual change', *Applied Psychology: An International Journal*, **41**, 347–57.
Vygotsky, L.S. (1978) *Mind in Society. The Development of Higher Psychological Processes*. Cambridge, MA: MIT Press.

Chapter 6

Self-regulated Learning by Talented Children
Pieter Span

Even by the beginning of this century the phrase 'Help me to do it myself' epitomized the philosophy of Montessori education; but it is only within the last two decades that the capacity for self-regulated or autonomous learning has become recognized as a major area of concern in educational psychology. Simons (1989) and Simons and Beukhof (1987) offered this brief and succinct description: 'Self-regulation pertains to the extent to which one is able to be one's own teacher. Self-regulation thus means: being able to prepare one's own learning, to take the necessary steps to learn, to regulate learning, to provide one's own feedback, and to keep oneself concentrated and motivated' (p. 4).

The use of such skills is so important in children's development that many are of the opinion that they should be taught to all pupils; as the influential American psychologist, Robert Glaser wrote:

> Transitioning the control of learning from teachers to students is a fundamental problem for educational research. Studies have revealed that children are ingenious in controlling their own learning. This capability develops early, to various extents, and it can be significantly enhanced with appropriate conditions of instruction and learning. Learners actively explore their environments, test beliefs and theories by their actions, and modify their approaches. The gradual refinement and tuning of these skills and learning strategies should be a major outcome of the school experience. Schools should give close attention to developing 'expert novices' who, although they may not possess sufficient background knowledge in a new field, know how to go about gaining that knowledge.
>
> (Glaser, 1987, p. 5)

In order to bring about autonomous learning, however, an essential two-part question must be answered: What are the most appropriate conditions of instruction, and are these conditions the same for average and highly able pupils? This chapter is concerned with the answers.

EUROPEAN HISTORICAL FOUNDATIONS

Several European countries have had a long tradition of psychological research and theory in intellectual meta-activities, if under a variety of terminologies – learning techniques, learning-to-learn, learning-to-think, and recently, self-regulation. However, because so much of this material has not been published in English, it was rarely referred to outside a relatively small group of academics. In fact, studies of self-regulation had started in Europe by the 1920s. The German psychologist Lobsien (1917) began by carrying out experiments with 9- and 10-year-old pupils, in which the subjects had to memorize texts. Some, he found, read the text as a whole, others divided it into parts, and yet others used either method depending on the text. Additionally, some studied very actively, trying to structure their learning and repeating salient parts, while others were passive in their studies, just reading the text over and over again. Lobsien suggested that because each pupil used his or her own method to memorize, it would not be possible to allocate a best method to all of them. He attributed the differences between their styles of memorization to personality differences.

Continuing Lobsien's work, his compatriot Herrmann (1929) gave 14-year-olds the task of memorizing history texts. He agreed that about 50 per cent of the pupils not only used more than one method, but that they adjusted their method to the structure of the text. Most importantly, those who used a variety of methods achieved better results than those who only used one method. Herrmann introduced the phrase 'learning technique' to describe the different intellectual ways in which the children worked. In his view, such learning techniques were a matter of spontaneous development, although he did accept that they could be stimulated and acquired.

The inspiring experimental work of Otto Selz (only known about and influential after it was described by George Humphrey in English in 1951) suggested that Herrmann's 'learning techniques' offered a way to gain insight into learning problems. Further, because intelligence certainly could be defined in terms of problem-solving, it should be possible to raise children's intelligence by teaching them learning techniques or activities (German: *Verhaltensweisen*). This hypothesis was tested by the German psychologists G. Sand and J. Andrae (referred to by Selz, 1935). In one experiment, Andrae gave children of 11, 12, and 13 years of age an intelligence test composed of five subtests. Then he trained half the pupils (the experimental group) on just one subtest, after which he tested the whole sample again with all the subtests. He found that, in fact, although both groups did better because of the overall practice effect, the trained experimental group did very much better than the non-trained – not only for the subtest for which the subjects had received training, but also for the other subtests. Andrae's conclusion was that the learning techniques had been transferred from the selected task to the four others: in other words, a child's score of measured intelligence could be enhanced through training.

This conclusion was very influential in such countries as the Netherlands, Belgium and South Africa where psychologists could read Selz's work in German; the move to practise his theories spread widely within education, even resulting in a school dedicated to such teaching in Ghent. Indeed, between 1930 and 1950, this movement strengthened the argument for 'nurturism' in the nature-or-nurture debate about differences in intelligence.

During these two decades, several further experiments were carried out in real classroom situations in these countries with 10- to 12-year-olds (Prins, 1951). It was found that their achievements, in subjects such as geography and history, could be improved by guiding the pupils to practise learning techniques. But it became apparent that in mixed-ability classes the experimenters used the better-achieving pupils as 'models' to help the others learn. Today, this situation in which the pupils learn from each other is called cooperative learning. On the whole, the researchers concluded that, certainly at that age, learning ability, which they equated with intelligence, could indeed be fostered by teaching those techniques. The outstanding finding, however, was that although most of the children benefited by this cooperative learning method, some of them did not need it at all, because they were already using efficient means of their own.

TEACHING–LEARNING ARRANGEMENTS

There is now ample scientific evidence demonstrating that in order to learn autonomously most pupils need help from their teachers (Paris and Byrne, 1989). But until recently, there have been few reliable indications as to the optimum teaching–learning arrangements for its promotion. When the Belgian educational researcher Joost Lowyck was looking for evidence of ways in which teachers adapted their teaching to help highly able pupils towards autonomous learning, his findings threw him into a state of 'disillusion' (Lowyck, 1988). A typical example of neglect in this area, Lowyck wrote, was Paul Torrance's (1986) chapter 'Teaching creative and gifted learners' in the third *Handbook of Research on Teaching*, which failed to offer a single word about the interaction of teachers with the highly able. Lowyck probably overlooked Donald Treffinger's work (Treffinger, 1975; Treffinger and Barton, 1979).

Yet even before discussing what teachers do (or do not do) in their teaching, it is pertinent to consider the activities which the learners themselves have to carry out during the teaching–learning process. These activities are not only influenced by the teacher but also by the nature of the task and the pupil's individual abilities.

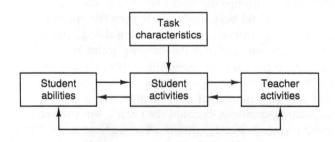

Figure 6.1 *Influences on student activities*

Educational researchers agree that there are at least three phases in the teaching–learning arrangements, each one including several regulating activities, called by the present author 'meta-activities', as follows:

1. The preparation of learning
   - orientation on goals, strategies and time
   - anticipation of problems and choice of strategies
   - actualizing prerequisite learning
2. The regulation of learning
   - monitoring the process of change
   - testing and questioning
   - revision
3. The evaluation of the learning process
   - looking for feedback
   - judgement of performance

In schools, the influence of the task or goal is a much-neglected aspect of the learning process, although its characteristics inevitably influence the styles of learning the pupil uses. It is the task itself which determines whether surface learning will be adequate to reach the goal, or whether deeper learning is needed. Deep learning differs from surface learning with regard to the attention devoted to the underlying meaning, and to the use of constructive or creative activities (Marton and Säljö, 1984). But deep learning is not always the most appropriate, such as in the learning of simple texts which have to be remembered only for a short time. However, it is the individual differences between pupils, their capabilities, which influence the selection of possible routes of learning. Although most are only capable of using the most superficial procedures, the highly intelligent can more often perceive and use the indications of the goal to choose between them.

In America, Robert Sternberg (1985) has recognized the value of styles of learning in his theories about intelligence. He proposes three mechanisms of intelligent functioning: 'metacomponents' – the considerations about styles – as well as 'performance components', and 'knowledge acquisition components' – this last mechanism being a popular research area for cognitive psychologists. These metacomponents, he says, characterize intelligent performance, and they are in large part responsible for the 'general factor' in mental ability tests. They are also seen as responsible for figuring out how to perform a particular task, and making sure that the task is done correctly. This is said to be true for the entire learning task, including the phases of planning, monitoring and evaluation – in which he is in agreement with Simons (1988). Relatively simple models have the tendency over the course of time to become more and more complex. In the reality of school life, self-regulation is a complicated and dynamic process including many, interacting factors. In an attempt to encompass all the significant factors Simons (1992) referred to the work of Borkowski and Muthukrishna (1992) who combined seven simple models into one complex one. The simple models relate to: the idea of 'strategy', knowledge about alternative strategies, the use of strategies, emotional and motivational conditions, general and area-specific knowledge (extremely important: compare Glaser, 1984, and Howe, 1991), and self-concept. In view of this complexity one can understand the difficulties with regard to guiding the process of development and learning of meta-activities. How do these meta-activities develop, and how could they be trained and taught?

THE DEVELOPMENT OF META-ACTIVITIES

In his cultural-historical theory, derived from experimental work in the 1920s, the Russian Lev Vygotsky stressed the idea that the so-called higher mental functions in babies and children, such as thinking and memory, develop in interaction with other human beings. The essential foundation of human interaction means that the development of intelligent behaviour is dependent on the passing on of culture (Vygotsky, 1978). Yet ironically, it was just because of difficulties in communicating these ideas across languages and cultures that they only became available in Western Europe in the early 1960s, and did not become familiar to English-speaking scholars until the 1970s, via sources such as the publications of Michael Cole (see Vygotsky, 1978).

Working with young children with the cultural-historical model, the American James Wertsch tried to provide some answers to the question of how some pupils find learning strategies for themselves, without having being taught them, while others do not. One of his experiments (Wertsch, 1979) did indeed demonstrate the substance of Vygotsky's theory, while providing an answer to the question of autonomous learning in middle childhood. He had presented young children of about 2½ to 4½ years old with a difficult problem, that of constructing a wooden truck carrying a load of six boxes. The mothers were present and were encouraged to help the children by asking questions, such as 'Did you look at the example?', 'Where are you going to start?', 'What kind of piece do you need now?' It seemed that the mothers did not need to ask the older ones these kinds of questions, because the children asked and answered the questions of themselves in monologue – a self-guiding function of speech. The younger children, though, needed their mothers to formulate the questions.

Wertsch concluded that the monologue had developed – become interiorized – from the dialogue begun in earlier years by the mothers. He went on to generalize that children's acquisition of learning techniques does in fact come from their social context, and that parents and teachers are responsible for the passing on of thinking strategies to children. The children's use of the self-guiding function of speech represents a shift from regulation by others to self-regulation; thinking does not develop spontaneously, but instead has to be actively promoted by adults in their interactions with young children. Some children (and some parents) are more successful in this respect than others, developing to a higher level of intelligent functioning at an earlier age.

Yet, when Gerhard Lehwald (1989; 1990) worked with highly intelligent children in Leipzig, he found that even with their advanced abilities, some used efficient meta-activities while others did not. Searching for the explanation, he put forward the idea of what he calls the 'missing link' of curiosity or quest for knowledge. By this he referred to the way that some children have a thirst or motivation to accumulate and consider more information. He then compared two groups of highly able adolescents (eighth grade), who differed only in their levels of measured curiosity, on the style of their attempts to solve science problems. Firstly, the findings showed that when the children were compared on a measure of motivation, those with high scores planned and evaluated their solutions (as Simons could have predicted), and what is more, they often made the decision not to ask for help from the experimenter (as Wertsch had also found). Secondly, the high scorers did not try to find solutions for the several isolated problems, but instead looked for rules or laws which would be valid for a category of problems. He found similar results for younger adolescents (6th grade) who were confronted with physical balance problems. Lehwald's 'quest for knowledge', thus appears to be an important condition for self-regulated learning during problem solving by highly able adolescents.

Lehwald also gave problems to 4-, 5- and 6-year-old children, who were asked to build a motorway from wooden blocks. Even by that age, the highly intelligent and motivated children showed that they were able to systematically explore the task using the kind of meta-activities discussed above. In line with the theories of both Vygotsky and Wertsch, Lehwald hypothesized that the parents of these young children offered them meta-cognitive hints while they were solving problems together during play, instead of simply giving them the solutions. It looks as though it is as a result of favourable social processes that children acquire the confidence to explore the environment, which in turn encourages the development of their problem-solving behaviour. As a result, such children are able to expand their cognitive abilities independently, on the basis of their own activities, i.e. self-regulated learning.

TRAINING PROGRAMMES FOR SELF-REGULATED LEARNING

The Israeli psychologist Reuven Feuerstein (1980) is one of the few who have attempted to systematize instruction for improving learning along the lines of Vygotskyan theory. He says that the role of the teacher, whom he calls the 'mediator', is to assist the passage of information and style of thinking from the culture by modifying it in such a way that it is acceptable to the child. In an overview of Feuerstein's outlook and his Instrumental Enrichment (IE) programme, Frances Link explains:

> The core of the IE programme is a three-year series of problem-solving tasks and exercises that are grouped in 14 areas of specific cognitive development. They are called instruments rather than lessons because in and of themselves they are virtually free of specific subject matter. Their purpose is to serve as the means or vehicle for cognition-orientated reactions between teacher and students. Each instrument's true goal is not the learner's acquisition of information, but the development, refinement, and crystallisation of functions that are prerequisite to effective thinking. In terms of behaviour, IE's ultimate aim is to transform retarded performance by altering their characteristically passive, and dependent cognitive style so that they become more active, self-motivated, independent thinkers.
>
> (Link, 1991)

Feuerstein says that in order for autonomous learning to become part of a student's repertoire, it is vital that the process of mediation (i.e. what passes from mediator to learner) should be concerned with 'regulation and control of behaviour', 'goal seeking', 'goal setting', 'goal planning' and 'challenge: the search for knowledge and complexity'. Although Feuerstein (1990) has outlined how the programme could be used for the highly able, he has not in fact tried out these ideas in practice. So far, the growing volume of research on IE has shown it to be effective when it is used for 'backward' children (Savell *et al.*, 1986; Blagg, 1991) although Feuerstein's theory has been particularly criticized with regard to the supposed 'unlimited plasticity of cognitive functioning' (Frisby, 1993). It is possible the programme would be helpful with young highly able children, because what he is presenting is fundamental and essential for high-level cognitive development (in line with the research and conclusions of Wertsch and Lehwald).

Frisby (1993) also refers to Arthur Jensen's First Law of Individual Differences: when a wide range of individuals are exposed to a systematic cognitive intervention programme, the intervention will have the effect of increasing the average scores of all subgroups, as well as individual differences. In other words, advanced children would profit more. However, research indicates that because older highly able children are convinced of the effectiveness of their meta-activities, they do not feel the need to change them. For them, notably detailed directions given by a teacher can actually interfere with their self-regulation capacities (van der Sanden *et al.*, 1988) – a situation which Richard Clark (1989) has captured succinctly in his phrase 'teaching kills learning'. He explained that the need for the teacher to provide all kinds of mental structures to foster the development of complex thinking should fade as pupils develop and show their capacity to handle these processes autonomously. Highly able pupils do not profit from detailed prompts by teachers: on the contrary, they are obstructed by them. (This is also described by the young people themselves in Joan Freeman's [1991] longitudinal British study.)

This development of autonomy in the learning of the highly able is in clear contrast to that of lower-ability pupils, for whom the external teacher regulations often compensate for their lack of internal regulation. For them, when external regulation is missing they often fall back on simple trial and error. The equation is relatively straightforward: the more able an individual is the more self-regulation will be needed for high achievement: the less able the individual is the more teacher regulation is needed. This is an example of the mechanism of 'aptitude-treatment-interaction' (Cronbach and Snow, 1977), meaning that the teacher's style has to interact with the child's aptitude for the best individual results, the understanding of which provides the basis for successful mixed-ability teaching (see Figure 6.2).

Because of the demonstrated and clear importance of early mediation to the development of autonomous learning, several researchers are somewhat sceptical about the value of learning-to-learn programmes in later life. One or two hours a week at school seems inadequate to repair the damage done during several years of neglect in early life. The currently available learning-to-learn and learning-to-think programmes (such as de Bono, 1976), often have no robust research evidence to back them, and in spite of their commercial success, are decidedly controversial. There is thus a recognized need for some well structured and reliable means of helping children towards improving the independence of their learning and thinking. Experimental work is vital for the development of cognitive training methods which could provide the means of helping the essential processes for performance, not only

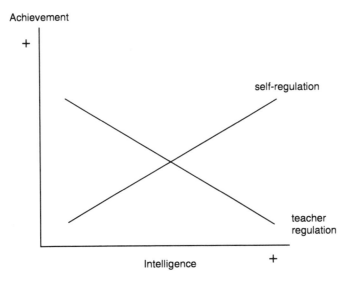

Figure 6.2 *The effect on achievement of the interaction between intelligence and kind of teaching*

in tests of mental ability, but in life problems. Researchers in this area are not only interested in getting improvement on a single task in a single situation, but also in showing the durability of training over time, as well as the transfer of training from the task on which performance is trained to other similar tasks (Sternberg, 1985).

During the last decade the debate as to whether meta-activities are context-free has become intense. Although programme designers, such as de Bono and Feuerstein say the 'tools', as de Bono calls them, are independent, both are generalists and believe in very broad transfer effects, which they say can spread from one domain to another. Others, such as Brown, Campione and Palincsar, disagree, choosing rather to provide instructional strategies in carefully selected domains, such as reading comprehension. This kind of specific skill teaching goes under the name of 'infusion' (Brown and Palincsar, 1987). All agree though, that there are general learning skills which are often used in specific situations, and that within such a specified situation they can be transferred to new problems by the pupil, even by the ages of 3 and 4. But this is only when the following conditions prevail:

- they are familiar with the problem domains;
- their attention is directed to the underlying goal structure;
- pupils are shown how problems resemble each other;
- examples are accompanied with rules, particularly when they are formulated by the pupils themselves;
- the learning takes place in a social context – 'reciprocal teaching'.

Regardless of the conditions necessary for the transfer of learning within specific areas, there are at least three arguments that favour the views of the generalists:

(1) 'Some people seem generally smart, not just knowledgeable, but insightful, no matter the subject' (Perkins and Salomon, 1989).
(2) It is important to recognize that general skills are an essential component of high-level behaviour, and in fact '... it may be that gifted people are gifted because they are more likely to use such skills to build up and use their knowledge' (Rabinowitz and Glaser, 1985).
(3) Experts often fall back on the application of general strategies if they are confronted with unfamiliar problems. If knowledge fails, the difference in approach between experts on the one hand and novices on the other becomes clear – the novices do not have access to the general strategies. In unfamiliar tasks, however, the approach of highly able novices resembles the approach of experts (Schoenfeld and Hermann, 1982; Elshout, 1988; 1995).

It can be supposed that for highly able pupils, because of their expert strategies, their deep-level information processing, and sometimes their expert knowledge, they themselves create the above-mentioned transfer conditions. They look for analogical problems, try to find the underlying goal structure and formulate the rules themselves. In other words, they regulate their own learning. In this respect, Gavriel Salomon (1987) speaks of the 'high road' of learning. High road transfer is a result of what might be called mindful abstraction. This involves the deliberate metacognitively guided removal of all the irrelevant principles and procedures from context of the problem – defining, extracting and working with only those points which are needed for solving the problem. When equipped with such abstractions, high road transfer enables the thinker to apply ideas from any one area to another entirely different one, e.g. applying thermodynamic principles to the analysis of family relations.

TEACHING SELF-REGULATION IN SCHOOL

With regard to systematic instruction in school, Paris and Byrne (1989) distinguish three types of instruction.

(1) *Direct instruction and explanation of learning strategies.* The present author holds the view that this type of instruction (treatment) does not match the learning style (aptitude) of highly able pupils.
(2) *Peer tutoring and dialogues about learning.* For example reciprocal teaching, Socratic discussion, apprenticeship models and dialogical learning.
(3) *Cooperative learning*, including group discussion, argument and co-construction of appropriate learning strategies.

It is not difficult to explain why some parts of types 2 and 3 do match the learning of highly able pupils.

(a) In modern cognitive apprenticeship (Collins *et al.*, 1989) two issues are emphasized. Primarily the teaching is aimed at demonstrating the processes that experts use to handle complex tasks. Conceptual and factual knowledge are exemplified and situated in the context of their use, and there is a dual focus, on expert processes and situated learning. Secondly, cognitive apprenticeship refers to the learning, through guided experience, of cognitive and metacognitive skills and processes. This necessitates the externalization of these skills and processes in the teacher, which makes it possible for the pupil to observe a model of a complex skill.

(b) Socratic teachers (Brown and Palincsar, 1989) try to reach their goals by a variety of questioning activities that force pupils to elaborate, justify and provide warrants and backings for their statements. The method models modes of scientific thought, rather than conveying a particular set of content material.

(c) The cooperative learning method allows the pupils to explain their reasoning to each other (Brown and Palincsar, 1989), and is directly connected to Vygotsky's theory. Cooperative teaching–learning interactions in the classroom are ideal for helping pupils take the leap to higher levels of understanding, stimulating shared expertise, and fostering cognitive conflict and reflection.

However, the likelihood of introducing all or even some of these methods for stimulating self-regulation in regular education seems to be slight. In the 1990s the complaints of Reis and Renzulli (1984) are still valid:

> We found that many students in advanced classes said that there was never time within their classes for independent or small group study or opportunities to pursue avenues of interest that were frequently sparked by reading assignments or teacher-led discussions . . . there was never time for in depth excursions into self-selected topics because there was always more content to cover. What happens in many secondary schools is that the processes of independent study and self-directed learning are caught in a tidal wave of content and eventually drowned. Instead, the student is cast as a perceptual 'consumer of information' day-after-day and year-after-year.

Because they need to transmit information, teachers come up against several barriers to implementing instructional methods for autonomous learning for their highly able pupils (Clark, 1990). Although they try to allocate different methods to different pupils in the same classroom (in line with the aptitude-treatment-interaction model) they lack the measuring instruments to find out the quantity and quality of their pupils' meta-activities. So, the usual method in classroom practice of finding the optimal 'match' between the teacher's behaviour and the highly able pupil's learning is more or less by trial-and-error. Unfortunately, since the 1970s there has been accumulating doubt about the teacher's capacities in this respect. Doyle (1986) argues that certain 'intervening variables' should be distinguished between the behaviour of the teacher and the learning of the pupil. He mentions two kinds, cognitive and situational (see Figure 6.3).

Cognitive variables concern the pupil's cognitive processing in the teaching–learning situation. This occurs during the solving of problems, the scanning of designs, during actualizing prerequisite knowledge and so on. Attempts by cognitive psychologists, however, to adapt the instruction directly to the learning of the pupils turned out to be far too optimistic. It is not justifiable to expect teachers – lacking the time, the adequate skills and instruments – to be able to diagnose the particularities of cognitive processing in their individual pupils (de Jong, 1992). The two favourable methods of instruction mentioned earlier did not demand this, but are concerned mainly with the externalization of the way of thinking of the teacher, or in

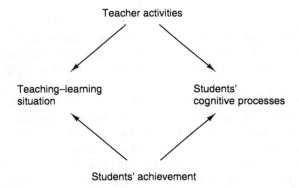

Figure 6.3 *Intervening variables between teacher and student*

Feuerstein's terms, of the mediator. It is only during discussion that a teacher can gain an idea about the quality of the pupil's thinking; therefore it is the task of the teacher being the second intervening variable, to optimize the teaching–learning situation.

Current literature on the curriculum for highly able students often refers to 'the learning environment', i.e. the psychological and physical environment in which learning is to occur; this includes work by the American, June Maker (1982a; 1982b), which is entirely in line with the theme of this chapter. However, the teaching–learning situation also includes the content of the curriculum, the activities of the pupils evoked by the curriculum, and the product which emerges as a result of the activities. These four aspects should be adapted to the characteristics in the learning of highly able children.

Content. The major focus of discussions should be on abstract concepts and generalizations, ideas that have a wide range of applicability or that transfer both within and across disciplines or fields of study. (We have already explained the preference for autonomous transfer activities by highly able students.) The abstract ideas need to be as complex as possible. The complexity can be determined by, for example, the diversity of the disciplines that must be integrated to comprehend the idea. These requirements mean that the learning tasks often should exceed the regular curriculum.

Process. The curriculum should include more open-ended than closed tasks, because openness stimulates divergent thinking. Tasks which require inductive reasoning should be stressed, so methods of instruction that make the use of meta-activities explicit can be used by the teacher during guided discovery, individually or in small groups.

Product. The products should differ from the average student's products. They should address real problems in line with the quest for 'situated learning'. They should represent transformations of existing information, more or less originally. This does not mean that the outcome should be left to the pupil, with no involvement by the teacher. The teacher remains responsible for the level of processing and the quality of the skills (HMI, 1992).

Learning environment. This environment should allow the implementation of the mentioned characteristics of content, process and product, as well as – the subject of this chapter – the self-regulation of the pupil. If teachers do not provide the opportunity for self-regulating activities, pupils cannot practise them. Consequently, the teachers may complain that the pupils are not able to learn independently, and the like. This certainly not only refers to moving in and out of the classroom and having access to the materials and equipment, but particularly to the aspects of the teaching–learning situation mentioned at the beginning of this chapter: preparation, regulation and evaluation of the learning process.

De Jong (1992) distinguished seven distinct environments in which self-regulation activities can be learned:

- discovery learning
- guided discovery
- observational learning
- guided participation
- content independent courses
- direct explanation by a teacher
- dyadic instruction

He located the research concerning self-regulation in these seven environments and recorded the amount of pupil success. It appeared that, first – independently of the kind of environment – the self-regulation process should be made explicit. Secondly, responsive social-interactive learning situations give the best results. Although these findings do not specifically concern the highly able learner, they concur with the chain of reasoning in this chapter. The general conclusion could be, therefore, to start teaching in – preferably – interactive situations early, and make meta-activities explicit as soon as possible.

DISCUSSION

It should be emphasized that this chapter only sets out to deal with the metacognitive aspect of information processing in highly able learners, as distinct from information acquisition *per se* – although both are necessary for the learning of complex matter. There is little argument that individuals who have an extensive knowledge of a specific domain will achieve at a higher level than those with a limited knowledge (Chi et al., 1988; Elshout, 1995). It is likely that the demonstrable ease with which the highly able acquire knowledge is in part explained by their high-level system of meta-activities.

Research in the area of metacognition has mostly been limited to children's learning from about the age of 4, and although we have general guidelines, still too little is known about the precise nature of influences on its development during infancy (but see Freeman, 1995). However, such findings that do exist lead to the conclusion that there is support for Vygotsky's line of thought. It is highly probable that the learning of meta-activities during infancy can be understood as interiorization of cognitive activities through social interaction, as well as through his concept of the 'zone of proximal development' – the child's potential area of development which needs mediation by others to function. But it is also certain that the metacognitive activities of children are influenced by their innate potential. The complexity and interweave of innate and acquired cognitive skills and metacognitive activities has been clearly demonstrated in recent work on linguistic development (Gombert, 1992). Hence, in spite of the theoretical standpoint of Vygotsky and his followers, Piaget's support for so-called innate intelligence structures which motivate children to interact with the environment is still valuable, particularly with regard to the motivated autonomous learning of highly able infants.

A major goal of this chapter is to warn against the neglect of the teaching and learning of meta-activities for the highly able. Metacognition is not only intellectual, but is a mixture of attitudes and strategies. The attitudinal aspects are, for example, the elements of curiosity, persistence and confidence; general strategies include planning, monitoring and evaluation. For example, work with highly achieving, intellectually gifted young adolescents showed that on multiple indices of psychological adjustment, the intellectually gifted were comparable to older adolescents with similar cognitive skills, but differed from their age-mates (Luthar et al., 1992). It is clear that those who make use of both 'will and skill', those who are not only persistent, but who also plan and evaluate, will be more successful than those who do not regulate their own learning.

REFERENCES

Blagg, N. (1991). *Can We Teach Intelligence?* London: Erlbaum.
Borkowski, J.G. and Muthukrishna, N. (1992) 'Moving metacognition into the classroom: "working models" and effective strategy teaching', in M. Pressley, K.K. Harris and G.T. Guthrie (eds), *Promoting Academic Competence and Literacy in School*. San Diego: Academic Press.
Brown, A.L. and Palincsar, A.S. (1987) 'Reciprocal teaching of comprehension strategies: a natural history of one program for enhancing learning', in J.D. Day and J. Borkowsky (eds), *Intelligence and Exceptionality*. Norwood, NJ: Ablex.
Brown, A.L. and Palincsar, A.S. (1989) 'Guided, cooperative learning and individual knowledge acquisition', in L.B. Resnick (ed.), *Knowing, Learning and Instruction*. Hillsdale, NJ: Erlbaum.
Chi, M.T.H., Glaser, R. and Farr, M.J. (1988) *The Development of Expertise*. Hillsdale, NJ: Erlbaum.
Clark, R.E. (1989) 'When teaching kills learning: studies of mathemathanic effects', in H. Mandl, E. De Corte, N. Bennett and H.F. Friedrich (eds), *Learning and Instruction*. Oxford: Pergamon.
Clark, R.E. (1990) 'A cognitive theory of instructional method'. A paper presented at the American Educational Research Association Conference, Boston.
Collins, A., Brown, J.S. and Newman, S.E. (1989) 'Cognitive apprenticeship: teaching the crafts of reading, writing and mathematics', in L.B. Resnick (ed.), *Knowing, Learning and Instruction*. Hillsdale, NJ: Erlbaum.
Cronbach, L.J. and Snow, R.E. (1977) *Aptitudes and Instructional Methods*. New York: Irvington.
de Bono, E. (1976) *Teaching Thinking*. London: Temple Smith.
de Jong, F.P.C.M. (1992) *Zelfstandig leren: Regulatie van het leerproces en het leren reguleren: Een procesbenadering*. Tilburg: Diss. K.U.B.
Doyle, W. (1986) 'Classroom organization and management', in M.C. Wittrock (ed.), *Handbook of Research on Teaching*. New York: Macmillan.
Elshout, J. (1988) 'Intelligence and a correct start', in G. Kanselaar, J.L. van der Linden and A. Pennings (eds), *Begaafdheid: Onderkenning and beinvloeding [Individual Differences in Giftedness, Identification and Education]*. Amersfoort/Leuven: Acco.

Elshout, J. (1995) 'Talent: the ability to become an expert'. Chapter 7, this volume.
Feuerstein, R. (1980) *Instrumental Enrichment*. Baltimore, MD: University Park Press.
Feuerstein, R. (1990) 'The gifted underachievers and mediated learning experience'. Paper given at the 2nd conference of the European Council for High Ability, Budapest.
Freeman, J. (1991) *Gifted Children Growing Up*. London: Cassell.
Freeman, J. (1995) 'Where talent begins'. Chapter 2, this volume.
Frisby, C.L. (1993) 'Feuerstein's theory of mediated learning: all things to all people?' *Contemporary Psychology*, **38** (11), 1169–71.
Glaser, R. (1984) 'Education and thinking: the role of knowledge', *American Psychologist*, 93–104.
Glaser, R. (1987) 'Teaching expert novices', *Educational Researcher*, **16**(9), 5.
Gombert, J.E. (1992) *Metalinguistic Development*. New York: Harvester/Wheatsheaf.
Herrmann, A. (1929) 'Über die Fähigkeit zu selbständigem Lernen und die natürlichen Lernweisen zur Zeit der Volksschulreife', *Zeitschrift für Psychologie*, **109**, 116ff.
HMI (1992) *The Education of Very Able Children in Maintained Schools*. London: HMSO.
Howe, M.J.A. (1991) 'A fine idea but does it work?' *Education Section Review*, **15** (2), 43–7.
Humphrey, G. (1951) *Thinking*. London: Methuen.
Lehwald, G. (1989) 'Curiosity, metacognition, and transfer performance of gifted children'. Madrid: EARLI conference.
Lehwald, G. (1990) 'Curiosity and exploratory behaviour in ability development', *European Journal for High Ability*, **1**, 204–10.
Link, F.R. (1991) 'Instrumental enrichment: a strategy for cognitive and academic improvement', in S. Maclure and P.Davies (eds), *Learning to Think: Thinking to Learn*. Oxford: Pergamon Press.
Lobsien, M. (1917) *Die Lernweisen der Schüler*. Leipzig: Ernst Wunderlich.
Lowyck, J. (1988) 'Research into the teaching and learning of the gifted', in G. Kanselaar, J.L. van der Linden and A. Pennings (eds), *Individual Differences in Giftedness: Identification and Education*. Amersfoort/Leuven: Acco. [in Dutch]
Luthar, S.S., Zigler, E. and Goldstein, D. (1992), 'Psychosocial adjustment among intellectually gifted adolescents: the role of cognitive-developmental and experiential factors', *Journal of Child Psychology and Psychiatry*, **33**, 361–73.
Maker, C.J. (1982a) *Teaching Models in Education of the Gifted*. Arizona: Aspen.
Maker, C.J. (1982b) *Curriculum Development for the Gifted*. Arizona: Aspen.
Marton, F. and Säljö, R. (1984) 'Approaches to learning', in F. Marton, D.J. Hounsell and N.J. Entwistle (eds), *The Experience of Learning*. Edinburgh: S.A. Press.
Paris, S.G. and Byrne, J.P. (1989) 'The constructivist approach to self-regulation and learning in the classroom', in B.J. Zimmerman and D.H. Schunk (eds), *Self-regulated Learning and Academic Achievement: Theory, Research and Practice*. New York: Academic Press.
Perkins, D.N. and Salomon, G. (1989) 'Are cognitive skills context-bound?' *Educational Researcher*, **18** (1), 16–25.
Prins, F.W. (1951) *Een experimenteel-didactische bijdrage tot de vorming van leerprestaties volgens denkpsychologische methode*. Groningen: Wolters.
Rabinowitz, M. and Glaser, R. (1985) 'Cognitive structure and process in highly competent performance', in F.D. Horowitz and M. O'Brien (eds), *The Gifted and Talented: Developmental Perspectives*. Washington, DC: APA.
Reis, S.M. and Renzulli, J.S. (1984) 'The secondary triad model'. Unpublished paper.
Salomon, G. (1987) 'Beyond skill and knowledge: the role of mindfulness in learning and transfer'. Invited address, EARLI Conference, Tübingen.
Savell, J.M., Twohig, P.T. and Rachford, D.L. (1986) 'Empirical status of Feuerstein's Instrumental Enrichment (FIE) technique as a method of teaching thinking skills', *Review of Educational Research*, **56** (4), 381–409.
Schoenfeld, A.H. and Hermann, D. (1982) 'Problem perception and knowledge structure in expert and novice mathematical problem solvers', *Journal of Experimental Psychology* (LMC), **8** (5), 484–91.
Selz, O. (1935) 'Versuche zur Hebung des Intelligenzniveaus', *Zeitschrift für Psychologie*, Band 134, 236ff.

Simons, P.R. (1989) 'Learning to learn', in P. Span, E. De Corte and B. van Hout-Wolters (eds), *Onderwijsleerprocessen: Strategieen voor de verwerking van informatie [Teaching–learning Processes: Strategies for Information Processing]*. Amsterdam/Lisse: Swets and Zeitlinger.

Simons, P.R. (1992) 'Ruimte geven voor zelfstandig leren [Giving opportunity for autonomous learning]', in P.R. Simons and J.G.G.Zuylen (eds), *Actief en zelfstandig studeren in de tweede fase [Active and Autonomous Study in the Second Phase of Secondary Education]*. Tilburg: Mesoconsult.

Simons, P.R. and Beukhof, G. (eds) (1987) *Regulation of Learning*. Gravenhage: SVO, Selecta Books.

Sternberg, R.J. (1985) *Human Abilities: An Information Processing Approach*. New York: Freeman.

Sternberg, R.J. (1986) *Intelligence Applied: Understanding and Increasing Your Intellectual Skills*. London: Harcourt Brace Jovanovitch.

Torrance, E.P. (1986) 'Teaching creative and gifted learners', in M.C. Wittrock (ed.), *Handbook of Research on Teaching*. New York: Macmillan.

Treffinger, D.J. (1975) 'Teaching for self-directed learning: a priority for the gifted and talented', *Gifted Child Quarterly*, **19**, 46–59.

Treffinger, D.J. and Barton, B.L. (1979) 'Fostering independent learning', *Gifted Child Quarterly*, **7**, 3–6 and 54.

van der Sanden, J.M.M., Schouten, A., van Oirschot, P. and Hornman, G. (1988) 'Performing technical psychomotor task: external regulation and action control', in P. Span, E. De Corte and B. van Hout-Wolters (eds), *Metacognitive Strategies*. Lisse: Swets and Zeitlinger.

Vygotsky, L.S. (1978) *Mind in Society: Development of Higher Psychological Processes*. Cambridge, MA: Harvard University Press.

Wertsch, J.D. (1979) 'From social interaction to higher psychological processes, a clarification and application of Vygotsky's theory', *Human Development*, **22** (1), 1–22.

Chapter 7

Talent: The Ability to Become an Expert

Jan Elshout

Until very recently, progress in understanding high ability and talent was much hampered by a lack of an agreed theoretical foundation for the concepts involved. However, during the past few years, this situation has changed. Now, a still-growing body of knowledge on the development of expertise is giving us a fresh perspective on such old questions as the meaning of talent and how it can be recognized (Chi et al., 1988; Ericsson and Smith, 1991; Ericsson and Charness, 1994). From this new perspective, to have talent in a certain domain means having the ability to become an expert in that domain. Some, though, hesitate to accept this new equation because expertise implies a large amount of experience, and high ability and experience can be regarded as belonging to different categories. However, there is no excellence without expertise – indeed, the terms imply much the same thing psychologically.

An expert is someone who has spent five years or more, full-time, working in some particular field of activity, ultimately at an advanced level. One may refer to the expert in general, because there are many features in common between experts operating in different domains – science, the arts, sports or cooking. In all such domains excellence can only be gained by actively working on skills and knowledge for thousands of hours. Expertise is easily recognized. We all marvel at the ease and assuredness of experts, at their mastery and creativity, whether they are writers or athletes or mathematicians, and we forgive them their superior ways and demands for high pay.

The concepts of expert and of expertise are natural and easy to comprehend. The scientific interest in expertise, however, is of recent date only. For the greater part of this century psychological interest was not so much in expertise and excellent performances *per se*, but rather in a person's ability or potential to excel. Actual performance can be observed and measured, while ability and potential are constructs that we have to abstract out of the raw givens of actual performance. Put into the form of a rough formula: how good someone actually is, is a function of the potential, the past opportunity to learn and the past and present motivational state. Thus, to obtain a good measure of potential, the other factors must be kept at a constant. This entails certain experimental and conceptual procedures to ensure that our view of people's potential is not obscured by the differences in opportunity, experience and schooling, nor by variations in interest and motivation. The abstract nature of concepts that refer to dispositions (such as high ability, talent) makes them difficult to understand. At least part of the controversiality of the concept of intelligence stems, in my view, precisely from its abstract nature. That someone who is less intelligent may perform better intellectually than someone of greater ability (because the latter is younger) is not easy to grasp. Compared with expertise, intelligence certainly is not a natural and easily assimilated construct.

THE QUEST FOR PURE POTENTIAL

Psychologists use two strategies to study ability, without interference from differences in motivation and previously acquired knowledge. To keep differences in motivation under control, subjects are given tasks of such short duration that most find them challenging. The second objective is achieved by using tasks which are knowledge-lean, i.e. relatively free of the sort of knowledge that is dependent on formal schooling. Tasks that ask for no knowledge at all are difficult to imagine, but many tasks can be found that demand only knowledge that everybody has had an equal opportunity to acquire. For example, every child has at least once tried to put trousers on over its head – and failed – but only some can later explain what happened exactly. According to the principle of equal opportunity, this difference in observable performance then must reflect a difference in the potential to understand and to profit from experience.

Though many critics insist that pure potential is only to be found at the neural level, these two strategies-of-abstraction have taken us quite far. Tests of intelligence which have been constructed along those lines allow us to make predictions that are far from trivial. We can predict, for instance, that of two children who perform at the same level on the test, it will be the younger one who will get further, profit more by instruction and show more transfer of learning. The study of thinking, too, has greatly profited by such strategies of abstraction. In the 1970s this approach culminated in the monumental work of Newell and Simon on human problem-solving (Newell and Simon, 1972). They described problem-solving or productive thinking as a process of search, in which the problem is decomposed step by step into more manageable sub-problems, until a level of decomposition is reached where one can proceed unproblematically to the goal. This view of problem-solving as a goal-directed search governed by heuristic rules has continued to be very influential and successful. In the late 1980s Newell and his co-workers expanded the 1972 theory in a manner that was meant to incorporate human learning in what they proposed as a universal theory of general human intelligence (Laird et al., 1987; Newell, 1990).

For all this success in 'abstracting away' the influence of differences in experience, schooling and motivation, there is a price to pay – that of generalizability. To keep experience a constant is one thing, but to keep it a constant at such a low level as is done concentrating on puzzle solving, where, by definition, no other knowledge is needed to reach the goal than the information provided by the instruction given at the start, means that one leaves the whole area of knowledge acquisition and knowledge application in problem-solving out of consideration. Problem-solving in real life – think of medical diagnosis as an example – clearly involves both experience and formal knowledge to a marked extent. But how readily can the theory of problem-solving – studied in the form of knowledge-lean puzzle solving – be expanded to cover real life problem-solving? Indeed, is puzzle-solving just a simplified form, or is it qualitatively different?

The first to raise this question within the Newell-Simon tradition (outside critics never took studying puzzle-solving seriously to begin with, for many different reasons) was Simon himself. In 1970 he published a study on learning puzzle-solving, that is, learning to do a puzzle better by doing it several times (Anzai and Simon, 1979). His conclusion was that gaining expertise by repeated doing was in itself a knowledge-lean process, as much as puzzle-solving itself. Later, Simon turned to problem-solving in physics, posing the question whether problem-solving in such a complex knowledge-rich domain could be described in terms of the same theory of goal directed search that had proved successful for puzzle solving. His conclusion was that it could. In Simon's view, complex problem-solving (e.g. in physics or medicine) was not qualitatively different from puzzle-solving (Bhaskar and Simon, 1977). Both involve goal directed search, a process of approaching the solution step-by-step; the choice of steps (operators) being guided by the same general heuristics. The only differences between them concern the nature of the operators. Each problem area has its own domain specific operators, and with knowledge-rich, realistic problems, these tend to be knowledge-rich themselves; also there are simply a great many more of those specific operators potentially applicable in realistic problem-solving than with laboratory puzzles. Thus the generalizability of Newell and Simon's theory was seen as having been preserved: the complex can indeed rise in a simple way out of the simple. The implications of this view are clear: we can safely study thinking in the laboratory, concentrating on puzzle-solving, and do not need to get involved with problems that call for a high level of expertise, which has to be gained outside the laboratory.

THE NEW ERA

By the time of this work, however, the study of interesting real-life problem-solving had already gained ground. Many took their point of departure from the work of de Groot on the thought and perception of chess grandmasters (de Groot, 1965). Grandmasters are experts who have spent several thousands of hours analysing chess positions. De Groot's intuition was that it could not be that thinking and perceiving are totally different processes, each governed by its own set of principles. There had to be a common ground. It was in the context of this intuition that de Groot was struck by the remarkable speed with which the chess expert takes in a new complex chess position presented to him. He describes an American grandmaster who, glancing in passing through the window of a chess cafe, noted that in the game going on there, White could be lost in one move! So the expert 'sees' in a glance what the less experienced has to compute in a slow process of deliberate thought.

In the 1960s, such feats of expertise were brought under the heading of pattern-recognition. We speak of pattern-recognition when a number of perceptually distinct elements (e.g. a number of pieces on a chess board) become recognized as one whole, as one new element, as a result of repeatedly having been processed as a whole. So a certain configuration of chess pieces that repeatedly turns up in different games and is repeatedly analysed as a whole can end up as an old friend, a known identity, recognized at a glance. Later research has shown that chess experts have (during their thousands of hours of study) developed a repertoire of several tens of thousands of such identifiable patterns of chess pieces.

The development of pattern recognition is a feat of both perception and memory. We come to see as a whole what in our knowledge base has come to be one concept, one node of meaning. What holds for chess is also true of other fields of expertise, though the patterns that are to be formed may be not figural, but symbolic or semantic in nature. The general phenomenon of pattern recognition can be diagnosed when there is fast, automatic and effort-free recognition of an identity, which a person without expertise has to discover after a slow process of effortful deliberate cogitation.

The advantages of pattern recognition to the expert are tremendous. What takes neither time nor effort will keep our mind (our working memory!) free for deliberate thought that would perhaps have been impossible otherwise. Furthermore: the recognized pattern is a direct point of entry (retrieval cue) to other information that has come to be associated with it in memory store. For instance, once you are able to recognize the sequence of symbols <1>, <2>, <1> as your old friend the number 121, you can organize around it the information that 121 is the square of 11 and divisible by 11 only and so forth; all this information is at your easy disposal, again without explicit computation.

EXPERTS: MORE, DIFFERENT, BETTER

The essence of pattern recognition is the formation of wholes out of what, to the beginner, are discrete elements. When the pattern has more of a conceptual nature and the perceptual aspects are less important, it is called a schema. We all have a great many patterns and a great many schemata in our repertoires. However, the expert in any particular domain not only has a great many more relevant recognizable schemata and patterns than the ordinary person, but those structures are at an intellectually higher level. They are more intelligent, so to speak, in two different ways; the schemata of the expert are both more operationalized, better organized for use in the actual practice of solving problems; and they are based on deeper understanding of the subject matter.

Someone who starts out learning in some realistic domain, such as medical diagnosis, typically has a large amount of recently acquired theoretical knowledge about the structures and workings, and failings, of the body. However, using such a vast store of bookish learning in actual medical diagnostic problem-solving is by no means easy (Boshuizen, 1989). Each patient presents the student with many specific data of potential importance – background data, medical history, complaints, laboratory data – that have to be connected to medical theory in order to arrive at one or more plausible explanations. Connecting the specific (this patient's particular pain) to the general (all the theoretically possible causes of such pains) is difficult.

According to Boshuizen, medical students need several years of experience to form the schemata that help in making this connection. These schemata – called 'illness-scripts' – connect patterns of patient data to certain descriptions of particular malfunctions, resulting in an AIDS-script, a pancreatitis-script, and so on. An illness-script is different from a syndrome, which is a scientific construct describing recurring clusters of symptoms. The illness-script is a knowledge structure a physician personally has built up over years of both studying and practice with real patients. This knowledge structure develops gradually. Each script details a description of a particular illness in the form of a causal chain and its possible variations. Often, one patient's history can function as the nucleus around which the schema is organized. In the later stages of gaining expertise these illness-scripts are more and more operationalized ('compiled'). That means that the chain of causal reasoning no longer comes fully to mind – the expert seems to jump to conclusions.

To give an example: a patient, a young male, out of work, presents himself with a complaint of recurring pain in the right side. The specialist, seemingly without thought, offers the (correct!) diagnosis that this complaint stems from pancreatitis. As a typical expert she does not have to bring to mind the full causal chain from the patient being a young male and without a job, through probable chronic overconsumption of alcohol, to its physiological and pathological effects. This may seem dangerous because it resembles reasoning by association and that certainly is one of the poorest forms of reasoning. Indeed, rushing to conclusions is typical beginner behaviour – 'pseudo-expert' behaviour. The point, of course, is that the short-cut is only as good as the longer chain of reasoning from which it is derived. The expert starts out from the correct chain of reasoning, while the novice just leaps by association.

Our daily functioning is full of short-cut behaviour. It essentially amounts to stimulus-response activity. For instance, if the temperature indicator of some device we know well enters into the red zone, we unthinkingly turn some wheel or knob – indicator red, wheel left – but what this action accomplishes (e.g. closing a valve) does not enter our mind. There is great mental economy in such short-cuts. For the novice, however, the short-cut typically is all there is; he or she will be in great trouble when the temperature indicator remains in the red after the wheel has been turned. On the other hand, although great expertise and the use of short-cuts go hand in hand, the expert at all times is able to revert to principled reasoning based on deep understanding. The expert knows what makes the temperature of the device go up, how that makes the indicator move, and why it is important that the temperature stays within certain limits and how turning this wheel to the left closes a valve, so cutting the fuel supply. Using short-cuts backed up by deep understanding is typical of expertise in any field.

The availability of a vast number of patterns of information that can be recognized as old friends, the structuring of knowledge about the domain into schemata that bring together the conceptual and the practical about the domain, the possibility of switching between levels of elaboratedness and attention, from the stimulus-response level to real explicit know-why, all make the expert-at-work qualitatively different from the not-so-expert of the same level of intelligence and motivation. An illustration of that is provided by the work of Crombach et al. (1977), who asked a judge of the Dutch High Court to evaluate some cases of civil law while thinking aloud: the think-aloud protocols began with much incomprehensible mumbling interspersed with many silences. After a while, however, the reasoning became more explicit. From their protocols Crombach *et al.* concluded that at this very high level of juridical expertise a verdict is first reached on the basis of a fast process of pattern recognition, of recognizing the presented case as a case of a certain well-known legal type; then a process begins of painstakingly constructing a justification of the verdict already reached 'intuitively'. Staff members of a faculty of law, who were also studied, worked the other way around, starting with an elaborate analysis and a process of systematic elimination that culminated in a verdict. When more and more experience results in such a drastic change in style of reasoning, we must conclude that the expert differs from the beginner not only quantitatively but also qualitatively.

ON WHAT DOES EXPERTISE/EXCELLENCE DEPEND?

Until now, the many studies on the development of expertise have concentrated on the cognitive aspects; the author is not aware of any that have also looked at the affective and motivational aspects of growing expertise (see Stedtnitz, 1995). In the 1960s and early 1970s, there was great interest in identifying people with potential for scientific and technological creativity – part of the Sputnik effect – but unfortunately no longitudinal studies resulted. The next-best approach, however, was to study scientists with roughly equal experience and to correlate measures of their scientific excellence – judged creativity, number of publications – with biographical data, self-ratings on relevant aspects of personal functioning, and scores on tests of cognitive abilities. In this type of research a particular pattern of relationships is consistently found: scientific excellence goes together with early and deeply felt interest in the particular scientific field one works in, with a somewhat higher intelligence, a liking for intellectual challenge, persistence, intellectual independence, and a very high level of professional self-confidence. As far as their particular field of expertise is concerned, experts are fully convinced of their ability to excel again and again (Taylor and Barron, 1963).

What is remarkable about these results is that they strongly suggest that above a certain level of expertise, non-cognitive factors (like professional self-confidence) contribute much more to excellence than intellectual factors. This may appear surprising because creative problem-solving in the sciences clearly taxes the intellect, and differences in intelligence should therefore show up in differences in the level of performance. They do indeed, but such differences are small. The clue to this riddle is that scientific creativity, which is recognized as such, is always situated at the highest levels of expertise – and even scientists of the same age may greatly differ as to their expertise in a given problem area. This, however, fails to explain why the other personal characteristics listed above are so highly predictive of future scientific excellence. It is through the many decision-making processes of the individual concerning the expenditure of time and effort that non-cognitive factors make their contribution to the judged level of creativity. The human costs involved in reaching the pinnacle of expertise are considerable. Given a certain equal level of expertise the more intelligent will somewhat outperform their less intelligent peers. In real life, however, a level of expertise is never 'given', but must be conquered, and in that process other factors make the greater difference.

From these studies of scientific excellence and expertise, a conclusion may be drawn that holds for the prediction of excellence in general – excellence and expertise are the same thing. They have the same causal background, depending on two factors. One is the opportunity to learn, and, over thousands of hours, to really master a domain; the other is what the person brings to it – the ability to profit from opportunity, and the characteristics needed to hold on to opportunity. If one leaves the field early, there is no expertise and no excellence. In real life, most people do leave; but those who stay will become expert, and be recognized as the talented.

THE ROLE AND NATURE OF BASIC ABILITIES

It would be incorrect to conclude that all talent amounts to is staying power. Recent experiments have shown that in certain areas (e.g. mental calculation, memory for numbers), given a great many hours of training, ordinary persons, without any obvious special talent, can learn to perform on a level comparable to that of most famous 'savants' and 'prodigies' described in the literature (Chi *et al.*, 1988; Chase and Ericsson, 1982). So at least in these areas which are low in inherent task complexity, expertise and excellence can be produced at will. No special talents are needed. But it is also true that in the experiments referred to, individual differences were found in the rate of progression. So, though these experiments do discredit the notion of extraordinary talents in these areas, they do on the other hand confirm that some people are more talented than others for acquiring the mnemonic structures these tasks call for. However, the mistake should not be made of thinking of memory talent, for example, as the central explanatory factor behind the astounding feats of memory shown, by the more and less talented alike. Talent is best characterized as that combination of personal qualities, cognitive and non-cognitive, that brings about specialization to an exceptionally high level of expertise.

The fact that tests of intelligence do not have much predictive validity for those who do achieve high scientific expertise, we have already established. Still, scientists do live by their brains, or don't they? Scientists of all sorts are all very intelligent. There is, however, enough variance in intelligence left between them (40 to 45 per cent of the variance in the unselected population is a reasonable guess) to eliminate restriction of range as a major cause of the disappointingly low correlations. The real cause is that gaining expertise follows the laws of practice, and practice needs opportunity and time. Therefore, time-related factors will increasingly come to dominate performance, leaving less time-related factors, such as inborn capacities, a smaller and smaller proportion of the variance.

The important thing with basic ability is to have enough of it – and that might be quite a lot! – to gain a foothold in the learning process, especially at a high level (see De Corte, 1995). As the building up of expertise progresses, the speed of progression at each further stage (N) will correlate less and less with basic ability and the level of performance in the starting phases, and more and more with the level just reached in the stage (N−1). This relationship has been found to hold in all developmental or learning processes. It even holds for the 'development' of IQ over the years. This

Table 7.1 *Correctly solved problems on a retention test after extensive practice (absolute and gain scores)*

	Absolute scores		Gains	
	High	Low	High	Low
Advanced	30.0	27.7	3.4	2.5
Novice	23.5	17.5	8.5	5.5

Maximum score = 38; S.D. = 4.4.

correlational pattern, though most impressive in its ubiquity, is just an empirical law; it does not explain why, for instance, measures of intelligence gradually lose their predictive power.

The author's position on this matter is that intelligence consists of a repertoire of basic skills useful for gaining expertise in intellectual domains. Furthermore, this basic repertoire is fundamentally not different from a domain-specific expertise. They are psychologically similar: both are repertoires, consisting of various pockets of more or less specialized procedural and declarative knowledge, depending on the same brain faculties for the speed and the precision of their deployment and execution. What makes the empirical law of the increase of the relative predictive power of the most recent advances also hold for explaining the building of expertise is that apparently domain-specific expertise gradually takes over the functions of the basic repertoire which we try to measure with tests of intelligence. Intelligence is proto-expertise and domain-expertise is domain-intelligence! These repertoires are completely one of a kind. They fully compensate for one another. The findings from a study on gaining expertise in solving a certain type of physics problem may serve to illustrate this relationship (Elshout et al. 1993). The selection of subjects was performed on the basis of their intelligence (High vs Low), and their expertise in physics (Advanced vs Novice), resulting in a two-factor design with four groups (n = 28). Table 7.1 gives the relevant results.

The correlation between intelligence and number of items solved on the retention test proved to be 0.26 in the advanced group, while it was a very significant 0.61 in the group of novices. This difference in correlation squares with the fact that the difference between the Highs and the Lows is much larger in the inexperienced group than it is in the advanced group. This is the law of diminishing correlations at work. Also note that experience compensates for intelligence: experienced Lows outperform Highs of less experience. Also we see that progression becomes slower the further one gets, but it never stops. Our Novices obviously have gained much more from their experience, but the Advanced also managed to learn, and they indeed still have a way to go because no subject reached the ceiling of 38 problems correctly solved.

Intelligence and domain-specific expertise are both best seen as complex repertoires of strictly the same psychological nature. Their difference lies in the phase in the development of expertise in which they perform their roles, the roles being no different. They serve the same functions: they aid learning and building up more expertise, mostly through a process of learning by doing. Domain-specific expertise quickly becomes more important than intelligence in this process, performing those functions better, often much better. But every time a new route to excellence is embarked upon, we may expect the basic repertoire to gain in importance for a while. Then experience will again regain the upper hand.

CONCLUSIONS

The concept of excellence refers to a certain exceptionally high level of performance. As we have seen, such excellence implies a most high level of expertise, achieved through many years of hard work. As the predictive power of tests of basic abilities for reaching such high levels is so low, one might wonder whether a person's capacity for sustained hard work is indeed all we need to know. The high predictive validity of certain biographical measures concerning, for instance, early and passionate interest in the particular domain of adult excellence, might seem to confirm this impression. Also, we might wonder from this pattern of results how intellectual the feats of great scientists really are, just as some theorists are not convinced that the memory performances of memorization experts have much to do with memory proper. The answer to these questions is that intelligence and other basic abilities are best considered to be repertoires of skills and knowledge useful for building more domain-specific repertoires, increasingly bound to the specific task environment, that gradually take over the functions (e.g. problem-solving, learning) of the original basic repertoire. Expertise is domain-specific intelligence. The people who will have most of it, after the many years necessary for achieving the level of excellence, the really talented, are those with traits most favouring the generous investment of time in the enterprise.

REFERENCES

Anzai, Y. and Simon, H.A. (1979) 'The theory of learning by doing', *Psychological Review*, **86**, 124–40.
Bhaskar, R. and Simon, H.A. (1977) 'Problem-solving in semantically rich domains: an example from engineering thermodynamics', *Cognitive Science*, **1**, 193–215.
Boshuizen, H.P.A. (1989) 'The Development of Medical Expertise' [in Dutch]. Doctoral dissertation, University of Maastricht.
Chase, W.G. and Ericsson, K.A. (1982) 'Skill and working memory', in G.H. Bower (ed.), *The Psychology of Learning and Motivation*. Vol. 16. New York: Academic Press.
Chi, M.T.H., Glaser, R. and Farr, M.J. (1988) *The Nature of Expertise*. Hillsdale, NJ: Erlbaum.
Crombach, H.F.M., de Wijckersloot, J.L. and Cohen, M.J. (1977) *A Theory of Juridical Decision Making* [in Dutch]. Groningen: Tjeenk Willink.
De Corte, E. (1995) 'Acquiring high-level learning skills: a perspective from instructional psychology'. Chapter 5, this volume.
de Groot, A.D. (1965) *Thought and Choice in Chess*. Den Haag: Mouton (first publication 1946).
Elshout, J.J., Veenman, M. and Van Hell, J. (1993) 'Using the computer as a help tool during learning by doing', *Computers and Education*, **21**, 115–22.
Ericsson, K.A. and Charness, N. (1994) 'Expert performance: its structure and acquisition', *American Psychologist*, **49**, 725–47.
Ericsson, K.A. and Smith, J. (1991) *Toward a General Theory of Expertise*. Cambridge: Cambridge University Press.

Laird, J.E., Newell, A. and Rosenbloom, P.S. (1987) 'SOAR: an architecture of general intelligence', *Artificial Intelligence*, **33**, 1–64.

Newell, A. (1990) *Unified Theories of Cognition*. Cambridge, MA: Harvard University Press.

Newell, A. and Simon, H.A. (1972) *Human Problem-solving*. Englewood Cliffs, NJ: Prentice Hall.

Stedtnitz, U. (1995) 'Psychological dimensions of talent: some major issues'. Chapter 4, this volume.

Taylor, C.W. and Barron, F. (eds) (1963) *Scientific Creativity: Its Recognition and Development*. New York: Wiley.

Part 3

High-level Achievement

Chapter 8

Actualizing Creative Intelligence

Arthur J. Cropley

To adapt a conclusion of Baldwin (1985), it is possible only in a few extreme cases to speak of actual talented performance in children. Although their achievements can be remarkable in contrast with those of other children, this is usually a case of precocity, since the performances of children are frequently, although not always, surpassed by adults or the children themselves when they become adult. Both adults and children can be described as 'extraordinary', but in the case of children the extraordinariness often takes the form of a potential rather than of concrete talented achievements, since such achievements frequently require highly developed technical skills or extensive experience of life, and thus often take years to bring to fruition. For this reason, it is important to view talent as either observable performance or as yet unrealized potential. Otherwise, in addition to the young, those who are in any way blocked or inhibited in their development (such as the physically handicapped, or the chronically ill, and members of disadvantaged groups) would be dismissed as lacking talent. Nonetheless, the idea of potential without performance raises not only theoretical, but also practical problems (e.g. identification, remediation). Some of these issues are touched upon later.

Traditionally, the notion of high ability has focused on the cognitive domain (e.g. feats of memory, exceptional achievement on learning tasks, outstandingly clever thinking, and the like). In particular, it has been associated with school settings or school-like situations. Thus it is traditional to speak of 'gifted students' or 'talented mathematicians' or 'gifted linguists'. This approach has often been expanded somewhat to include performances in music, the fine arts and, perhaps surprisingly, chess (Elshout, 1995). More or less parallel to interest in outstanding performance of the kind just described, has been an interest in exceptional sporting performance (Rowley, 1995), although these two areas – the cognitive, on the one hand and the sensori-motor, on the other – have not usually been discussed in a single context. Apart from exceptions, such as the conferences and symposia of the European Council for High Ability or the present volume, books and conferences on gifted education and related topics have rarely concerned themselves with the teaching and learning of skills in putting the shot or swimming, while coaches of outstanding athletes have seldom concerned themselves with the fostering of talents in chess or music.

A major tendency in recent discussions, however, has been a broadening of the definition of giftedness to include not only 'schoolhouse' giftedness, but also non-school high achievement. This tendency has been greatly facilitated by increased interest in not only the cognitive aspects of gifts and talents, but also in the personal, affective and motivational elements. An example is to be seen in the discussion of self-concept and attitudes in high academic achievement, or record-breaking athletic performances (Süle, 1990). Another example is to be seen in the area of leadership. Many recent discussions emphasize the need for individuals to use their talents in an ethically desirable way, not applying them, for instance, to self-aggrandizement and personal enrichment, but rather to the solution of societal problems such as poverty, prejudice or environmental destruction (see Cropley et al., 1986, for several relevant papers).

In the cognitive domain there has been a move away from a quantitative (How much of some particular skill does a particular gifted person possess?) to a qualitative approach (What kind of abilities constitute giftedness? How are they organized and how do they interact with each other?). It has been suggested (Shaughnessy, 1990) that even traditional cognitive tests should be used to define not only levels of ability but also patterns of organization; for example, 'cognitive structure'. Allied with this development has been an increasing emphasis on cognitive processes, especially on the activities which define them and the mechanisms which direct, accelerate or decelerate, and guide them. Among others, achieving insight or developing special tactics for solving problems have been investigated. The metacognitive approach to giftedness (see, for instance, Sternberg, 1985; De Corte, 1995; Span, 1995) emphasizes elements such as the selection of 'good' problems, the distinction between promising lines of attack and dead ends, the evaluation of partial solutions, or the identification of more promising alternative lines of attack when evaluation shows that progress to date has not been satisfactory.

Non-cognitive approaches to the defining of giftedness emphasize motivation, values and attitudes, and personal characteristics such as self-image (Stedtnitz, 1995). Great expertise requires not only skills and abilities, but also fascination for a particular area, a feeling that it is worthwhile to dedicate oneself to this area, and confidence in one's own ability to master the area in question (Elshout, 1995). The achievement of exceptional expertise also frequently requires investment of large amounts of energy (see also later discussions). Amabile (1983) discussed a number of these factors. Finally, it has become apparent that giftedness has a strong social element (see Sternberg, 1985). The society or its subgroups play a major role in deciding which achievements will be regarded as prodigious and valuable (and hence talented), which, by contrast, could be dismissed as crackpot, dangerous, subversive, destructive or even criminal (and hence not talented).

CREATIVITY AS AN ELEMENT OF GIFTEDNESS

The 'Sputnik shock' of the late 1950s led to a period of national soul-searching in the USA, and to the conclusion that the country's educational system had failed to produce enough talented scientists, blamed on the lack of emphasis on creativity. The wave of creativity research which followed set the stage for intense international interest in the topic. The late 1970s saw the emergence of a second wave of research, which is still continuing, once again largely set in motion by renewed interest in fostering giftedness. In retrospect, it is apparent that, from the very beginning, creativity was seen as an element in high academic achievement.

The purpose of the American National Defense Education Act, calling for more emphasis on creativity, which was passed shortly after the successful launching of Sputnik I, was production of scientists and engineers capable of matching the achievements of their counterparts in the Soviet Union. Studies such as Gibson and Light's (1967) investigation of scientists at Cambridge University, which showed that many students had IQs of under 130, a traditional cut-off point for identifying giftedness, indicated that intelligence alone was not sufficient for academic achievement. In a major review of research on IQ and creativity, Milgram (1990) showed that, despite occasional findings to the contrary, IQs and similar scores do not adequately predict real-life creativity. Apparently, talented achievement demands something more than simply high IQ.

Wallach and Kogan (1965) looked at children high in both intelligence and creativity, while in studies of schoolchildren in Canada and university students in Australia, Cropley (1967a; 1967b) showed that, although the highly intelligent–low creative subjects obtained good marks, they were consistently outstripped by students high in both characteristics. This superiority of achievement among people combining conventional intelligence and creativity became more pronounced as the level of education increased (i.e. from grade 7 to first-year university, to final-year university, to honours-level studies). In a longitudinal study in the Federal Republic of Germany, pupils of very high intelligence but without corresponding creativity surpassed those merely high in creativity, but in all other cases those higher in creativity achieved better (Sierwald, 1989). As Facaoaru (1985) showed in a study of engineers in Romania, talented achievement depends on a combination of conventional abilities (good memory, logical thinking, knowledge of facts, accuracy, etc.) and creative abilities (generating ideas, recognizing alternative possibilities, seeing unexpected combinations, having the courage to try the unusual, and so on). This combination defines what Cropley (1981) has called 'true giftedness'.

The psychological components of creativity

The initial impulse in modern studies of creativity came from the work of Guilford (1950), and derived from his distinction between 'convergent' and 'divergent' thinking. Early theorizing adopted a relatively undifferentiated approach (intelligence = convergent thinking; creativity = divergent thinking), but this has since been expanded by a number of authors. Torrance and Hall (1980), for instance, concluded that creative thinking involves:

- uniting disparate ideas by putting them into a common context;
- being able to imagine, at least as a theoretical possibility, almost anything;

- enriching one's own thinking through the application of fantasy;
- adding spice to one's thinking through the use of humour.

Although Necka's (1986) 'triad' model of creativity goes beyond thinking to encompass motives and skills, thinking is still of great importance in this approach. The aspects he emphasized include:

- forming associations;
- recognizing similarities;
- constructing metaphors;
- carrying out transformations;
- selectively directing the focus of attention;
- seeing the abstract aspects of the concrete.

Simonton (1988) advanced what he called the 'chance-configuration' model of genius. His approach can, however, be applied to creativity. He concluded – somewhat adapted for present purposes – that creativity involves production of a large number of associations, more or less randomly or blindly with the chance occurrence of 'configurations' – happy combinations which represent just what is needed to solve the problem in question. The creative person is especially good not only at producing associations, but also at recognizing that a configuration has occurred, and grasping that it offers a solution. Weisberg (1986) examined self-reports and case studies of famous creators, and combined this information with data obtained in experimental studies. He concluded that creativity arises not from random combinations, but from 'chains' of ideas connected associatively in a long series of strictly logical small steps, for which knowledge of the field is vital.

However, an analysis based on thinking alone cannot offer an adequate explanation of creativity. Studies of famous highly achieving individuals of the past have confirmed that, among other things, motivation plays an important role. For instance, Cox's (1926) retrospective studies of geniuses, such as Newton, Copernicus, Galileo, Kepler, and Darwin showed clearly that in addition to high intelligence these people were marked by tenacity and perseverance. In a similar vein, Biermann (1985) concluded, on the basis of a study of creative mathematicians of the seventeenth to nineteenth centuries, that fascination with the subject matter and consequent extreme motivation was one of the major features of his subjects. Hassenstein (1988) also commented on the obsessive nature of the work of gifted individuals, while Goertzel et al. (1978) showed the importance of motivation in their case studies of historical figures.

One of the early findings in studies of creative mathematicians, scientists, architects, painters and writers was that these people seemed to possess special personality characteristics which set them apart from less creative colleagues; they included flexibility, sensitivity, tolerance, a sense of responsibility, empathy, independence and a positive self-image. Heinelt (1974) studied schoolchildren identified on the basis of test scores as highly creative, and came to the conclusion that they were – significantly more frequently than uncreative youngsters – introverted, self-willed, intellectually active, flexible and possessed of wit and a sense of humour. Reviewing a substantial number of studies in this area, Farisha (1978) concluded that a relationship between personality and creativity is one of the most consistently emphasized findings in the literature.

Investigations related to studies of personality and creativity emphasize interactions with other people, i.e. social factors. Heinelt's (1974) study showed, for instance, that schoolchildren identified as creative tended to remain aloof from their classmates, and preferred to work independently. They were often described as socially isolated and unpopular, and this phenomenon was associated with a tendency to feel superior to their classmates to the point of arrogance. However, a recent sociometric study (Gebart-Eaglemont and Foddy, 1994) showed that creative youngsters belonged predominately to the 'neglected' group in the classroom, not to the 'rejected', 'popular' or 'academic' groups. Other studies (e.g. Neff, 1975) showed that creative youngsters are often uninterested in making a good impression on others or in conforming. In accord, Freeman (1991), in an in-depth follow-up study, found that it was the more creative youngsters who had the best social life, and the high academic achievers who had the poorest quality. Anderson and Cropley (1966) studied the reactions of schoolchildren in situations where a number of alternative courses of action were possible and concluded that the children were guided by social 'stop rules' which forbade most reactions in favour of the socially approved one. Societies have 'filters' (Fromm, 1980) through which not only behaviours but also ideas must pass, and carry out constant 'surveillance' (Amabile *et al.*, 1990) in order to detect and deter deviance.

Indeed, being creative must involve thinking or behaving differently from others, otherwise the element of originality would be missing. Consequently, creative individuals must display 'the courage to create' (Motamedi, 1982; Landau, 1985): they must risk the censure and rejection often associated with failure to conform. C.G. Jung (1964) has, in fact, written about an innate human fear of novelty, providing a reason why it requires courage to be creative, although Horn (1988) distinguished between two basic styles of reaction to novelty, the one involving avoidance, the other attraction.

The interaction of creativity and intelligence in talented performance

The question which now arises is that of how creativity and intelligence interact to produce exceptional achievement. An early approach was that of MacKinnon (1962), who proposed the threshold theory. In essence, this argues that a certain minimum level (threshold) of intelligence is necessary before creativity is possible. Bringing out a different aspect of the same idea, McNemar (1964) pointed out that high IQ is no guarantee of creativity, but a low IQ means that it is impossible. Guilford and Christensen (1973) took a somewhat different position, suggesting that there is a 'one-way relationship' between creative potential and intelligence, i.e. an IQ test provides an indicator of the upper limit for performance, but does not indicate the likelihood of creativity. Their interpretation is based on the argument that IQ indicates the extent to which an individual possesses relevant information and can call it out of storage upon demand. Without information there is nothing to be retrieved and divergently processed.

A more dynamic interpretation along similar lines is to regard the individual as a communication channel. Channel capacity, in the sense of an upper limit on the number of 'bits' of information that can be assimilated, is intuitively compatible with the concept of intelligence. The versatility and extent to which an individual can manipulate, reorganize and recombine those bits is compatible with the notion of originality, creativity or divergent productive thinking.

Creativity can be conceptualized as a qualitative aspect of mental functioning. Over 20 years ago, on the basis of data showing substantial correlations between creativity test scores and IQ scores, as well as between 'creativity' and 'intelligence' factors, Cropley (1969) described creativity as a 'style' for applying intelligence, rather than as a separate ability. More recently, Gardner (1983) referred to it as the highest form of application of intelligence, and Runco and Albert (1986) defined it as 'intelligence in action'.

In essence, the 'style' approach argues that people may deal with situations which demand intelligence, either by trying to reapply what has already been learned, concentrating on proven tactics, and relating the new situation to the familiar, or by searching for the novel, backing intuitions, taking a chance, and so on. For brevity's sake, the first kind of tactic will be called 'convergent', and the second 'divergent', although these are obviously stereotypes. In daily life few people function permanently at one or the other extreme, most tending towards a greater or lesser degree of divergence/convergence according to the particular situation.

Actual creative behaviour seems to call for an interacting combination of psychological properties. As a result of convergent thinking or intelligence (knowledge acquisition, development of skills), human beings possess a range of what Simonton (1988) called 'mental elements'. When confronted with a situation which demands action (problem-solving in the broadest sense of the term), the individual works through the available mental elements, selecting or discarding, bringing them into juxtaposition, etc., until a 'configuration' (see earlier discussions) occurs. This configuration could involve an idea, a model, an action, a way of arranging words, musical notes, or shapes or forms. The divergent thinker is able to combine elements in ways which are remote and unexpected, and thus produce configurations that others regard as creative. However, construction of divergent configurations demands more than divergent and convergent thinking. Creativity needs motivation (for instance a drive to produce better solutions), appropriate personal characteristics (e.g. openness to the new), social elements (willingness to be nonconforming), and communication skills. This interactive process is also accompanied by emotions. This model of gifted achievement is shown in Figure 8.1.

OVERVIEW

What emerges from the above considerations is a more comprehensive definition of talent than in the past. It is not confined to school-related activities, but also involves areas such as sport and leadership. It derives not merely from possession of a high level of cognitive skill, but also involves the nature and organization of abilities and emotions, and it is best regarded as a process. The nature, direction and speed of this process depends partly upon cognitive factors, but is also strongly influenced by personality and motivation, and has strong social elements including, among other things, an ethical dimension and an important communication aspect. Finally, it is important to adopt the apparently paradoxical position that a high proportion of the

Actualizing Creative Intelligence 105

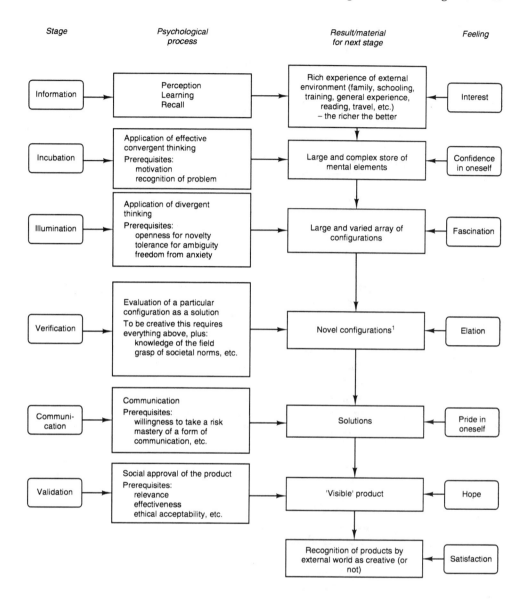

[1] Such configurations can also occur through chance. Some theorists argue that they need not involve divergent thinking at all, but can result from purely convergent thinking of a particularly persistent and thorough kind. Nonetheless, without communication and evaluation they cannot lead to an acknowledged creative product.

Figure 8.1 *The process of achieving creative solutions*

population is (at least potentially) capable of talented performance, even if only a few actually display it.

This approach involves a move away from a quantitative model of talent to a qualitative one: giftedness is defined not by its frequency of occurrence, but by the quality of performance. A gift or talent can manifest itself not only in the form of a statistically uncommon performance, but also in a special kind or quality of performance. Despite the fact that giftedness has, in the past, been regarded as confined to a small proportion of the population, far more people than suggested by the quantitative approach possess the potential to develop high levels of expertise and display especially effective performances. Howe (1995) goes so far as to argue that with trust in themselves and sufficient effort (for instance, practice), most people are capable of talented performance.

FOSTERING THE DEVELOPMENT OF TALENTS

The fact that talented performance is often related to gender (for instance, superior performances in school of boys in mathematics and girls in languages – although this is changing rapidly in the West as girls are now challenging boys in all areas – and lower incidence of women among famous achievers, such as scientists, writers, artists), and birth-order effects (for instance, a higher proportion of first-born Nobel prize winners; a higher proportion of later-borns among artists, poets or actors) suggests that the realization of talent is related to life circumstances. The alternative is the assumption that males' abilities are genetically different from those of females and that early and later-borns are differently oriented by nature alone. (For a more detailed discussion of these differences see Cropley, 1992; Freeman, 1995a.) Even more compelling is evidence of the connection between peak performance and age. Despite criticism over the years, the classical study by Lehman (1953) is still widely supported (see Simonton, 1988, for a detailed analysis of this relationship, with examples of famous people).

The age at which peak performances occur differs somewhat from discipline to discipline, mathematicians tending to become famous particularly early, but it is generally true that most outstanding achievements occur between 30 and 40, somewhere around 40 being the most productive age. Nonetheless, many famous talented people continue to produce until well into later life: Darwin, Freud and Einstein became famous in their twenties and remained active into their seventies. Those who start youngest seem to continue longest. Mumford and Gustafson (1988) offered a model which helps to make sense of the apparent discrepancy between the findings that peak performances occur young and that productivity often persists into old age. They distinguished between two forms of productive creativity, 'major' and 'minor' creativity. Significant breakthroughs (major creativity) tend to occur up to about 35 or 40, and broadening and consolidation (minor creativity) after that.

Concentrating on 'ordinary' people who had not become famous for outstanding performances, various authors (see Cropley, 1992 for a summary) have concluded that there is a curvilinear relationship between test-measured creativity and age up to about 30. Scores increase until about age 6, followed by a trough between about 6 and 16, and increase again until about 30; after 30 there is a steady decline. Cropley concluded that this pattern results from aspects of cognitive development, such as passage from the pre-operational stage (thinking focuses on concrete attributes of objects and events) to the operational (thinking begins to take account of abstract 'meaning'), the influence of school norms (emphasis on logic and accuracy), social pressures (the demands of the job), and physiological factors (for example, reduced speed of thinking with increasing age).

Factors affecting high levels of performance

Many of the findings which underlie the accepted wisdom of creative production have been derived from the psychological testing of schoolchildren. But recently, biographical and autobiographical studies of living or historical gifted individuals have begun to play a more important role in identifying the important developmental conditions for the emergence of gifts and talents. Although many such studies existed before the First World War, after a period of neglect, recent years have seen a resurgence in case studies of exceptional achievers, past and present, e.g. Nobel prize winners, Olympic gold medallists, persons rated as exceptional by their colleagues (Simonton, 1988; Weisberg, 1986; Berry, 1990).

These studies have been extremely fruitful, as they have contradicted a number of common beliefs about talented individuals. For example, most talented people do not show strikingly precocious performance, despite the existence of exceptions such as Mozart. Achieving success is often a very long process: famous pianists, successful scientists and even Olympic swimmers typically require 15 years or more of intense effort before they are accepted as gifted (see Elshout, 1990; 1995). During much of this learning time their performances may be merely good average or only somewhat above average. However, because of the influences of personal and motivational factors, some work and practise so hard that they eventually become outstanding. If intense dedication usually starts at about 15 to 20 years of age, it is apparent why peak performances frequently come no earlier than 30 to 40 years of age.

What is clear is that the development of talents does not involve the emergence in a more or less pre-programmed way of God-given potentials. On the contrary, their emergence depends on a process which may or may not reach a successful conclusion; it is possible, for instance, to speak of unrealized talents. (It is also possible to identify talents which have emerged from apparently unpromising beginnings.) Quite apart from the possible possession of inborn advantages involving the sense organs, the central nervous system, or other physical features, the development of talents depends upon the circumstances of life. It also depends upon the individual's personality, values, interests, self-image, motives and so on, and these are themselves shaped by the circumstances of life.

Opportunity is necessary for the development of gifts and talents, such as contact with a particular field, its contents, activities or materials. In most cases, long and concentrated practice is also necessary; case studies have shown that highly achieving individuals cannot succeed without this element (Howe, 1995). Fascination with an area, motivation to dedicate oneself to the area, belief in oneself as capable of high levels of achievement, and the like, are not only important prerequisites encouraging willingness to practise (possibly for thousands of hours), but are themselves partly acquired through crucial experiences provided by the environment. As various studies have shown (for instance, Bloom, 1985), contact with models or mentors is of great importance. Mentors may be parents, siblings, teachers or coaches. They display skills within the area of giftedness, the values and attitudes associated with it, and the self-image required for success. They need not themselves be gifted – the 'crystallizing' person is sometimes someone in a more humble, encouraging role, such as a primary school teacher.

The fact that the emergence of gifts and talents involves a developmental process guided by 'environmental enablers' raises special problems for children from disadvantaged backgrounds. This is not only for social out-groups such as the poor or immigrants, but also for groups from whom giftedness is not usually expected, or who by virtue of some special characteristic are denied contacts with a field of endeavour, opportunities for practice, interactions with crystallizing persons, or other crucial experiences (e.g. girls in some cultures, the physically handicapped, the sensorily handicapped). Not only may a stigma or a handicap limit contact with environmental enablers, but it may also inhibit recognition of an emerging potential (e.g. because of prejudice, or even a well-meaning desire to 'protect' the child in question), and thus further reduce opportunity, introducing a downward spiral of unrealized potential. The problem of recognizing gifted potential in disadvantaged groups has received intensive interest in recent years (e.g. Baldwin, 1985; Butler-Por, 1993), and is one of the most important issues in contemporary gifted education.

Identification

If the very simple definition of talent or giftedness is made in terms of high conventional intelligence, its identification is necessarily dominated by intelligence tests. Although a number of writers have argued for an extension of the mental test approach by incorporating creativity tests, research has shown that only moderate progress has been made: intelligence tests still predominate (see McLeod and Cropley, 1989). In any case, use of current creativity tests represents only an improvement of the existing, cognitively oriented, socially biased approach.

More recently, there has been a call for 'identification by performance' (Shore and Tsiamis, 1986). The basic idea is that children who display high achievement are deemed to be talented or gifted and are offered special educational provision. One can see, though, that if this approach were limited to high marks in traditional school subjects, it would be fraught with problems. For instance, young children would scarcely be identified at all, since they have had no chance to display high achievement. The well-known correlation between home background (social class, ethnic origin, mother tongue, etc.) and school marks would mean that identification would be limited almost exclusively to children from the dominant social class (usually middle-class speakers of the official language of the society in question). For these reasons, 'performance' should be understood as something more than school grades.

The extended definition of talent presented here provides many ideas for the redefinition of 'performance', and hence offers new impetus for identifying those of any age who possess this quality. Unusual skill or high levels of talent can be expanded to include content areas going beyond those of the traditional classroom (photography, music, debating), or even those which lie outside the school altogether (hobbies and clubs, sports organizations, part-time work). Furthermore, performance need not be confined to finished products, but can be expanded to include non-cognitive aspects. These would be, for example, intense interest in a field of endeavour, sustained effort stretching over months and years, willingness to make sacrifices in pursuing an interest, confidence in oneself as capable of 'making it', willingness to stand up for something in the face of peer group pressure, and similar properties. The areas of activity need not be those conventionally prized in the dominant social group. Indeed, the recognition of the differences in talents is very important for youngsters from out-groups (the social underclass, migrants, native speakers of 'foreign' languages – in many cases these are the same people, since there is a strong interaction among the three conditions). What is important in identifying the gifted is exceptional performance in areas of activity prized by the social subgroup to which a particular child belongs. Naturally, excellence in conventional schoolhouse areas should not be devalued, but the focus should be expanded (see McLeod and Cropley, 1989).

A variant of 'identification by performance' of gifted children, is 'identification by provision' (Shore and Tsiamis, 1986). For this, children who wish to (or whose parents or teachers nominate them) can participate in special 'gifted programmes'. If they flourish, they have, in fact, identified themselves; if they do not do well, they have demonstrated its inappropriateness for them, and they can return to normal provision. Children 'identified' by provision succeed about as frequently as those identified by other procedures such as IQ testing.

These methods focused on the usefulness of parent, teacher, and even self-nominations for identifying gifted children. Self-selection, especially through performance, as outlined earlier, as well as via nomination by parents, is not significantly less accurate than identification via test procedures – although both approaches have substantial weaknesses. The ability of teachers to identify gifted children has often been sharply criticized, on the grounds that they tend to identify boys, conformers, and generally likeable youngsters at the expense of girls, quiet, self-effacing children and troublemakers. However, large-scale studies have shown that when teachers are given a clear definition of the properties they are looking for and a certain amount of training, they can select with a satisfactory degree of accuracy (Denton, 1986).

Special education

Identification of the talented is pointless unless it leads to special treatment aimed at facilitating the development and continuance of their special abilities. The expanded definition of talent and giftedness outlined above provides guidelines for such special provision. In order to promote the acquisition of high levels of expertise, it should offer opportunities for intensive work in a particular area. In addition it should promote interest in the area, conviction about its importance and worth, familiarity with the values and ethics of the area, confidence in one's own ability to do outstanding work, and willingness to make long and sustained effort to achieve success.

Traditionally, discussions of special provision in schools have distinguished between 'acceleration' (completing the work specified in the curriculum in less time than usual) and 'enrichment' (going into material more deeply than usual). Speeding-up by covering contents quickly or entering school, high school or university early may simply mean that a child finishes a part of education at an early age, leading, for instance, to people graduating from university at 13, 14 or 15, or achieving a PhD at 18, 19 or 20. However, in school settings in several countries, such as the USA or Australia, enrichment takes place, typically involving children spending time in a 'resource room' or with the 'gifted' teacher. The activities carried out there would normally involve a more intensive treatment of the standard material, often accompanied by attempts to promote creativity. It is apparent that acceleration and enrichment are, for all practical purposes if not in theory, two sides of the same coin.

More recent work on special provision for gifted children has emphasized other forms of organization in which the acceleration/enrichment dichotomy has become blurred. For example, elementary schools may cooperate with secondary schools to allow gifted pupils to spend some class time with age-mates in subjects where they are working at the 'normal' level, possibly with an enriched intensity. They may also work with older students, in areas where the gifted pupil has shown a thirst for acceleration. Outstanding examples of such patterns of special provision involve youngsters who may be in grade 5 or 6 in, let us say, mother-tongue and social studies, in grade 11 or 12 in chemistry and biology and in third-year university in mathematics and physics. Such forms of provision answer a number of the objections made to acceleration, such as removal of a child from social contact with age-mates, and that they offer great promise which may not be fulfilled. They also require a high level of cooperation among segments of the education system, and are only possible when administrators and teachers are flexible.

Other organizational forms of special provision include cooperation between schools and industry; for instance, highly motivated students can work in a firm's laboratory at weekends or during vacations. Saturday schools and vacation camps may occur with or without the cooperation of schools. In many Western European countries gifted education is almost entirely confined to such non-school activities, because education ministries, teachers' unions, and even teachers are opposed to special provision for the gifted on ideological grounds (Freeman, 1995b).

A second area in which there have been marked changes in gifted education in recent years involves the definition of who is a teacher. Not only may schools invite successful practitioners to give talks to pupils, but contact between gifted youngsters and such people may go beyond occasional visits to include regular opportunities to work with them (for instance, at the practitioner's place of work), intense tutoring from such people (for instance, at weekend seminars or vacation camps), or even establishment of an informal or sometimes formal mentorship. In the last example, practitioner and pupil plan a project together and the child carries it out under the watchful eye of the expert, who provides advice, encouragement, criticism, concrete help, and collegial feedback. Such contacts are particularly important in helping gifted youngsters develop not only skills but also attitudes, values and identity, and, perhaps most importantly, a feel for the ethics and brotherhood/sisterhood among practitioners of a particular discipline. In view of recent research revealing the important role of a crystallizing person in the childhood of people who later became highly successful, this latter aspect should not be undervalued.

Recent political events in Central and Eastern Europe raise a number of interesting issues. Communist regimes were generally strongly in favour of gifted education (even if the political status of the parents played a major role in deciding which children were identified as gifted). Several of these countries (including the Soviet Union) had well-developed systems, including, for example, special schools, organized and effective holiday camps and children's villages, as well as university clubs for children gifted in special subjects. Although participation in competitions at national level (such as the national science, language and music competitions in Germany) or international level (such as the International Mathematics Olympiad) was by no means restricted to the formerly Communist countries, the latter supported such forms of special provision for the gifted with great vigour. It remains to be seen whether these traditions will be maintained and strengthened under new governments, or if they will be swept aside in the course of reform.

Fostering creativity

One aspect of the rise in interest in creativity as an integral element of talent has been increasing research on encouraging bright people to be more creative. Although Torrance (1972) evaluated 142 studies on the enhancement of creativity, and concluded that many of these had a positive effect, several authors have challenged this. Among others, Mansfield *et al.* (1978) argued that even the more famous creativity training procedures are of doubtful value. Rump (1979) showed that the effects of creativity training are at their strongest when the criterion most closely resembles training procedures, and at their weakest when these elements are most dissimilar.

Figure 8.1 shows that conventional programmes and procedures for fostering creativity are too narrow, concentrating as they usually do on loosening up attitudes and work habits, and facilitating the development of divergent thinking skills. This largely takes place through working with unconventional materials, at least in comparison with traditional school materials. Furthermore, such programmes are limited to a particularly short period of time, for instance an hour a week for a year or so during the school years, and they commence when the children have already had a number of years' exposure to convergent ways of operating.

Ideally, what is needed is an effort embracing not only school, but also the family and the wider community. The holistic approach is essential, not only involving the promotion of skills and abilities (as in most existing programmes), but also the promotion of personal properties (courage, determination, independence, conviction of one's own rightness), and motivational states (dissatisfaction with the imperfect, willingness to take risks). Fostering these requires that children have early contacts with ambiguity, puzzlingness, uncertainty and imperfection, and that they have experience both in seeking solutions and also in making errors free of negative sanctions, or even in being praised for a bold but unsuccessful attempt rather than a tame correct solution.

SPECIAL QUESTIONS AND RESEARCH NEEDS

A number of issues still need further clarification. Among these is a set of 'conceptual' issues. What is a talent, and how can the origins and development of talents be accommodated within existing psychological models (or, what changes to such models are made necessary by the phenomenon of giftedness)? What forces and factors alter, facilitate or impede, accelerate or slow down, or change, the forms in which talents emerge?

Also important are questions about the phenomenology of exceptionally high ability. What does it 'feel like' to possess a special talent? What tactics are developed for coping with the situation, and what meaning do they have for the identity and self-image of talented individuals?

There are also practical questions, for instance, about the way in which potential for talented performance signals its presence. This question is especially important with regard to disadvantaged and deprived groups, the physically handicapped or the chronically ill: what are the signs of excellence in such groups? A further major practical question involves the part played by parents in the emergence of talents. Many are unsure of how to act in the best interests of their children, and are afraid of making mistakes. Others fear that they will be laughed at by family and friends. There may be a need for family counselling to help parents cope with the situation in a constructive way, as well as to help talented individuals deal with ambivalence about themselves, such as the feeling in adults of having been denied a 'normal' childhood for the glory of achievement.

REFERENCES

Amabile, T.M. (1983) *The Social Psychology of Creativity*. New York: Springer.
Amabile, T.M., Goldfarb, P. and Brackfield, S.C. (1990) 'Social influences on creativity: evaluation, coaction, surveillance', *Creativity Research Journal*, 3, 6–21.
Anderson, C.C. and Cropley, A.J. (1966) 'Some correlates of originality', *Australian Journal of Psychology*, 18, 218–27.
Baldwin, A.Y. (1985) 'Programs for the gifted and talented: issues concerning minority populations', in F.D. Horowitz and M. O'Brien (eds), *The Gifted and Talented: Developmental Perspectives*. Washington, DC: American Psychological Association.
Berry, C. (1990) 'On the origins of exceptional intellectual and cultural achievement', in M.J.A. Howe (ed.), *Encouraging the Development of Exceptional Skills and Talents*. Leicester: British Psychological Society.
Biermann, K.-R. (1985) 'Über Stigmata der Kreativität bei Mathematikern des 17. bis 19. Jahrhunderts', *Rostocker Mathematik Kolloquium*, 27, 5–22.
Bloom, B.S. (ed.) (1985) *Developing Talent in Young People*. New York: Ballantine.
Butler-Por, N. (1993) 'Underachieving gifted students', in K.A. Heller, F.J. Mönks and A.H. Passow (eds), *International Handbook of Research and Development of Giftedness and Talent*. Oxford: Pergamon.
Cornelius, S.W. and Crespi, A. (1987) 'Everyday problem-solving in adulthood and old age', *Psychology and Aging*, 2, 144–53.
Cox, C.M. (1926) *Genetic Studies of Genius: The Early Mental Traits of Three Hundred Geniuses*. Stanford: Stanford University Press.
Cropley, A.J. (1967a) *Creativity*. London: Longmans.
Cropley, A.J. (1967b) 'Divergent thinking and science specialist', *Nature*, 215, 671–2.

Cropley, A.J. (1969) 'Creativity, intelligence and intellectual style', *Australian Journal of Education*, **13**, 3–7.
Cropley, A.J. (1981) 'Hochbegabung und Kreativität: Eine Herausforderung für die Schule', in W. Wieczerkowski and H. Wagner (eds), *Das hochbegabte Kind*. Düsseldorf: Schwann.
Cropley, A.J. (1982) *Kreativität und Erziehung*. München: Reinhardt.
Cropley, A.J. (1994) 'Kreativität', in K. Pawlik and M. Amelang (eds), *Différentielle Psychologie*. Vol. 2, *Enzyklopädie der Psychologie*. Göttingen: Hogrefe.
Cropley, A.J., Urban K.K., Wagner, H. and Wieczerkowski, W. (1986) (eds) *Giftedness: A Continuing Worldwide Challenge*. New York: Trillium.
De Corte, E. (1995) 'Acquiring high-level learning skills'. Chapter 5, this volume.
Denton, F.C.J. (1986) 'Identifikation durch Lehrer', in W. Wieczerkowski, H. Wagner, K.K. Urban and A.J. Cropley (eds), *Hochbegabung, Gesellschaft, Schule*. Bad Honnef: Bock.
Elshout, J. (1990) 'Expertise and giftedness', *European Journal for High Ability*, **1**, 197–203.
Elshout, J. (1995) 'Talent: the ability to become an expert'. Chapter 7, this volume.
Facaoaru, C. (1985) *Kreativität in Wissenschaft und Technik. Operationalisierung von Problemlösefähigkeiten und kognitiven Stilen*. Bern: Huber.
Farisha, B. (1978) 'Mental imagery and creativity: review and speculation', *Journal of Mental Imagery*, **2**, 209–38.
Freeman, J. (1991) *Gifted Children Growing Up*. London: Cassell.
Freeman, J. (1995a) 'Review of current thinking on the development of talent'. Chapter 1, this volume.
Freeman, J. (1995b) 'Towards a policy for actualizing talent'. Chapter 13, this volume.
Fromm, E. (1980) *Greatness and Limitations of Freud's Thought*. New York: New American Library.
Gardner, H. (1983) *Frames of Mind: The Theory of Multiple Intelligences*. New York: Basic Books.
Gebart-Eaglemont, J.E. and Foddy, M. (1994) 'Creative potential and the sociometric status of children', *Creativity Research Journal*, **7**, 47–57.
Gibson, J. and Light, P. (1967) 'Intelligence among university scientists', *Nature*, **213**, 441–3.
Goertzel, M.G., Goertzel, V. and Goertzel, T.G. (1978) *300 Eminent Personalities*. San Francisco: Jossey-Bass.
Guilford, J.P.(1950) 'Creativity', *American Psychologist*, **5**, 444–54.
Guilford, J.P. and Christensen, P.R. (1973) 'The one-way relation between creative potential and IQ', *Journal of Creative Behavior*, **7**, 247–52.
Hassenstein, M. (1988) *Bausteine zu einer Naturgeschichte der Intelligenz*. Stuttgart: Deutsche Verlags-Anstalt.
Heinelt, G. (1974) *Kreative Lehrer – kreative Schüler*. Freiburg: Herder.
Horn, J.L. (1988) 'Major issues before us now and for the next few decades'. Paper presented at Seminar on Intelligence, Melbourne, Australia.
Howe, M. (1995) 'What can we learn from the lives of geniuses?' Chapter 3, this volume.
Jung, C.G. (1964) 'Approaching the unconscious', in C.G. Jung (ed.), *Man and His Symbols*. London: Aldus Books.
Landau, E. (1985) 'Creative questioning for the future', in J. Freeman (ed.), *The Psychology of Gifted Children*. Chichester: Wiley.
Lehman, H.C. (1953) *Age and Achievement*. Princeton: Princeton University Press.
MacKinnon, D.W. (1962) 'The nature and nurture of creative talent', *American Psychologist*, **17**, 484–95.
McLeod, J. and Cropley, A.J. (1989) *Fostering Academic Excellence*. Oxford: Pergamon.
McNemar, Q. (1964) 'Lost: our intelligence? Why?' *American Psychologist*, **19**, 871–82.
Mansfield, R.S., Busse, T.V. and Krepelka, E.J. (1978) 'The effectiveness of creativity training', *Review of Educational Research*, **48**, 517–36.
Milgram, R.M. (1990) 'Creativity: an idea whose time has come and gone?', in M.A. Runco and R.S. Albert (eds), *Theories of Creativity*. Newbury Park, CA: Sage.
Motamedi, K. (1982) 'Extending the concept of creativity', *Journal of Creative Behavior*, **16**, 75–88.

Mumford, M.D. and Gustafson, S.B. (1988) 'Creativity syndrome: integration, application, and innovation', *Psychological Bulletin*, **103**, 27–43.

Necka, E. (1986) 'On the nature of creative talent', in A.J. Cropley, K.K. Urban, H. Wagner and W. Wieczerkowski (eds), *Giftedness: A Continuing Worldwide Challenge*. New York: Trillium.

Neff, G. (1975) *Kreativität in Schule und Gesellschaft*. Ravensburg: Maier.

Rowley, S. (1995) 'Identification and development of talent in young athletes'. Chapter 10, this volume.

Rump, E.E. (1979) 'Divergent thinking, aesthetic preferences and orientation towards arts and sciences'. Unpublished PhD dissertation, University of Adelaide.

Runco, M.A. and Albert, R.S. (1986) 'The threshold theory regarding creativity and intelligence: an empirical test with gifted and nongifted children', *Creative Child and Adult Quarterly*, **11**, 212–18.

Shaughnessy, M.F. (1990) 'Cognitive structures of the gifted', *Gifted Educational International*, **6**, 149–51.

Shore, B.M. and Tsiamis, A. (1986) 'Identification by provision: limited field test of a radical alternative for identifying gifted students', in K.A. Heller and J.F. Feldhusen (eds), *Identifying and Nurturing the Gifted*. Bern: Huber.

Sierwald, W. (1989) 'Kreative Hochbegabung – Identifikation, Entwicklung und Förderung kreativer Hochbegabter'. Paper presented at 2nd Meeting of the Educational Psychology Section of the German Psychological Society, Munich.

Simonton, D.K. (1988) *Scientific Genius. A Psychology of Science*. Cambridge: Cambridge University Press.

Span, P. (1995) 'Self-regulated learning by talented children'. Chapter 6, this volume.

Stedtnitz, U. (1995) 'Psychosocial dimensions of talent: some major issues'. Chapter 4, this volume.

Sternberg, R.J. (1985) *Beyond IQ: A Triarchic Theory of Human Intelligence*. New York: Cambridge University Press.

Sternberg, R.J. and Lubart, T.I. (1992) 'Creative giftedness in children', in P.S. Klein and A.J. Tannenbaum (eds), *To Be Young and Gifted*. Norwood, NJ: Ablex.

Süle, F. (1990) 'Imaginative psychotherapy in the psychological care of top athletes', *European Journal for High Ability*, **1**, 162–5.

Torrance, E.P. (1972) 'Predictive validity of the Torrance Test of Creative Thinking', *Journal of Creative Behavior*, **32**, 401–5.

Torrance, E.P. and Hall, L.K. (1980) 'Assessing the further reaches of creative potential', *Journal of Creative Behavior*, **14**, 1–19.

Wallach, M.A. and Kogan, N. (1965) *Modes of Thinking in Young Children*. New York: Holt, Rinehart and Winston.

Weisberg, R.W. (1986) *Creativity*. New York: Freeman.

Chapter 9

The Emergence of Pictorial Talents
Norman H. Freeman

The arts are a prime way in which people relate both to other people and to situations, as well as providing a means of creating imaginative fiction. But there are specific questions about the emergence of pictorial talents. In what way can a picture realize imagination? What sorts of desires do pictures satisfy? What beliefs about pictures do people hold? Is there an irreducible character trait called 'artistic talent', of which some people have more than others? Once, 'influenced by the romantic tradition, art was thought to be extraordinary, a result of rare genius... Now we see art as less rare' (Smith and Fucigna, 1988). Although there can be no doubt that some people are highly gifted artistically, the current view is that it is possible to actualize a wide, general pool of talent to a far greater extent than had previously been accepted. Since the field of enquiry and its literature are vast, this chapter concentrates on two strands of enquiry, so as to focus on the actualization of pictorial talent.

Theory

An articulated theory is a set of concepts embedded in a network of beliefs, directed to a particular domain; this can put constraints on creativity, so as to channel it in a particular direction. What is the role of such theory as a mediator between potential and its actualization? Statements about theory often begin simply, but rapidly become complex, e.g. 'we have knowledge about our art processes; we have knowledge about our knowledge. Perhaps the most meaningful communication to the artist is, "here's how we see you seeing us conceiving of you doing your art"' (Beittel, 1972).

Constraints

The constraints themselves are typically of 'genre', i.e. the style of production and interpretation of a work. 'The creation of ... works of art such as novels and paintings, is typically carried out within the conventions of an existing genre' (Johnson-Laird, 1987). Some individuals are decidedly talented at 'genre-spotting'. Pictorial talent is actualized by an interplay which involves social constraints between aesthetic desires and beliefs. In order to make a picture, the artist will not only have to investigate how best to generate visual effects, but also test how best the effects can be put into being within a particular social context. For this, theory alone is not enough; the artist has both to acquire and value intuitive-practical knowledge of which he or she may only be dimly aware, perhaps being simply conscious of the feeling that aesthetic desires are at one time satisfied and at another aroused. Educators must work with this complex situation.

Can one see talent directly expressed in a picture? Certainly one can in the public display of the performing arts. Spectators watch a process whereby dance movements or chord sequences reveal something of how the performances are generated, although spectators may not always be aware of the hard work of rehearsal and preparation. Without personal practice (at any level), some of the performance of dance or playing an instrument may be incomprehensible, even if it is admired. Pictorial talent, though, appears to uninitiated spectators (perhaps most spectators) to be even more mysterious. Typically, the finished products are put on exhibition but the details of how they were made remain hidden, so that art historians are effectively detectives – notably in the case of dead artists. It is only on television that most people get a chance to see an artist in action. The sheer speed, dexterity and certainty of television cartoonists in making images leap out of a few lines actually reinforces the impression that drawing is mysterious – one either has the talent to do it, or one has not. And the social nature of the visual arts is much less apparent than with those arts where people perform together.

As Johnson-Laird (1987) succinctly observed: 'Any process that does not depend on magic can be modelled'. But to do this, 'A creative process must start with some existing "building blocks", and our working definition entails that it must be both non-deterministic and meet some criteria'. Pictorial talent looks like magic, but that appearance is something that will have to be explained one day, rather than built into an account at the outset. The high-point of the 'mystery movement' came in the 1960s, when many educators took up the idea that all that was necessary for actualizing talent was to provide children with stimulating environments, opportunities for 'creative' adventures and plenty of paint, from which the innate creativity – the birthright of all children – would evolve to generate exhibition products. However, during the last 20 years or so, both researchers and educators have had to first recognize and then emphasize the constraints that artists work with, which stem from many sources. Artists put some constraints upon themselves, while other constraints come from the contexts within which their pictorial discoveries are made.

An artist is someone with both the disposition to do a particular kind of visual research and the tenacity to generate and resolve pictorial problems. Currently, the most useful new approach to the actualization of pictorial talent is to examine what it means to do successful pictorial investigation. It is not only artists, however, who conduct pictorial experiments. There is now sufficient evidence, seen in normal developmental milestones in art, to suggest that all human beings are endowed with the talent needed to begin successful art work. But many hopeful beginnings fail to be followed through. Another part of the study of pictorial talent, which particularly concerns educators, is the investigation of what happens when talent appears to dry up, even to the extent that people feel inadequate to act as gifted spectators because they believe that they 'have no eye for art' or 'cannot draw'.

TOWARDS A THEORY OF PICTURE-MAKING

Imagination, tenacity and pictorial experimentation

It has often been noted that the actualization of talent is intimately bound up with a person's tenacity in exploring the effects of combining and reworking marks on the picture surface. Deregowski (1984, p. 112) observed that:

> visual artists like to explore patterns by transforming them again and again in search of the 'elements of visual experience'. Such elements ... can be distilled and reshaped, so that by redrawing, a ball can be derived from a tree-stump and a pebble.

This quotation captures something of what it is like to do pictorial research: derivative play is a major source of the free use of imagination. Indeed, such repeated transformations of surface markings are an essential aspect of artistic production, so that all marks on a page can take on many guises and functions – a circle can denote a sphere, disc, hoop, hole, and so on.

Once a mark is in place on a page, it sets up relations with other marks. In one respect, the marking affords a possible direct relation to a possible scene. It has relationships with other marks in two respects. In one, the mark can be examined for its likeness to an object, such as a ball, tree-stump, or pebble, i.e. a projective relationship to a referent. Pinning down and reworking the mark in that way offers insight into a kind of visual thinking about how forms in the world can be related via possible shapes that are projected.

In the other respect, there may not be a specific referent object; the mark on the page takes its relationship possibilities from secondary sources of drawings of an object, made in different ways. Thus, if a rough circle is being drawn to describe a potato, the circular line cannot be found by looking at the real object, but instead denotes a region of curvature on the surface of the largely smooth object (such a line is technically called an 'occluding contour'). If the potato is sprouting, a shoot might be represented by a single line that now represents an extended object by collapsing the contours, just as one does in representing the limbs and trunk of a stick-figure in human-figure drawing. Such different line-usages are called 'denotations'; every drawing can be analysed in terms of a 'calculus' of denotations (Willats, 1995).

There is now a growing literature on the analysis of interrelations between denotation and projection, which together make a referent recognizable in the picture. Willats (1985) presents some worked examples of young children's discoveries of denotional possibilities. Indeed, it is now becoming possible to be precise about the pictorial discoveries that young artists make, and thereby to specify what sort of pictorial experimentation is characteristic of talented individuals who commit their intelligence to the experimentation. Although it is easy to recognize a vegetable it is not so easy to draw it, and attempting to do so alerts one to the painful fact that it can be drawn differently according to whatever graphic solution one is attempting. A striking finding of Smith and Fucigna (1988) was that:

> Children join outlines and interior lines such that one line fades, joins, and is occluded as it follows a contour. This ability appeared early (first grade) and its use grew steadily, whereas the use of curving obliques to imply form was a later and more abrupt development ... this suggests the presence of relatively independent drawing systems. (p. 74)

An excellent study by Reith (1988) on increasingly complex moulded smooth forms, confirmed the use of contours by children below the age of 5 years, as well as illustrating how contour systems can be used in subdividing the form after the age of 8.

Thus, progress is being made in describing the types of pictorial experimentation that guide talent: 'The search for a profoundly original idea ... will succeed only if it is guided, at least in part by constraints of some sort' (Johnson-Laird, 1987, p. 128). Experimentation with combinations of marks and colours is an exploration of setting up and breaking constraints; talented individuals are those who find the enterprise intrinsically interesting and are prepared to let new visual effects emerge. As Winner (1982) put it: 'The moment of "insight" is simply the final step in a chain of reasoning' (p. 46).

Pictorial discoveries, however, do not come easily, and tenacity occurs in fits and starts, so that artists do not usually show it by settling down to an eight-hour day with regular tea breaks. But beneath the chaos and unpredictability of artistic success lies a kind of long-term commitment that psychologists are beginning to analyse. Wolf (1989) describes psychologists' change of direction as a turning away from the pictorial products to the life of the producers:

> Creative adults ... go about life and work in particular ways: notably they find personal projects and sustain interest ... as much as creating theories or paintings, they create a 'path of enquiry' where questions are revisited, answers refined, and new questions unearthed. The development of this capacity for cutting a path should command our attention. (p. 2)

The 'path' can be thought of as a sequence of generating pictorial problems – good art challenges the viewer to undertake much intelligent visual work.

What inspires tenacity?

Is it true that children have to be caught when young, when their minds are open, to be recruited for picture-making? Many educationalists believe that it is important to collaborate with young children and to secure their pictorial attitude before the turmoil of adolescence. Yet many retired adults have turned to the relatively solitary pursuit of making pictures very late in life, and whilst talent normally flourishes amongst the young it is not necessary to be young to become committed to visual experimentation. There is reason to be wary of any account which fails to recognize how artistry can develop at any stage in the life-span: youthfulness is an asset but not a prerequisite.

Nor does a person have to be in a particularly good psychological state to discover his or her artistic talent. There are many reports of people who were suffering or in extreme peril who turned to the making of pictures: if that were not so, there would be little chance of art therapy having any meaning for patients. This is a good place to start to analyse the nature of pictorial imagination, since in 'crisis management' there is a chance of seeing in dramatic form something which occurs quietly and often invisibly in the activities of normal healthy people – the committed construction of pictorial meaningfulness.

Dreyfus (1983) noticed how attached cancer patients could become to their pictures. In a way that is odd, for in a life-threatening situation people can become self-protectively drawn in on themselves. Yet a picture that has been made can achieve the status of a 'transitional object', normally associated with early childhood – the pink blanket or dog-eared teddy bear that is comforter and mediator of emergence into a social world (Shmukler, 1985). Dreyfus (1983) argued that the picture is the result of the patient's creative illusion, the space between the subjective world of the patient and outside reality that is represented by the presence of the art therapist. Thus, patients take up their relationship with the life-supporting therapist and embody it in art.

There has never been any evidence to suggest that human beings lack the artistic resources necessary to assimilate art to any existing relationships that they find important; this includes relationships with nature and with the mundane objects that sustain life in routine fashion. The earliest depictions of 'Still Life' – maybe a few apples and a spoon on a rough table interestingly displayed – opened people's eyes to how visually stimulating the most apparently conceptually boring of objects can be. Brook (1983) caught the essence of this: 'Pictures are the most potent of ... non-verbal representations by means of which we ambivalently seek to open and close the gap between the actual and what is possible' (p. 180). There are three approaches to closing that gap between the actual and the possible, and accounts of the ingredients of pictorial talent may therefore contain statements referring to them – what is depicted, how it is depicted, and why the depiction makes you think in particular ways.

What is depicted: artistic talent can employ imagination to develop pictorial fiction in the same way as literary fiction, which bears an uneasy relationship to what is possible, by exploring and depicting what can never be seen. But on the one hand, if the fictional distance is too small, the imagination too poor, the picture may appear rather prosaic and unbelievable, almost as though it had a cautious pictorial message tacked on, saying 'this is fiction'. This is what 5-year-olds seem to have done in an experiment where they were asked to draw a 'man who doesn't exist' (Karmiloff-Smith, 1992). On the other hand, if the fiction is too well done, too explicit, it means that there is no interesting work for the spectator to do in investigating the 'gap between the actual and what is possible'. Talent in teasing the spectator about what he or she is looking at demands an insight into the relationships between facts and fictions.

How it is depicted: one can focus on the truth that all depictions are fictions, no matter how well they are presented as representations of reality. The fictional quality arises from the dual reality of the picture, as either an object in its own right or as an 'intentional' object which refers to and represents a state of affairs outside itself. Thus, although a brick is an object, its picture on a flat surface is also an object, but at the same time it is a token of a different type. Somehow, people are able to respect this distinction psychologically, regarding the picture as an object which depicts another object – it is a picture of a brick. This dual reality creates an intriguing tension in the mind of the spectator who is prepared to apply his or her visual intelligence to the picture. That tension has psychological effects that play out as a drama. It also provides the raw material for aestheticians, who divide broadly into those who regard depictions as objects upon which the aesthetic spotlight happens to play (e.g. Hospers, 1946), and those who regard aesthetic experience as inherently tied to the peculiar properties of pictures (e.g. Goodman, 1968).

The effect of the depiction on thinking: the third approach to possibility is to focus on what people say about pictures and picture-making. Whenever judges inspect a picture that a hopeful artist has sent in for exhibition, it is expected that they will do more than just express their taste – 'I rather like that one'; they have to act as critics, explaining their judgements. Artists also often explain their pictorial ideas – 'If I were to darken that yellow, then perhaps the sky would lighten' – before, during, or after they make pictorial experiments. Judges are often sensitive to pictorial experimentation, and couch their explanations in terms of what they think 'the picture is trying to do'. Thus, both artists and spectators have theories of what is pictorially possible; these may be more or less articulately expressed in words, but are often in metaphor – 'That nervous line is saliently cutting across the composition in a provoking way'. Everyone has the capacity to be an art critic (for the early stages see Golomb, 1992).

Artistic talent can be seen as a commitment to investigating links between the above three approaches in a (literally) productive manner. There are roles to be taken up of producer, perceiver and critic (see Winner, 1982, for an extensive analysis of role-play and art). In the course of taking up these roles and relating each to the others, the artist involves herself in creative visual research, problem-solving and problem-generation. Research involves essentially the same kind of mental work, whatever its domain of application – 'The popular and mistaken identification of the arts with creativity and of science with problem-solving may partly arise from the way in which psychologists have gone about investigating these domains' (Hargreaves, 1989, p. 5). Although it is no accident that psychological researchers do stress what is particular to the pictorial domain, it is possible that the reference to aesthetics and imagination is too limiting if one wants an account of pictorial potential which traces the roots of pictorial experimentation.

Origins of pictorial potential

Morris (1962) records that he once worked with a group of young chimpanzees, taking them one by one and helping them make a mark on paper. The fourth chimp needed no help – 'she grabbed the pencil from me and started to work without any hesitation' (p. 34). That chimp had been observing what was going on and needed no extrinsic reward to engage with the new endeavour: even monkeys have been observed to draw with chalks (Kluver, 1933), and individuals seem to have pictorial preferences: about a quarter of the productions of Morris's chimp Congo were of fan shapes. For Congo's first scribble, he was given a card with a blot on it and he aimed straight for it. Given large 'abstract' shapes like squares and circles, Schiller's chimpanzee Alpha roughly filled them in for 22 out of 25 drawings (Schiller, 1951). Morris was able to diagnose a set of rules that Congo employed in placing marks in relation to what was already on the page, from aiming at the mark to offsetting it to give an asymmetrically balanced design. Human children in the scribbling stage investigate patterns without any teaching in how to do it.

Using evidence such as this, it seems probable that basic pictorial aesthetics and a willingness to work at art-making evolved long before our own species arose, so that every member is endowed with the ability to produce an artefact that he or she finds of aesthetic value. Indeed, there is not a shred of evidence that any normal human being is by nature aesthetically 'tone deaf'. But there are things that human beings do spontaneously with pictures that apes do not – propensities which appear to be biologically primed in our species, and which do not need any tuition for their actualization.

Gardner and Wolf (1987, p. 310) summarized one route into the pictorial attitude – 'Consider when the child of 1½ or 2 is asked to draw a truck . . . a typical child will grab a marker, move it across the paper back and forth rapidly, and then say "Vroommm, Vroommm" as if the marker itself is a vehicle' (see also Wolf, 1989). The child is using the crayon to visually record the activity, but once the caption is forgotten, the record loses its power as an interpretation of what it was meant to represent. This simple example shows how records are not 'pictorially fixed' – they cannot independently trigger any recognition in a spectator that is based on normal experience, either of trucks or of depictions. But limited though recording may be, the activity is important in being a mode of discovering how the properties of the medium can yield a representation via exploration that is bound up with functional play. The child discovers how a type of play can yield a meaningful mark – a mark that stands for something – though the connection between the marks and the reality is too direct to generate an imaginative picture. It is the next step in the sequence which does achieve pictorial fiction, and again its emergence appears to be biologically primed in all normal members of our species. In this the child pretends to be an artist and pretends that the resulting scribble represents a situation or object.

Leslie (1988) has argued that in pretend play, the child automatically sets up mental models that are alternatives to reality. Consider how remarkable pretence is as a specifically psychological achievement. The young of many species play at life-tasks, like mock fighting; but what characterizes our species is that in early childhood, something switches on automatically (except in autistic children) which enables us to divorce our minds from reality. Real things in scenes are used as stage-props in constructing and following through an alternative mental model. Somehow, this does not confuse children: pretence operates on 'decoupled' representations, so that one can safely pretend a banana is a telephone without thereby getting odd ideas about the edibility of telephones. Indeed, it has been claimed that expertise with pretence, the setting-up of mental models by a mental act with stipulation, is a forerunner of a theory of mind – the understanding of the mental models of others, and of the 'key component' of make-believe in art (Harris and Kavanaugh, 1933).

When children play at being artists, they accept pictorial fiction. Pretence and play are often identified as essential for the young child's creativity and autonomy, and many teachers encourage pre-schoolers to spill it over into art works. Indeed, it is not easy to overestimate the early importance of 'playing pictures'. Pretence works by attribution. If a child attributes the quality of a 'cake' to some clay and of 'plums' to some beads, then it is a 'truth', at least to the child, that the bead-studded blob of clay is indeed a 'plum cake'. That 'truth' is vital if the child is to make 'as-if' deductive discoveries from it, discoveries which are as rigorous as in any scientific system, and as creative a stipulation as in any of the arts. The natural next step up from simple recording is to broaden the focus (decentre) from the marker to the picture-plane, and define that a scribble is, for example, a drawing of a person. If a horizontal line at the bottom of the page is then said to be the ground, then the pictorial 'truth' is produced of a person standing on the ground. Long before the child can exhibit differentiated graphic skills, she can logically describe different kinds of art and meaning in a picture. And within the constraints of pretend play in her world, she will be right.

It is as much of an innate gift to show imagination in pictorial fiction as it is to take aesthetic pleasure in patterning. Each aspect is enough in itself to account for the enterprise and tenacity that characterizes the early years: 'the ages 5–7 seem to us a very special time, one that deserves to be termed the flowering of symbolism' (Gardner and Wolf, 1987, p. 314). But of course, that is not enough to guarantee that successful products will emerge, for such an outcome depends on the child embracing the right sort of constraints within which to perform.

But how do constraints become represented in the minds of aspiring artists? Human beings work well with an intuitive theory that is expressed in the language of desires, beliefs, intentions and traits (Wellman, 1990); picture-making becomes embraced by such terminology, and people develop a theory of pictorial art (Freeman, 1990; 1991). Such a theory channels their creativity into a set of constraints. No conscious theory of art can magically make one who holds it creative, but it does provide a means of communicating about the purposes and functions of art-objects. For example, the theorist becomes intellectually aware of the critical work that a spectator can do.

That is the rational kernel of the upheaval in art education that has occurred in our generation. In the USA, the importance of the opportunity to act as art critic in explaining how art exerts its effects was stressed by the Discipline-Based Art Education Movement (DBAE), and in the UK, a later less centralized movement now termed Critical Studies has a similar emphasis (Thistlewood, 1989). The argument is that high ability in pictorial art should not be identified solely with the outcome of studio work: individuals can be highly talented as art critics. Indeed, critical non-producers play an active role in a visually positive (iconophilic) culture, providing the essential medium in which able and committed producers can flourish in their intuitive pictorial reasoning that leads to insights and success.

The emergence of a theory of art

How would one know whether an individual had a productive theory of art or not? There are several sources of evidence that educators detect and amplify for the child during the early school years. In those years, do children believe that someone can draw a picture to make you think or feel in one way or another? That would be a causal-explanatory link between artist's intentionality and spectator reaction. Do children believe that you can find out what someone is thinking or feeling from the picture he or she makes? That would be an inference from product to producer. Do children believe that a happy artist will necessarily make a more beautiful picture than a sad artist? That would be a causal-explanatory link from producer to product. Do children understand that someone can intend to make an interesting picture and mistakenly make a dull one? That would be an inference about unfulfilled intentions, an 'honest mistake' – a concept that serves to puzzle pre-schoolers when they try to work out the explanatory role of mental representations (Wellman, 1990). As yet, however, research evidence is scanty (see Freeman, 1995, and Freeman and Sanger, 1993, for discussion).

Parsons' (1987) basic argument is that people respond to paintings differently because they understand them differently. They have different expectations about what paintings in general should be like, and what kinds of qualities can be found in them:

> Young children start with much the same basic understanding of what paintings are about, and they restructure that understanding in much the same ways as they grow older ... to make better sense of the works of art they encounter ... where individual people wind up in this sequence depends on what kinds of art they encounter and how far they are encouraged to think about them. (pp. 1–5)

The beginning is in mundane visual experience, the end-point is presumably the interconnectedness of aesthetic and social aspects of art-objects: the task is to chart the theory in between.

Two examples will show how the research is not merely a matter of describing 'understanding', but rather of testing hypotheses about the underlying generative theory in between visual experience and successful art work.

The first example comes from interviews with adolescents on a visit to the Tate Gallery in London, reported by Turner (1983). One group unanimously disliked Derain's Fauvist *Pool of London* (1906), which they criticized for its lack of naturalism. Taylor (1989) subsumed the example under a demonstration that 'all distortions are bad' – an intolerance of deviation from the visually 'given' of a possible scene. He went on to argue that intolerance is a symptom of children inheriting 'aesthetic attitudes from their parents' reactions to photography, snapshots especially ... a belief in verisimilitude is taken for granted by the majority of the population'. Children do indeed have a naïve-realist theory of depiction (Freeman, 1991), but Taylor also noted that children improve in their technical skills, and that Turner's children regarded Derain's work as 'amateur'. In the original report, it is clear that the children could not see what kind of visual research had gone into the picture-production, so that they saw it as carelessly dashed off. It is seemingly a part of the vernacular theory of art that artwork should not be easy to produce – 'If anyone could do it like that it cannot be good art'. What is needed is a study that pits apparent ease of execution against naturalism: only that type of analytic work would expose both the child's underlying theory of the artist's labour and the form of the product. From Turner's report, one cannot quite tell what theory gave rise to the surface criticism of 'a shoddy work produced by a non-professional'.

However, there is another strand to the children's criticisms that needs exposing. The children focused on the picture and the individual artist, which is understandable in the interview situation, but they seemed to lack an understanding of the cooperative nature of art production. They fail to grasp that Derain was an agent for a cultural system trading in signs. In Johnson's (1982) interviews with children aged between 4 and 18 years, they, too, believed implicitly that an artist works alone. A major thrust of the Critical Studies movement is to counteract that position. There is indeed much to counteract in popular cultural stereotypes about art – 'the general hostility to modern art which is endemic in the general population will already have been transmitted to the child of 5 or 6 and upward' (Taylor, 1989). The term 'hostility' is not overstated, and artistic talent often has to be actualized in a hostile environment.

One of the tools for actualizing talent at the educators' disposal is a fostering of reflective awareness about works of art. Naïve realism is an obstacle to the actualization of talent that should be overcome in order to help aspiring artists regain access to their natural understanding of pictures as fictions. But the matter must be handled sensitively, for the insight that has become unproductively 'hardened' in a naïve-realist theory is that depiction is anchored in the visible world. However, disregarding that insight would be to throw out the baby with the bathwater, because it provides the bedrock of the category of depictions itself (Freeman, 1991). A productive theory of the pictorial is one which recognizes that a picture inspires thinking in a particular way about mundane objects, as well as thinking in a particular way about pictures.

CONCLUSIONS ON A THEORY

Like other aspects of art, pattern-making is older than our species. Human infants who take such pleasure in gesturing and making marks and forms within soft materials, spontaneously take pleasure in making marks on paper. They need no tuition to recognize referents in depictions, nor in applying pretence and imagination to picture-making. All that is our biological heritage, and it is no misuse of language to assert that we are a highly talented species in basic visual aesthetics.

But like all talents, the potential only becomes actualized if a person invests the right sort of research effort into the domain. Tenacity is essential in exploring the combination and recombination of shapes that both satisfies and arouses aesthetic desires. The investment of such effort can be an intensely isolating affair, since the pictorial is largely a private, non-performing mode. However, some people find it meaningful and satisfying to appropriate picture-making for their own 'path of enquiry', undertaking their personal investigations of themselves (as did Dreyfus (1983) with cancer patients).

Our species spontaneously develops theories about various aspects of life, and the pictorial domain is no exception. The advance of the past few years has been for researchers to pay closer attention to what children say about picturing. Although the evidence has to be filtered through an understanding that some children have greater verbal fluency than others, there is a new understanding that talent as art critic is both valuable and easily worked with. Whilst collections of children's studio-work probably have not changed all that much in the last generation, collections of children's critiques of art have become radically more sensitive (see, for instance,

Parsons, 1987). It is too early to be sure of success, but it is worth persevering with the new line of education, discussing art with children in such a way that the issues encourage them to articulate their theory of art and challenge them to develop their ideas further.

It may be said that any decent curriculum automatically allows high-ability individuals to emerge. There is a vast literature on the subject of how to engage children's energies in picture-related activities, and an even greater number of working papers and local curricula. From this, a rather simple conclusion emerges – that there is not a single activity, in or out of school, which cannot be used by a skilled adult to energize children's productions and foster a love of art at all ages and stages. It is a two-way process – all aspects of art can be worked with to provide benefit from the activities. 'Art is issue saturated. The making of art is a reaction to experience . . . experience demands understanding, it teases the great issues of life' (King, 1987, p. 38).

Many educators, like MacGregor (1977), write simply about the kinds of messages which depictions can convey. These range from a propaganda poster, which emphasizes the specifics of a conflict and, by drawing the protagonists as mirror-images of one another, delivers a powerful graphic message to the alert viewer, to a possible association between a blue prize-ribbon and the colour of the sky. As van Sommers (1984) observed, many aspects of graphic production are either social acts 'or contribute to graphic social acts. The man who gives a tradesperson a meticulous drawing is issuing a request for a meticulous job' (p. 265).

Researchers have also been seeking out propositions on which to found general accounts of how children benefit from joint enterprises. When the Design Research Team of the Royal College of Art (1975) came to articulate principles, it settled on people's 'desire and ability to mould [their] physical environment to meet [their] material and spiritual needs'. They thus identified a motivation which is far greater than aesthetic motivation in providing the energy and resource to be focused by educators. At that level, the child's emerging theory of art is in a subclass of her general theory of control over her environment.

If one is looking for clues about where adults can foster aptitude for problem-generation in visual art, the literature is packed with arguments that any joint enterprise can be shaped to those ends. On the one hand, that appears to be excellent, since anything can be used in the process of creating a social context for the expression of ability. But on the other hand it is rather depressing, because the greater the claim for generality, the harder it has been to know precisely how to set about the teaching task. For example, different methods may be required to focus on joint enterprises as 'education through art', or as 'education in art' (Loeb and Fullick, 1979). Another reason for confusion is that there are no grounds for believing that different kinds of art-aptitudes are highly correlated. The preliminary study to the Leonardo Project for Developing Curricula for Visual Arts Education (Karpati, 1988) reports a very weak correlation between art-critical skills and do-it-yourself studio work: 'The traditional approach of Hungarian art educators – most of them with the ambition to be accepted as creative artists – to focus mainly on studio art will clearly not result automatically in high achievement in art criticism' (p. 133). This means that a generation is growing up who are inarticulate at helping each other with art and using peer-group language to explain how pictures can be the object of an intelligent gaze.

How closely can one work with children to implant a theory of 'how art can be done'? Although that implantation would provide a door for the fostering of one aspect of a theory of art, many educators are wary of pushing the door open. Harris (1982) questions 'the assumption which some teachers take for granted . . . that art teachers can know the most fruitful direction for an individual pupil's work . . . from looking at work in progress and perhaps talking with the pupil'. Similarly, the North Eastern Region of the Art Advisers Association (1978) expressed the view that 'the child needs to be allowed to draw in his own way, and might easily lose confidence through the misplaced intervention of an adult' (p. 13), while Brook (1983) suggested that 'it is intolerably frustrating for the child-victim of the art class as we know it, who repeatedly re-learns what he/she takes to be "the game" only to have the rules of play up-ended by the next institutional judge' (p. 44). He adds that 'radically new models can only be recognised as such after they have been generated'. All these comments reflect a valid concern that the child's spontaneous innovations should not be interfered with, lest their source dry up, as well as a recognition of the psychological complexity of picture-production. The debate continues on how best to enlist the producer's point of view, expressed through her theory of art, in the interests of finding her a safe niche for her research into how to push her path of enquiry forward.

REFERENCES

Arts Advisers Association, North Eastern Region (1978) *Learning Through Drawing*. London: The Association.
Beittel, K. (1972) *Mind and Context in the Art of Drawing*. New York: Holt, Rinehart and Winston.
Brook, D. (1983) 'Painting, photography and representation', *Journal of Aesthetics and Art Criticism*, **42**, 171–80.
Deregowski, J. (1984) *Distortion in Art: The Eye and the Mind*. London: Routledge.
Design Research Team of the Royal College of Art (1975) *Programme for Design in Education Summer School*. July. London: Royal College of Art.
Dreyfus, E. (1983) 'Art therapy with cancer patients' in *The Healing Role of the Arts*. Rockefeller Foundation Report.
Freeman, N.H. (1990) 'Children's implicit theory of art', *Australian Art Education*, **14**, 31–9.
Freeman, N.H. (1991) 'The theory of art that underpins children's naive realism', *Visual Arts Research*, **17**, 65–75.
Freeman, N.H. (1993) 'Language and belief in critical thinking: emerging exploration of pictures', *Exceptionality Education Canada*, **3**, 43–58.
Freeman, N.H. (1995) 'The emergence of a framework theory of pictorial reasoning', in C. Lange-Keutner and G.V. Thomas (eds), *Drawing and Looking*. Hemel Hempstead: Prentice Hall.
Freeman, N.H. and Sanger, D. (1993) 'Language and belief in critical thinking: emerging explanations of pictures', *Exceptionality Education, Canada*, **3**, 43–58.
Gardner, H. and Wolf, D. (1987) 'The symbolic products of early childhood', in D. Gorlitz and J.F. Wohlwill (eds), *Curiosity, Imagination and Play*. Hillsdale, NJ: Erlbaum.
Golomb, C. (1992) *The Child's Creation of a Pictorial World*. Berkeley: University of California Press.
Goodman, N. (1968) *Languages of Art*. Indianapolis: Bobbs-Merrill.
Hargreaves, D.J. (1989) 'Developmental psychology and the arts', in D.J. Hargreaves (ed.), *Children and the Arts*. Milton Keynes: Open University Press.

Harris, A. (1982) 'The challenge of art education: the role of the teacher and the role of the student', in M. Ross (ed.), *The Development of Aesthetic Experience*. Oxford: Pergamon.
Harris, P.L. and Kavanaugh, R.D. (1993) 'Young children's understanding of pretence', *Monographs of the Society for Research in Child Development*, **58** (1), serial no. 231, pp. 1–110.
Hospers, J. (1946) *Meaning and Truth in the Arts*. Chapel Hill: University of North Carolina Press.
Johnson, N.R. (1982) 'Children's meanings in art', *Studies in Art Education*, **23**, 61–7.
Johnson-Laird, P.N. (1987) 'Reasoning, imagining and creating', *Bulletin of the British Psychological Society*, **40**, 121–9.
Karmiloff-Smith, A. (1992) *Beyond Modularity*. Cambridge MA: MIT Press.
Karpati, A. (1988) 'Art as a tool and conveyor of knowledge'. Paper given at the Congress of the International Society for Education Through Art, Stockholm.
King, G. (1987) 'The laundering of art: where have all the issues gone?' *Journal of the Institute of Art Education*, **11**, 37–41.
Kluver, H. (1933) *Behavior Mechanisms in Monkeys*. Chicago: University of Chicago Press.
Leslie, A.M. (1988) 'Some implications of pretence for mechanisms underlying the child's theory of mind', in J. Astington, P.L. Harris and D. Olson (eds), *Developing Theories of Mind*. Cambridge: Cambridge University Press.
Loeb, H. and Fullick, J. (1979) *Art as Learning* (Art Education Monographs No. 3). Birmingham: City of Birmingham Polytechnic.
MacGregor, R.N. (1977) *Art Plus*. Toronto: McGraw-Hill Ryerson.
Morris, D. (1962) *The Biology of Art*. London: Methuen.
Parsons, M.J. (1987) *How We Understand Art*. Cambridge: Cambridge University Press.
Reith, E. (1988) 'The development of use of contour lines in children's drawings of figurative and non-figurative three-dimensional models', *Archives de Psychologie*, **56**, 83–103.
Schiller, P. (1951) 'Figural preferences in the drawings of a chimpanzee', *Journal of Comparative and Physiological Psychology*, **44**, 406–14.
Shmukler, D. (1985) 'Foundations of creativity: the facilitating environment', in J. Freeman (ed.), *The Psychology of Gifted Children*. Chichester: Wiley.
Smith, N. and Fucigna, C. (1988) 'Drawing systems in children's pictures: contour and form', *Visual Arts Research*, **14**, 66–76.
Sommers, P. van (1984) *Drawing and Cognition*. Cambridge: Cambridge University Press.
Taylor, B. (1989) 'Art history in the classroom: a plea for caution', in D. Thistlewood (ed.), *Critical Studies in Art and Design Education*. London: Longman.
Thistlewood, D. (ed.) (1989) *Critical Studies in Art and Design Education*. London: Longman.
Turner, P. (1983) 'Children's responses to art: interpretation and criticisms', *Journal of Art and Design Education*, **2**, 185–98.
Wellman, H.M. (1990) *The Child's Theory of Mind*. Cambridge, MA: MIT Press.
Willats, J. (1985) 'Drawing systems revisited', in N.H. Freeman and M.V. Cox (eds), *Visual Order: The Nature and Development of Pictorial Representation*. Cambridge: Cambridge University Press.
Willats, J. (1995) 'An information processing approach to drawing development', in C. Lange-Kuetner and G.V. Thomas (eds), *Drawing and Looking*. Hemel Hempstead: Prentice Hall.
Winner, E. (1982) *Invented Worlds: The Psychology of the Arts*. Cambridge, MA: Harvard University Press.
Wolf, D.P. (1989) 'Novelty, creativity, and child development', *Society for Research in Child Development Newsletter*, Spring, 1–3.

Chapter 10

Identification and Development of Talent in Young Athletes

Stephen Rowley

The selection and development of talent has intrigued coaches and sports scientists in different countries for many years (Hebbelinck, 1988). Much time and effort has been spent trying to identify the particular physical and psychological characteristics which contribute to élite performance, and although considerable debate has surrounded the relative contributions of genetic, social, and environmental factors, most authors agree that talent has to be identified before potential can be reached. How can we identify the champions of the future as early as possible?

The identification of talent has gained in importance over the years, as performance standards have continued to improve and the age at which younger athletes reach the top has significantly reduced (Fisher and Borms, 1990). In sport, age is a critical factor in development – the earlier the start the better the results. In fact, there is some evidence that early advancement in motor skills within the first year of life may keep this advantage in later years (Lewis and Louis, 1991; and see Freeman, 1995). Those with exceptional physical talent share with other children of high ability the need for early identification and continual development and support if potential is to be reached. However, what really differentiates the physically able from children with abilities more commonly associated with giftedness, such as musical or intellectual excellence, is the relatively small window of opportunity available to actualize their talents in adult life. In many sports, athletes have to cram a lifetime's achievement into a relatively short period of time. For example, an analysis of the world's top ten tennis players indicates that the average peak age for men is 23.7 years, and for women 21.7 years. These players can expect only a further six or seven years at the top before diminishing motivation, injury, and of course the ageing process cause a decline in their performance.

This chapter will describe the results of a three-year longidutinal study which monitored the psychological development of 453 talented young athletes, aged between 8 and 19 years.

THE IDENTIFICATION OF TALENT IN SPORT

In sport, children are usually identified as talented on the basis of either results or potential, whereas adult competitors have to show a consistently high quality of performance, often whilst under tremendous physical and emotional pressure. Superficially, the identification of exceptional talent in sport seems to be a relatively easy matter (Kane, 1986). Most identification procedures rely heavily on performance as evidence of talent, so that the child who is achieving at a level well beyond that of his/her contemporaries can be easily identified by parents, teachers or coaches. However, the early assessment of talent may be confounded by social and environmental factors; the child's achievement being either the result of early opportunity and parental support or pressure, or of a biological advantage due to early maturation (Kane, 1986).

The main aim of any systematic search for talent is that children with potential should be given the opportunity to develop their sports skills, in the hope that an accelerated programme of intensive training will increase the likelihood of success at the senior level. However, much depends on matching the right children with the right sport. The process of matching is that:

> by which children are encouraged to participate in those sports in which they are most likely to succeed, based on the results of testing selected parameters designed to predict future performance capacity accounting for the child's current level of fitness and degree of maturity. (Thomson and Beavis, 1985, p. 31)

In her review of the assessment of giftedness, Freeman (1991) points out that the resources required for the development of any special ability must also be considered as part of the appraisal process when identifying talent, or as McQuattie (1986) put it, 'a potential long-distance runner cannot flourish in a confined apartment'. The physically talented young athlete needs to be matched with both the appropriate facilities and a coach who can develop his/her potential to the projected levels. Many Eastern European countries have employed selection processes for many years, and in fact specialist schools for languages, sport and music have been in operation there since the 1930s. Western nations, though, have been slow to develop structured identification programmes (Fisher and Borms, 1990). In Hungary, for example, Harsanyi et al. (1990) investigated the dynamics of the performance of male 100-metre sprinters, and found that even by the ages of 15 to 18, those whose development had been faster in performance, but not biological maturity, were significantly more successful. This integrated approach, measuring both ability and the efficacy of training, was suggested as a useful indicator for identification.

In the United Kingdom, for example, sporting potential is usually recognized by competition results (the Proof Principle) or by a coach's 'gut-feeling'; there is little in the way of any systematic search for talent based upon scientific tests. It is true, nevertheless, that many of the screening procedures available to the coach to predict performance potential have dubious reliability. When screening procedures are used, they usually consist of selected physical characteristics – height and weight, for example – and/or performance on tests of assessment which are thought to measure traits associated with performance in a particular sport.

In addition to those physical and psychological factors associated with performance potential, a child's familial, educational and general social background are also important factors. Probably the most important influence on a young person's capacity to be successful in sport (and most other domains) is the home environment (Freeman, 1993); parents with an active interest in sport will naturally expose their children to various activities at an early age as part of family leisure time (Thomson and Beavis, 1985; Fisher and Borms, 1990). It has been suggested that at least one of the parents of élite performers is often interested and/or active in the same or a similar area (Bloom, 1985; Ericsson et al., 1990). Further studies have shown that the family provides the main motivation for a child's participation in specific sports (Fowler, 1969), although little information is available on why children increase their involvement beyond an average level. However, a study of motivation in physical education found that perceived competence was positively associated with intrinsic interest, which in turn was determined by self-determination, that is, an absence of pressure for pupils to engage in sport which did not appeal to them. 'Further, intrinsic interest was a strong predictor of students' intentions to keep involved with the activities' (Goudas et al., 1994, p. 462). However, there are wider influences, such as national pride. In Australia, a sport-conscious country, for example, 'Going for Gold' represented a massive input of $4 per head of the population (15.6 million people) to develop sporting talent, in reaction to the country's poor performance in the Seoul Olympics (Gross, 1993, p. 58). Sport in previously communist Europe performed a propagandist function through the record-breaking efforts, which were well supported by identification and training.

Yet despite the problems associated with identifying talent, the search for potential champions at an early age has become a high priority within sport. Children of increasingly younger ages now compete in élite national and international championships, and often surpass performances that were once thought to represent the peak of adult achievement (Thomson and Beavis, 1985).

There is increasing concern among those involved in youth sport, though, about possible adverse effects of intensive training on the physical and psychological development of young athletes (e.g. Dudink, 1990). Anecdotal reports of overuse injuries to bones and joints, impaired growth, and both physical and psychological 'burn-out' have alerted many parents, coaches and sports scientists to the possible detrimental effects which prolonged intensive training may have upon a child's health. There is evidence that psychotherapeutic work with top athletes can be helpful to counter the pressure they may be under (Süle, 1990). Even without rigorous evidence, the Council of Europe (1982) recommended that specialization in sport before 12 years of age was not advisable, whilst there is still inadequate information on the biological consequences for the child's growth and development.

THE TRAINING OF YOUNG ATHLETES (TOYA) STUDY

The Training of Young Athletes (TOYA) study was a large-scale survey designed to look at the effects of intensive training on a sample of highly trained young athletes (Rowley, 1992). The specific aim was to determine the effect that accelerated programmes of coaching and training might have on the physical and psychological development of the growing child. Sport coaches from England and Wales were invited to nominate children aged between 8 and 16 years who were training intensively in football, gymnastics, swimming and tennis. A random sample of 453 young people was selected and monitored annually for three consecutive years. The data presented in this chapter are taken from interviews conducted at home with both children and parents.

Demographic variables and identification of talent

Despite the availability of higher standards of coaching, training and competition for the young (as outlined above), the opportunity to participate in sport is still determined by a number of social and environmental factors, including the gender of a child, social class background, race and the geographical location of the home (McPherson, 1982). These variables explain to some degree why children who may be physically and psychologically similar do or do not become involved in sport.

Gender. Because of socially bound behavioural expectations, participation in sports remains positively associated with the male sex-role (Duquin, 1978). Consequently, although the male's involvement in sport is associated with masculinity and conformity with gender role, the female who is physically talented may be seen either as losing her femininity or defying religious restrictions through her involvement, and thus manifesting gender abnormality (Anthrop and Allison, 1983). Female participation is still channelled into certain 'feminine' sports, such as gymnastics and figure-skating, which display the body in graceful balletic movements. The swimmer or tennis player may be faced with the dilemma that she must satisfy her needs for achievement in sport, whilst meeting the societal expectations of the feminine role. The mutual contradiction of these dual roles can be a cause of emotional strain (Del Ray, 1978), particularly when, as Anthrop and Allison (1983) have suggested, there is often a lack of emotional support, recognition or reward for the female's persistence or success.

This situation can be made more difficult for very young athletes when the incentives and social supports present before puberty are withdrawn in adolescence. Because of these constraints, many women in sport either remain underachievers or else drop out of sports altogether during early adolescence or young adulthood.

Social class. Many studies have shown that social class has a considerable effect on sports participation, usually concluding that the lower social classes are under-represented (Macintosh, 1982). Unfortunately, most of these studies have only examined the class background of successful adult athletes. It has been suggested that working-class children are less likely to make 'constructive' use of available leisure time, since there is less encouragement at home to do so (Scarlett, 1975). This may affect the opportunity for physically able youngsters from lower social classes to be identified as talented, other than in specific areas, such as 'blacks' in boxing.

An analysis of the social-class distribution of the families taking part in the TOYA study indicates that across all four sports there were fewer children from the lower socio-economic groups, classes IV and V (manual and unskilled occupations), when compared to the general population, indicated by census data (OPCS). Figure 10.1 illustrates the social-class distribution of the TOYA families.

132 *Actualizing Talent*

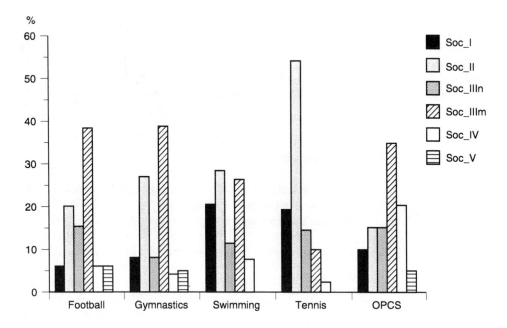

Figure 10.1 *Social-class distribution*

Such is the dominance of the middle class that in sports such as swimming and tennis there were no families representing unskilled occupations, class V in the graph. Even football, traditionally thought to be the preserve of the working class, has a distribution which is skewed toward the higher socio-economic groups.

The relationship between social class and intensive training indicates that there are inequalities in access to intensive participation in sports amongst young people. Reasons for this appear to be:

- Considerable financial support is required to enable children to participate in intensive training routines.
- Occupational flexibility and greater mobility of middle-class families allows parents more time to take their children to and from sports clubs.
- Parents play a significant role in introducing children into sport for health or safety reasons. It is more likely that the middle classes attach greater value to these attributes, and see sport as contributing towards them.

Cost of sports participation and parental support. Considerable financial demands are associated with participation at an élite level. The vertical axis of Figure 10.2 shows the cost per annum, and the horizontal axis the birth years of the children taking part in the study. Costs increase to meet the growing demands of training and competition as the young athlete's participation matures and develops. For example, a 10-year-old swimmer (born in 1975) cost the family on average £826 per annum, whereas by the time a child born in 1973 reached 14 years of age the costs had risen to £1,769 per annum.

The costs that these figures represent can be a source of financial strain. Table 10.1 displays the experiences of families involved in the study: with the exception of

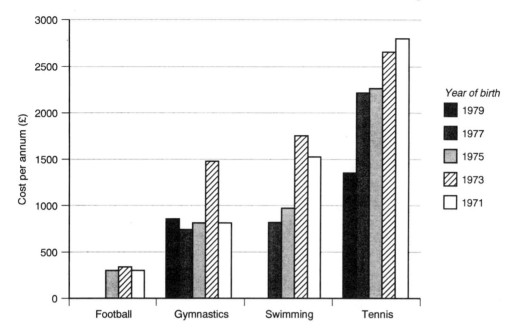

Figure 10.2 *Average cost of sports participation per annum*

Table 10.1 *Parental assessment of financial strain by sport (%)*

	Football	Gymnastics	Swimming	Tennis
No hardship	88	46	56	43
Mild hardship	9	31	26	19
Moderate hardship	3	19	12	23
Severe hardship	–	4	6	15
Total	100	100	100	100

football, many parents report some degree of financial strain from sport, and a small proportion of families, particularly those involved in tennis, described quite severe financial hardship. This involved forgoing holidays, new clothes, and in some cases finding additional employment.

Family type. There are several types of family – married/cohabiting, single parent, divorced/separated, or widowed; it is likely that each will affect a child's level of achievement in sport. Table 10.2 provides estimates of the numbers of different types of one-parent families, taken from a national sample (Haskey, 1989) and compared with TOYA one-parent families. From the table, it is clear that one-parent families are significantly under-represented when compared to the population trend within Great Britain (chi square = 27.37; $p < .001$). The reasons for this difference are probably financial, but may also be influenced by a lack of occupational mobility. Although the total distribution differs, the relative distribution of the different types of one-parent families are very similar.

Geographical area. Research findings suggest that an individual's place of residence has a significant influence on participation in sports (Knopp, 1972: Sofranko and

Table 10.2 *A comparison of the type of one-parent family with dependent children in Great Britain: numbers and characteristics*

Type of family	Sample UK	TOYA
	%	%
Total one-parent families	16.12	5.3
Single mother	23	29
Divorced/separated	59	46
Widowed	8	25
Single father	10	0
Total	100	100

Dependent children are defined as aged 16 or less, or 16 to 18 and in full-time education.

Nolan, 1972). If the child lives in an isolated rural area, certain activities may be precluded either because of the lack of facilities or the problems caused by the need to travel long distances for training. Consequently, despite their natural ability, children born in a particular geographical location may never have the opportunity to develop their sports potential.

Why children enter sport. Information provided by interviews with parents suggests that there are significant differences in the reasons why children start participating in sport, and how they are identified as talented.

The information suggests that regardless of the sport, the family played the most significant role in introducing children into these four sports, although there are sports-specific differences between parents as to which of them played the more significant role. Mothers played a far more significant role than fathers in socializing their children into swimming and gymnastics; this may be because mothers see teaching their child how to swim or developing movement skills as an extension of their child-rearing role. In football, the trend is reversed, with the father having more responsibility for nurturing the youngster's involvement. Comments by friends, relatives and neighbours ('Comments by other person' in Table 10.3) also account for some of the reasons why children entered a particular sport. Interestingly, very few parents perceived their child as unusually talented. Participation in sport was perceived either as a natural extension of family leisure time (most parents had taken part in sport when they were younger), as a particular interest of a parent, or – as is the case with swimming – parents wanted their children to learn how to swim mainly for safety reasons.

Identification of talent in sport. Looking at the identification of talent, a sports-specific pattern emerges. Only in football does there appear to be a positive search for talent.

The majority of young footballers who showed promise were identified by a club scout or schoolteacher ('Comment by other person' – 24 per cent, coach – 61 per cent). Unlike the other three sports, there was little reliance on either the parents or – more importantly – the children themselves. With the exception of football, schools appeared to play only a minor role; links between schools and sports clubs are generally poor and there is little evidence to suggest that coaches actively seek out talent in school.

Table 10.3 *Why children enter sport (%)*

	Football	Gymnastics	Swimming	Tennis
Comment by other person	15	32	15	12
Mother	3	26	29	16
Father	33	4	10	12
Both parents	3	3	23	17
Child – self-motivated	46	34	22	38
Coach	–	1	1	5
Total	100	100	100	100

Table 10.4 *Identification of talent (%)*

	Football	Gymnastics	Swimming	Tennis
Comment by other person	24	13	8	3
Mother	3	1	4	5
Father	9	3	1	8
Both parents	–	–	36	4
Child – self-motivated	3	34	–	34
Coach	61	49	51	46
Total	100	100	100	100

Summary of the research. The TOYA findings suggest that the identification of sport talent in Britain is overly dependent on parents and on the motivation of the children themselves. Sports clubs and coaches generally play a secondary role in identifying talent – they can only select those children who have already been encouraged to participate by their parents. There must be many more children who could enjoy the health-related benefits of participation, and who may also be talented, but neither parents, schools nor coaches have given them sufficient encouragement to take it up. On the one hand, children with potential are not being identified in sufficient numbers, and, on the other, some young athletes participating in intensive training may not merit specialized coaching to accelerate their development. Many children in sports like gymnastics, swimming and tennis are not identified by a professional as talented. This raises a number of questions as to whether the child is especially suited to a particular sport, and whether it is worth the time, effort and cost of intensive training if they stand little chance of reaching the goals of high-level performance.

When children enter sport. The age at which children should begin intensive training depends on two factors – the age at which top performance in a specific sport is normally achieved, and the period of training required for top performance. For most young performers there is a gradual increase in training until peak performance is reached, often between 16 and 25 years of age. The first stage in this process is for the child to be exposed to the sport before any learning or interest can take place. This exposure often occurs in the family – particularly where parents are also active – in the school playground, or through televised sport. In the second stage, the child begins active participation, which requires access to facilities and some instruction or coaching. Finally, the young athlete begins systematic or intensive training.

Table 10.5 *Mean age (in years and months) when children begin active participation and systematic practice*

	Mean age when started sports	Mean age started systematic training	Difference
Football	7.6	11.3	3.9
Gymnastics	6.3	8.6	2.3
Swimming	6.3	9.2	2.11
Tennis	7.4	9.5	2.1

The ages at which children in the TOYA study started active participation and intensive training, as well as the length of exposure to the sport before the young athlete started intensive training are illustrated in Table 10.5.

The average starting age across the four sports was uniformly young, on average between 6.3 and 7.6 years, although the sports did differ, with gymnasts and swimmers starting significantly earlier than either tennis or football players. The onset of intensive training in gymnastics, swimming and tennis started two to three years later, between 8.6 and 9.5 years of age. Football is the exception: intensive training did not start until after 11 years of age, possibly reflecting the later age when footballers reach the peak of their performance potential. The youngest child was a swimmer who was aged 6 months when he first started the sport! In the other sports, children often began some form of involvement at around 3 years of age. These data, together with the reasons why children became involved in intensive training, suggest a 'closed' system of identifying talent. If a child was not chosen at an early age, soon after being introduced to the sport, there was little chance of him or her re-entering the identification process.

FACTORS AFFECTING THE DEVELOPMENT OF TALENT IN SPORT

Psychologists have paid little attention to the study of children in sport. Where research has taken place, studies have concentrated upon establishing the psychological determinants of competitive success, rather than of the process-training — which allows potential to be actualized (Rowley, 1987). The following section describes particular areas of vulnerability for the young athlete, and provides examples of the psychological sequelae associated with intensive training.

Family functioning

Critics of youth sport have proposed that children are not developmentally prepared to cope with the emotional pressures of the sports environment (Brower, 1978; Roberts, 1975). However, as Freeman (1991) suggests, this is not a matter for children to cope with on their own, since progress along the road to excellence is heavily influenced by the parents, coaches or peer group. In addition, as she has found, a child is never termed 'gifted' without reference to others, and this labelling process is likely to affect the attitudes and behaviour of 'significant others' in the child's life. It has been argued that when adults become involved in youth sport, they have a tendency to place unreasonable demands on the young athlete, following ambitions of their own, and place an excessive emphasis on winning (Ogilvie, 1981; Sage, 1978). This can result in some young athletes developing unrealistic aspirations and commitment to training, as feelings of personal worth become equated with performance success (Rowley, 1987).

The emotional stress associated with this situation has been reported to cause psychosomatic complaints (Lask, 1986), loss of appetite (Smith and Smoll, 1981), and nervous exhaustion (Cratty, 1978). In its extreme form, this may result in some children developing injuries for which no physical basis can be found: these allow them a socially acceptable form of retreat from physical activities that are construed as socially, psychologically or physically threatening (Yaffe, 1983). The stability of the family may also affect the health and well-being of the gifted young athlete. It has been found that young players who had experienced life-events or long-term difficulties – such as family instability due to parental illness, separation, divorce or death – were more likely to sustain a significant injury (Coddington and Troxell, 1980).

It is clear that parents have the main responsibility for introducing children into sport and maintaining their involvement, but unfortunately many parents are not fully prepared for the extent or changing nature of their role. It is also possible that heavy parental involvement may have implications for marital disharmony – frequent absences from the home and a cessation of social life can magnify areas of dissatisfaction and increase the number of arguments between partners. Alternatively, having a child in sport can give purpose and direction to, and create greater cohesion between, family members. Parents report that taking the child to the training facility gives them time to talk, and improves their relationship; this involvement can strengthen and preserve the family. On the other hand, it does seem more than likely that sport can also highlight problems that already exist within a family, and these conflicts may prevent the physically able from reaching their potential. For example, the 'gift' may be labelled the problem, rather than identifying the real cause of disharmony within the home.

Sport and the family life cycle

Sport has a dynamic rather than a static effect on family life. The main challenge to the family system comes from having to adapt to the increasing financial, physical and emotional demands of the child's increasing participation in sport. Using terms more commonly associated with growth and maturation – childhood, adolescence, young adulthood and maturity – this effect can be conceptualized using a life-cycle or developmental model. The life-cycle model can be described as follows:

Childhood. When the child first starts sport, parents rarely understand the long-term implications: they are usually naïve and generally happy to let the coach direct both their child's and their own involvement. Few parents report that the coach explained what their role would or should be, or what level of commitment would be required.

Adolescence. As the child increases his/her involvement, parents have to give up more and more of their time, effort and money. This can result in some adopting a cost-effective equation of sports performance, which can result in emotional stress for both the child and parent. The father of a 13-year-old tennis player summarized this problem when he observed: 'In a match where she should have won, she played terrible. I told her there were so many sacrifices going on – all parents taking their kids miles and miles; when they don't do well (you) take it out on the kids.'

It seems the only way this father could articulate his disappointment was by making reference to the 'sacrifices' he and his wife were making – a comment which could only hurt his child and further increase her disappointment. This type of response suggests that some parents may not know how to deal with their own emotions after sporting defeat. Parental over-involvement can also rob the child of the enjoyment of participating in sport. A male gymnast who is ranked in the top ten in the UK commented: 'At first, gymnastics was something to enjoy; then, the only thing keeping me going was my Dad – still the same now – Dad's too overpowering – (he) always has to have his say.' Parental involvement of this kind can trap children in a sport. They may want to give up, retire or reduce their commitment, but feel guilty because of all the sacrifices parents have made, or the meaning sport has for the parents. The same gymnast said, on the prospect of giving up: 'It would break my Dad's heart if I gave up. It means everything (to him).' The only way this athlete could 'communicate' his needs to his father was by leaving travel magazines around the house to indicate his wish to travel – a metaphor for leaving sport.

It is also at this stage that parents can develop an abrasive relationship with the coach, who may be perceived as uncommunicative, distant and, in some cases, exploitative. Parents may become emotionally over-involved or enmeshed – sometimes in an effort to protect their children from disappointment.

There are cases where parents seem unable to separate their own identity from that of their children; sport begins to challenge the ability of the family system to adapt to change. The father of a girl gymnast described his response to his child's failure as: 'I would criticize her for cheating, for not giving her best. This would result in a row in the car coming home.' His wife would then use his criticism to bolster her argument for their daughter to give up. The family system fragmented, Dad aligning himself with his daughter, his wife with the other, non-sporting daughter. The decision to continue gymnastics became a struggle for power between husband and wife, and the needs of the young gymnast were largely ignored. It is at this stage that success or failure can affect the mood of the whole family.

Young adulthood. Parents begin to disengage from control as the child takes on more responsibility for directing his/her own sports involvement. More mature children can also take themselves to the training facility, so freeing the parents from this considerable supporting role.

Maturity. At this stage of the life-cycle, the individual entirely directs his/her own involvement. Parents are no longer so emotionally committed, and so may develop a more productive role in supporting their child's sport. The mother of an older swimmer commented: 'We're pleased for him (if he does well). It's not taken over our life: we have other interests.'

Using this life-cycle model, it is possible to develop educational programmes which deal with specific needs of families in sport. Current programmes tend to conceptualize a family's involvement as static, and so do not respond to their changing needs. The model also provides a means of identifying periods of risk. The transition from one stage to another, for example, can be very threatening to a young child. Kate, an 11-year-old swimmer, found that her training load had increased, and she had recently begun to feel anxious before training. Her main worry was that she would not be able to keep up with the other swimmers, and that the coach would ignore or reject her. This meant that for much of the time, she didn't want to go training, but felt that she must, because: 'If I missed one training session, I would get unfit and wouldn't be able to win.' Her mother reinforced this notion by saying she had to go, as 'You don't want to be unfit the next day.' Her mother's misunderstanding of what the change in training status meant to her daughter increased the girl's anxiety.

It is during the transition phase from one part of the life-cycle to another that parental education programmes would be most effective, because it is during these phases that the child and family are most at risk. The increased needs of sport then challenge the ability of the family to adapt to often considerable change.

It would be unrealistic to suggest that the life-cycle model implies that all families should adapt to the changing needs of their child's involvement in sport, and that they will eventually achieve a 'mature' attitude. Some parents can and do become 'stuck' in one particular part of the cycle; the ensuing discrepancy between the respective needs of the child, parent and coach can then cause friction and, in some cases, conflict.

Intensive training

The intensity of an athlete's training regime is usually determined by the number of hours he/she trains per week. This figure varies, depending upon the child's age, stage of biological maturity, and the training requirements of the particular activity: an 8-year-old gymnast aiming to compete at either national or international level would be expected to train for between 10 and 15 hours per week, whereas a swimmer or tennis player would not reach these levels until between 10 and 12 years of age. These figures then rise dramatically during early adolescence, when athletes can spend 28 hours a week training. For a young athlete to maximize his or her potential, while minimizing harmful effects, it is of increasing importance that coaches in particular, but also athletes and their parents, should have a shared understanding of what quality and quantity of training is appropriate for young people at different stages of physical and psychological maturation. Concern has been expressed that gifted athletes may be overtraining and at risk of physical injury, not to mention physical or mental exhaustion. But there is also the possibility of undertraining, with its own attendant problems. It seems that although the concept of intensive training is sufficiently general to be understood by both laymen and professionals, it is actually understood by very few, and by those few in very different ways (Rowley, 1991). The lack of any agreed standards which can be used as guidelines when developing training programmes to actualize talent not only poses a risk to the health and well-being of the athlete, but also interferes with the development of the potential itself.

School

Research into pedagogy for the gifted has tended to ignore sporting talent, as it appears to be less élitist and therefore less controversial than other kinds of giftedness, and is usually encouraged and supported in schools (Freeman, 1991). Traditionally, school has played an important role in introducing children to competitive sport (Campbell, 1990), but during recent years considerable publicity has suggested that sport in school has changed. Today in Britain, pupils between the ages of 12 and 14 have on average only two hours of physical exercise per week. Of the 5,161 secondary schools in the UK, 70 per cent have inadequate playing fields, and nearly half of all playing fields are sub-standard (Secondary Heads Association, 1988). There has also been a reaction against competitive sport from many local education authorities, who argue that it has been responsible for developing élitism and inequality, and that competition can lead to discrimination against the less able or physically underdeveloped child.

However, instead of replacing the traditional practices of competition by sports which are safe and equally accessible to children of differing age, shape, size and ability, the current approach to sport in schools has in fact extended discrimination by removing competition altogether. This means that it is equally unfair to the more able, as well as the less able (Rowley, 1989). The new National Curriculum in Britain and the introduction of statutory hours for teachers have limited the extra-curricular activity undertaken by teachers (Sports Council, 1991), and so have brought about a decline in traditional school sport. In addition, because many schools now have control of their own budgets (Local Management of Schools), within a period of four years about 500 school playing fields have been sold off. Consequently, there is less and less provision within schools to assist the development of the more able at sport. To counter this, some sporting organizations, like the British Lawn Tennis Association and the Football Association, have made considerable efforts to withdraw their élite young athletes from the state school system by providing tennis and football schools, so that training then complements rather than antagonizes the educational process.

CONCLUSIONS

Unlike the other talents more commonly associated with high ability, such as musical or intellectual excellence, children who excel in sports suffer less from a negative stereotyping than from a lack of recognition that they, too, may have special needs. Competitive children's sport is still regarded by many as a harmless recreational pursuit, and so the young athlete's special emotional, educational and interpersonal needs can suffer if parents, teachers and coaches fail to recognize or respond to them.

Family members in particular have an important function, since they maintain the child's interest and involvement by providing various kinds of supporting roles, and serve to maintain a balance between family functioning and the young athlete's training practices.

In her review of the emotional needs of the gifted child, Freeman (1994) pointed out that teachers, parents and other care-givers need to be more child-centred – to recognize the abilities of their children and the problems these may bring. Both the coach and the parent in youth sports have just such a similar responsibility and there needs to be a greater awareness of the specific emotional and interpersonal vulnerabilities associated with intense sports involvement. Unfortunately, too few studies have monitored the psychological effects of intensive training for any specific conclusions to be drawn about it.

In particular, attention needs to be directed towards those athletes, both young and old, who retire from sport after having actualized their talents; members of this group may need special help to cope with the possible blow to their self-esteem that retirement brings. Properly designed studies which are concerned with practical issues should assist the parents, coaches, teachers and the athletes themselves by identifying areas of special need and describing the level of expertise necessary to identify, develop and actualize physical talent (Coe, 1990).

The implications of this work are the following:

- All parents of young children need encouragement to introduce them to a range of sporting activities at a relatively young age. Such early activity need not be highly competitive to enable talent to be revealed.
- Campaigns to encourage children's participation in sport need to be designed with greater precision, targeting (especially) mothers of young children and parents who are not interested or active in sport themselves.
- Greater effort should be made to establish links between schools and sports clubs, to promote young children's involvement in sport and to establish systems of talent identification.
- Clubs need to reduce the demands on parents in supporting the development of talent. The formation of parents' associations could help to share the burden and cost of transport through the organization of rota systems.
- More information is needed on the identification of talent in various sports; little information exists on the pathways by which children reach the position of being identified.
- There is a need for more research on the role of the family and on correlates of giftedness in sport, in order to establish the relationship between family life, child development and sporting excellence.
- There is a need for sport science to examine the issue of talent identification. Properly designed studies which address themselves to the development of reliable sports-specific tests should assist the coach to identify exceptional talent. Such tests need to be sensitive to the expected performance potential associated with any child's physical and psychological stage of development.
- Coaches need better education and training to help them identify talent.
- There is a need for specialized care and counselling for young athletes, who are liable to be under pressure from intensive training and competitions.

REFERENCES

Anthrop, J. and Allison, M.T. (1983) 'Role conflict and the high school female athlete', *Research Quarterly for Exercise and Sport*, **2**, 102–11.
Bloom, B.S. (1985) 'Generalisations about talent development', in B. Bloom (ed.), *Developing Talent in Young People*. New York: Ballantine Books.
Brower, J.J. (1978) 'Little league baseballism: adult dominance in a child's game', in R. Martens (ed.), *Joy and Sadness in Children's Sport*. Champaign, IL: Human Kinetics.
Campbell, S. (1990) 'A proposal for integration', in Southern Council for Sport and Recreation (ed.), *School and Sport: The Way Forward*. Reading: Sports Council.
Coddington, R.D.S. and Troxell, J.R. (1980) 'The effect of emotional factors on football injury rates – a pilot study', *Journal of Human Stress*, **6**, 3–5.
Coe, S. (1990) 'The public's responsibility to promote excellence', *European Journal for High Ability*, **1**, 7–10.
Council of Europe (1982) Seminar on sport for children. Committee for the Development of Sport, Norway, September–October.
Cratty, B.J. (1978) 'Psychological health in athletics: model for maintenance' in W.F. Straub (ed.) *Sport Psychology: An Analysis of Athlete Behavior*. New York: Mouvement.
Del Ray, P. (1978) 'The apologetic and women in sport', in C.A. Oglesby (ed.), *Women and Sport: From Myth to Reality*. Philadelphia: Lea and Febiger.
Dudink, A. (1990) 'High ability in sport: a case study', *European Journal for High Ability*, **1/2**, 144–50.
Duquin, M.E. (1978) 'The androgynous advantage', in C.A. Oglesby (ed.), *Women and Sport: From Myth to Reality*. Philadelphia: Lea and Febiger.
Ericsson, K.A., Tesch-Romer, C. and Krampe, R. (1990) 'The role of practice and motivation in the acquisition of expert-level performance in real life', in M.J.A. Howe (ed.), *Encouraging the Development of Exceptional Skills and Talents*. Leicester: British Psychological Society.
Fisher, R.J. and Borms, J. (1990) *The Search for Sporting Excellence* (Sport Science Studies Vol. 3. International Council of Sport Science & Physical Education). Schorndorf: Karl Hoffman.
Fowler, W.F. (1969) 'The effect of early stimulation: the problem of focus in developmental stimulation', *Merrill-Palmer Quarterly*, **15**, 157–70.
Freeman, J. (1991) *Gifted Children Growing Up*. London: Cassell.
Freeman, J. (1993) 'Parents and families in nurturing giftedness and talent', in K.A. Heller, F.J. Mönks and A.H. Passow (eds), *International Handbook of Research and Development of Giftedness and Talent*. Oxford: Pergamon Press.
Freeman, J. (1994) 'Some emotional aspects of being gifted', *Journal for the Education of the Gifted*, **17**, 180–97.
Freeman, J. (1995) 'Where talent begins'. Chapter 2, this volume.
Goudas, M., Biddle, S. and Fox, K. (1994) 'Perceived locus of causality, goal orientations, and perceived competence in school physical education classes', *British Journal of Educational Psychology*, **64**, 453–63.
Gross, M.U.M. (1993) *Exceptionally Gifted Children*. London: Routledge.
Haskey, J. (1989) 'One parent families and their children in Great Britain: numbers and characteristics', *Population Trends*, no. 55. London: HMSO.
Harsanyi, L., Sebö, A. and Morvay, B. (1990) 'Identification of talent in sport', *European Journal for High Ability*, **1/2**, 151–61.
Hebbelinck, M. (1988) 'Talent identification'. Paper delivered at the Seoul Olympic Conference.
Kane, J.E. (1986) 'Giftedness in sport', in G. Gleeson (ed.), *The Growing Child in Competitive Sport*. Sevenoaks: Hodder and Stoughton.
Knopp, T.B. (1972) 'Environmental determinants of recreational behaviour', *Journal of Leisure Research*, **4**, 129–38.
Lask, B. (1986) 'The high achieving child', *Postgraduate Medical Journal*, **62**, 143–5.
Lewis, M. and Louis, B. (1991) 'Young gifted children', in G.A. Colangelo and G.A. Davis (eds), *Handbook of Gifted Education*. Boston: Allyn and Bacon.

Macintosh, D. (1982) 'Socio-economic, educational and status characteristics of Ontario interschool athletes', *Canadian Journal of Applied Sports Science*, 7, 272–83.
McPherson, B.D. (1982) 'The child in competitive sport: influence of the social milieu', in R. Magill and F. Smoll (eds), *Children in Sport*. Champaign, IL: Human Kinetics.
McQuattie, S. (1986) 'Giftedness in music', in G. Gleeson (ed.), *The Growing Child in Competitive Sport*. Sevenoaks: Hodder & Stoughton.
Ogilvie, B. (1981) 'The child athlete: psychological implications of participation in sport', *Annals of the American Academy*, 445, 47–58.
Roberts, R. (1975) 'Strike out little league', *Newsweek*, 11 July, p. 6.
Rowley, S.R.W. (1987) 'Psychological effects of intensive training in young athletes', *Journal of Child Psychology and Psychiatry*, 28, 371–7.
Rowley, S.R.W. (1989) 'Children in sport and inequalities in health', *Radical Community Medicine*, Autumn, 13–17.
Rowley, S.R.W. (1991) 'Intensive training: can it be defined?' *Coaches and Coaching*, 7, 10–14.
Rowley, S.R.W. (1992) *The Training of Young Athletes Study (TOYA): Project Description*. London: Sports Council Publication Unit.
Sage, G.H. (1978) 'Humanistic psychology and coaching', in W.F. Straub (ed.), *Sport Psychology: An Analysis of Athlete Behavior*. New York: Mouvement.
Scarlett, C.L. (1975) *Euroscot: The New European Generation*. Edinburgh: Scottish Standing Conference of Voluntary Youth Organisations.
Secondary Heads Association (1988) *The Provision of Physical Education in Secondary Schools in 1987*. London: Secondary Heads Association.
Smith, R.E. and Smoll, F.L. (1982) 'Psychological stress: a conceptual model and some intervention strategies in youth sport', in R. Magill and F. Smoll (eds), *Children in Sport*. Champaign, IL: Human Kinetics.
Sofranko, A. and Nolan, M.F. (1972) 'Early life experiences and adult sport participation', *Journal of Leisure Research*, 4, 6–18.
Sports Council (1991) Talent Identification (unpublished report).
Süle, F. (1990) 'Imaginative psychotherapy in the psychological care of top athletes', *European Journal for High Ability*, 1/2, 162–4.
Thomson, R.W. and Beavis, N. (1985) *Talent Identification in Sport*. Auckland: New Zealand Sports Foundation.
Yaffe, M. (1983) 'Sports injuries: psychological aspects', *British Journal of Hospital Medicine*, 20, 224–32.

Chapter 11

Complementary Approaches to Talent Development

Harald Wagner

It is generally assumed that human abilities develop from initial individual dispositions or potentials. Certainly we know that from the very moment of birth children differ considerably as to their sensory awareness, energy and curiosity to explore their environment, as well as their ease of learning and retention (Freeman, 1995). In order to fully develop these potentials into high abilities and subsequent excellent achievement it is essential that the child:

- has the opportunity to discover and try out his or her potential;
- develops a consistent, high motivation for achievement;
- gets optimal support and education from the environment (parents, teachers, trainers, mentors);
- is appreciated for his or her own achievement.

Insufficiently trained and exercised potential may deteriorate or even vanish, as is well known from speech development (Curtiss, 1977). For some fields of talent (gymnastics, ballet, violin or piano playing and chess) there seem to be critical periods of development, specific times when learning is most easily acquired. Even under optimal conditions, any training which only starts after that is unlikely to result in top-level performance. Therefore it is essential that children's potentials are tried and challenged as early and consistently as possible. This means providing opportunities for a child to acquire content-specific knowledge, to build skills and develop aptitudes as early and to the extent that it is needed.

A FRAMEWORK TO FOSTER POTENTIALS

In a German study, Weinert (Weinert and Wagner, 1987) proposed a framework for the development and fostering of potentials, concluding that effective measures for young people should be characterized by the following features:

- *Incitations*: Curiosity, a quest for knowledge and the interest in learning have to be incited by a multitude of attractive sources of information within easy access.
- *Offers*: A variety of options has to be available to engage in learning activities such as workshops, courses, summer programmes, competitions.
- *Challenges*: The difficulty and the level of the activities should match the level of ability so that very able pupils feel sufficiently challenged and have to exert considerable effort to reach the goal.
- *Incentives*: The activities should be exciting and attractive, they should provide the experience of success and personal recognition.
- *Counselling*: The young people, their parents and teachers should be able to obtain qualified information on existing and available support programmes and on the peculiarities of the talent potential.
- *Cooperation*: Very able young people, too, should be brought up and educated in a community of peers to experience a variety of social contacts in order to acquire social responsibility and to facilitate a harmonious development of their personality.

According to this study, at least in the domain of intellectual abilities, it seems to be quite unrealistic to strive for a comprehensive, valid and reliable system of early assessment of potentials followed by a closed system of support programmes. Instead, every effort should be made to provide a variety of measures to meet the needs of those who are eager to achieve and who show a high degree of motivation. Provision should be easily put into practice, easily accessible, differentiated and as open as possible.

IMPORTANCE OF NON-SCHOOL PROVISION

The most significant roles in the education and development of the highly able are played, without doubt, by both general and vocational schools. They are expected to make provision in order that each child may achieve the highest possible level of development according to his or her individual ability and willingness. However, in the main, this commitment is only met for the large proportion of average and below-average pupils and for children with the most varied handicaps and impediments. Of course no school can be suitable for every pupil to the same extent, and no pupil can expect his or her school to provide adequately for every type of talent, gift or specialized interest. But all too often children who are widely talented, highly perceptive, have a well-developed capacity for concentration and achievement, who are inquisitive and have broad interests at school, face idleness, too few challenges, boredom and lack of motivation. The consequences, lamented again and again, are a reduction in their willingness to make an effort, a decline in achievement, behavioural problems or apathy. The less the school is willing and able to meet the special requirements of its highly able students, the more important out-of-school provision becomes. Czikszentmihalyi *et al.* (1993) found that the best school lessons – those from which the students learnt most and with which they were most involved – were the closest in style to voluntary out-of-school activities.

THE PARENTS' ROLE IN TALENT DEVELOPMENT

The key principle for talent development in children is to provide a wide range of opportunities for intellectual, musical, sports and creative activities, and to carefully observe which of these activities are most readily adopted (see Freeman, 1995). The child should set the pace; compulsion and excess should be avoided along with those typical creativity killers – constant nagging, fault-finding, interrupting play, knowing better, indifference towards the child's games, punishment by taking away a favourite toy. For a more detailed discussion of the influence of the home atmosphere see Albert (1983), Elkind (1987), Heller (1991), Kulieke and Olszewski-Kubilius (1989), Ochse (1990) and Sloane (1985).

When the child enters school it may become necessary for parents to provide supplementary activities by introducing the child to exciting and fascinating subjects, such as archaeology, astronomy, chess and other strategy games, computers, dinosaurs, Egyptology, Eskimos, Greek mythology, Indians, nature, or space travel. Often nature trails, visits to historical sites, museums, exhibitions, technical installations, or concerts for children can stimulate the child's interest in that subject area.

Early introduction to the use of information sources, such as reference books and public libraries, can take the strain off parents of those children who are particularly eager to learn. This should be done with the aim of arming children with tools to enable them to learn independently by discovery and investigation. The main idea is not merely to accumulate knowledge – in which the highly able succeed with ease – but to develop intellectual depth and creative thinking by combining elements of knowledge. In addition to this, particular value should be placed on developing creativity in widely varied fields (languages, play-acting, music, art, dance, sports, handicrafts), and nurturing social responsibilities and social consciousness, in particular in those children whose intellectual development is far beyond their social-emotional development (Cropley, 1995). For many parents this task is rather intimidating. When they seek professional help and advice from kindergarten educators, paediatricians, teachers, school psychologists or educational counsellors they are more often than not confronted with ignorance and prejudice.

SELF-HELP GROUPS

Faced with the predicament of having to solve their problems more or less on their own, the parents of highly able children in many countries have established self-help groups in the form of associations such as the Gifted Child Society in the USA, the British National Association for Gifted Children (NAGC), the *Deutsche Gesellschaft für das hochbegabte Kind* in Germany, 'Pharos' in The Netherlands, 'Bekina' in Belgium, *Association Nationale pour les Enfants Intellectuellement Précoces* (ANPEIP) in France, or *Elternverein für hochbegabte Kinder (EHK) Schweiz* in Switzerland. Here follows a detailed description of a successful association for the highly able, whose aims and activities are similar to those of others: the National Association for Gifted Children (NAGC, UK), the largest European parents' initiative for highly able children, with approximately 4,000 members.

Its work with children and parents takes place throughout England and Wales in

35 branches (regional groups). Most of these organize Saturday Clubs which offer a wide range of activities. Their joint aims are:

- to provide an opportunity for highly able children to meet and pursue their intellectual or artistic activities or sports in company;
- to facilitate contact with interesting and informed adults offering children intellectual stimulus and an introduction to a wide range of interests;
- to provide and encourage companionship between children and adults, other than their parents and schoolteachers, in order to help them to integrate socially and develop in emotional maturity both at home and at school;
- to give help, advice and information to parents of gifted children;
- to increase community awareness and understanding of the need to develop links with, and information for, local agencies such as teachers, social workers and medical officers;
- to encourage their interest and to promote an extension of the work of gifted children.

The NAGC's education policy is twofold:

1 Not to compete with state-run educational programmes or to prescribe a more or less fixed special programme for gifted and talented children and
2 Not to relinquish the support or spontaneous cooperation of parents and other adults in favour of a more professional approach.

The NAGC does not organize programmes or other provision which require action or choices at school for implementation (such as class allocation, ability streaming). It aims rather to provide incentives as a supplement to formal educational provisions for children to test their strengths according to their wishes. The intention of Saturday Clubs, therefore, is to offer an enrichment programme. Courses held at the various branches are run in general by adult volunteers, often by a parent of one of the children, or by someone who is interested in these children's progress. The volunteers determine to a large extent the selection of activities available. One Saturday's programme could, for example, consist of:

- sports (badminton, football, gymnastics, table tennis, trampolining);
- arts and crafts (painting, pottery, sewing, doll-making, balsa modelling);
- courses on electronics, natural sciences and computers;
- foreign languages such as French;
- board games;
- making a newspaper.

The NAGC is funded by membership fees and donations from industry and foundations. State institutions provide support from time to time, for example, by granting the use of accommodation and facilities. The association's courses are suitable for children and youngsters between the ages of 5 and 17. Members should have an IQ of at least 140, although testing is not always demanded, because IQ assessment is recognized as an imperfect measure of a child's ability, in particular for children with disadvantaged or different cultural backgrounds. The following factors are therefore also taken into account when children are selected. They may be considered if:

- they have been highly recommended by social workers, medical officers etc.;
- they are from one-parent families;
- they come from poor homes;
- they are culturally deprived;
- they are causing problems at home or at school;
- they are lonely;
- they have parents who have offered skilled help.

Siblings are invited to join the Saturday Clubs because in many cases more than one child in a family is likely to be of high intelligence.

LONG-TERM COURSES

The programmes offered by parents' associations are dependent on many, often chance influences, such as the number of children of a certain age group interested and willing to participate, the availability of course instructors, special rooms, equipment, and materials. As a considerably more intensive form of provision, long-term courses are often intellectually more demanding. They can take place either in the afternoons or at weekends, or in the form of holiday courses, and allow for a more systematic approach to a specific subject area. As an outstanding example for this type of programme, the Hamburg Model of finding and fostering mathematically able pupils is now described in more detail.

Inspired by the work of Julian C. Stanley and his group at Johns Hopkins University (Benbow and Stanley, 1983), in 1983 a group of psychologists and mathematicians at the University of Hamburg, Germany, developed an annual regional search for mathematically able pupils at the end of grade 6 (12 year-olds) (Wagner and Zimmermann, 1986). Selection criteria were:

1 German versions of the mathematical parts of the Scholastic Aptitude Test (SAT);
2 a test of mathematical problem solving consisting of seven items.

Both were to be taken during an examination of three hours' duration. Pupils interested in the talent search received a preparation booklet in advance containing a complete version of the mathematical parts of the SAT to be worked through and attempted at home.

Over 2,400 pupils have taken part in the 12 talent searches carried out so far (1983–94), of whom 571 (about 24 per cent) were invited to participate in a long-term programme of tuition. During the 1994–95 school year approximately 160 pupils were attending classes at Hamburg University on Saturday mornings. The coursework consists of some 20 units during the school year. The pupils work in small groups on challenging mathematical problems, the topics varying from week to week. Expert secondary-school teachers, mathematics students and mathematicians serve as instructors.

Rather than cover future curriculum material, the mathematical areas selected are predominantly those which pupils would find interesting and appealing, which at the same time are important for the application of modern mathematics, e.g. graph theory, combinatorics, representation of numbers in connection with measuring, number theory, geometry, game theory. The problems are always chosen in such a way that they can be extended to allow the development of a small mathematical theory and put pupils in a research situation – albeit an elementary one. New problem areas are introduced by a short paper including a few initial questions which help to motivate the pupils. In addition to developing and practising strategies for problem-solving, special importance is attached to recognizing, formulating and perhaps solving subsequent problems.

Despite the considerable length of the course (participation is possible for up to five or six consecutive years) demanding a substantial investment of free time, and the challenging coursework, there is an extremely low dropout rate. The extraordinarily positive opinion the pupils have of the course shows that this type of programme is very successful in meeting such pupils' needs. On the one hand, this is largely due to the excitement generated by the assignments, as well as to the informal manner of working in small groups, in pairs or even alone, which is quite unlike that at the pupils' normal schools.

On the other hand, there is also an important social motive for taking part: in this group pupils meet others of the same age of a similarly high intellectual level and with mutual interests, without encountering incomprehension or even rejection. This type of separate provision for the highly able does not (as is sometimes implied) lead to social isolation, but rather causes participants to feel less like outsiders among their age-peers. For the first time, most of them have been faced with a challenge commensurate with their capability and aptitude. Funds from the German Federal Government initially helped to get the programme started, although after three years it became self-supporting through contributions from parents. Offshoots of the Hamburg project show that even when confronted with the typical transport and distance problems of rural areas, and despite the long journeys involved, the appeal of the programme prevails.

RESIDENTIAL PROGRAMMES

The difficulties of long-distance commuting can be overcome by residential programmes which typically last from one to several weeks. This setting allows total involvement in a certain subject with intensive tutoring and a multitude of social contacts. Particularly in the USA, such programmes have long been a fixed element of out-of-school provisions for highly able students (Olszewski-Kubilius, 1989). One of the most sound and consistent approaches was developed at the Johns Hopkins University in Baltimore. It has been emulated by several institutions in the USA (Duke University, North Carolina; Northwestern University, Illinois; Arizona State University; California State University at Sacramento) and Dublin City University, Ireland, and is presented here in detail.

With the Study of Mathematically Precocious Youth (SMPY), the psychologist Julian C. Stanley and some of his colleagues have been developing procedures for identifying and promoting gifted pupils since 1971. They used the Scholastic Aptitude Test (now the Scholastic Assessment Test, SAT) to identify students with outstanding abilities. This is a standardized test of mathematical and verbal reasoning abilities which was designed as a university entrance test for 16- to 17-year-old high-school students. Stanley's target group were 12- to 13-year-olds. The only pupils allowed to take part in the SAT talent search were those who, according to in-grade achievement tests, belonged to the top 2 to 3 per cent. Whoever then achieved results in the SAT comparable at least to average college-bound high-school seniors was qualified to take part in special academic programmes.

Since 1979, the Johns Hopkins University's Center for Talented Youth (CTY) has identified more than 400,000 highly able seventh-grade pupils by means of regional, national and international talent searches. They provide detailed educational and career guidance to pupils who have qualified for them. A network puts parents in touch with other parents of academically able pupils. The core activities for the able are, however, the three-week-long residential summer programmes which have been held since 1980. In the summer of 1993 over 4,000 pupils from all over the USA and from over 30 other countries participated in these programmes. They are located at six college sites in New York State, Maryland, Pennsylvania, Maine and California. Within the 15 years of its existence, over 30,000 students in seventh grade and above have completed CTY courses (CTY, 1994).

CTY's academic programme is based on three premisses:

1 Academically talented students should be provided with the opportunity to learn subject matter, and to develop skills at a pace and level appropriate to their abilities, rather than to their age and grade level.
2 Academically talented students require a rigorous, challenging course of studies in the liberal arts.
3 Students' academic accomplishments should be acknowledged and rewarded.
(CTY, 1992, 5)

The pupils work in one course on their chosen subject for five hours per day, five days per week. Each evening, they are expected to spend at least two hours preparing for classes the next day. The courses, with an average size of 15 participants, are tutored by an instructor and a teaching assistant. Each site offers a variety of 12 to 21 courses for the 300 to 500 residents. Courses cover humanities, writing, mathematics, science and computer science. Parallel courses are provided for the most popular subjects, precalculus mathematics and writing.

Time is allotted for socializing, sports and music to provide relief from the high-level academic programme. This, in addition to the actual work, contributes considerably towards the great success of the CTY programme. Many return to their home communities fortified, to achieve better than before, both academically and socially. Students between the ages of 12 and 16 repeatedly attend the programmes, some even taking two successive three-week courses. Some very bright pupils, even as young as 13 or 14, can become teaching assistants. This helps them develop even more academic and social maturity. Many of the home schools will acknowledge results and achievements from the summer programmes by giving credit and/or advanced standing to the pupils. In 1992 the talent search approach and the residential programmes were extended to fifth and sixth graders, while commuter programmes are already being offered to pupils in grade two with courses such as French, Mathematical Problem Solving or Introduction to Environmental Science. In 1993 the first non-American offshoot of the Baltimore programme was launched at Dublin City University, Ireland.

THE GERMAN 'SCHÜLERAKADEMIEN' (PUPILS' ACADEMIES)

In 1988, inspired by CTY's approach, Bildung und Begabung, a non-profit-making association, sponsored by the Federal Government, started residential summer programmes for 16- to 19-year-old secondary school pupils, thus filling a critical gap between the last school years and higher education. Within a few years these *Schülerakademien* (pupils' academies) have developed into an outstanding opportunity for academically highly talented and motivated adolescents, which seems to be quite unique in continental Europe (Bundesministerium, 1994a).

The main objectives are:

- to offer several fields for scientific endeavour in order to develop and improve methods and abilities of knowledge acquisition, interdisciplinary thinking, research techniques and autonomous learning;
- to challenge intellectual potentials to their limits;
- to provide role models through encounters with highly creative, able, motivated and inspiring teachers and scientists;
- to experience a community of equally able and motivated peers, to develop lasting friendships and thus to accept their own personality as valuable and 'normal'.

A 17-day Schülerakademie typically includes 90 boys and girls, each one participating in one of six courses covering a broad range of academic disciplines. The spectrum of courses offered in the academies has been extended considerably over the years, adding to the initial subjects of mathematics, physics and foreign languages new courses in creative writing, music, biology, chemistry, computer science, philosophy, history, economics, psychology, rhetoric and visual arts (Bildung und Begabung, 1994). The total amount of time spent on coursework within the 17 days is about 45 hours. The level of work is mostly comparable with advanced university seminars. Two teachers (scholars, expert *gymnasium* schoolteachers or freelancers) design and run each of the courses with a minimum daily duration of 4 to 5 hours. The rest of the day is filled with additional optional activities such as sports, music (instrumental, choir), excursions, discussions and drama.

Between 1988 and 1994 19 academies with more than 1,500 participants were held in boarding schools in Germany, which have proved to be ideal locations for these programmes. Within a few days, each of the academies develops an atmosphere which can hardly be described, filled with the enthusiasm and motivation of both participants and instructors, with intensive personal relations and incredible openness; discussions and gatherings go on until late into the night. The numerous overwhelmingly positive feedbacks and evaluations from participants, their home schools and parents confirm the immense impact the academy has on the participants.

The participants are expected to pay a fee that covers accommodation and food, the rest of the expenses being provided by the Government. Financial assistance is available for needy families so that nobody is excluded for financial reasons. Pupils are invited to apply for a place either on the basis of successful participation in one of the intellectually demanding competitions in Germany, or on individual recommendation by headteachers, classroom teachers, educational consultants or psychologists.

In 1994, 572 (or 73.5 per cent) of the 778 boys and girls who were invited applied for the 350 available places in four academies. This means that 61 per cent of the applicants could be accommodated that year. An expansion is planned for the years to come.

SCIENCE TRAINING PROGRAMMES

Another interesting option for those secondary pupils who are talented and interested in science, are training programmes at research institutions or at universities. They are designed to provide the pupils with educational opportunities in science, engineering and mathematics beyond school level. Within these programmes, outstanding pupils are brought into contact with the instructional staff, research personnel and general resources of colleges, universities and research institutions.

Programmes involve students as junior associates of a research team or as a principal investigator on a problem of appropriate difficulty, under the direct supervision of an experienced research scientist. Other programmes provide courses specially designed for the pupils or regular early college courses; and combinations of both are also possible. The *Directory of Student Science Training Programs for Precollege Students*, published annually by the Science Service Inc. in Washington DC lists (1994) more than 400 entries for the USA.

Other countries offer similar programmes. One of these is the highly reputed one month International Summer Science Institute for pre-university students at the Weizmann Institute of Science in Rehovot, Israel (Maoz, 1993). The Weizmann Institute is devoted to research and teaching in the natural sciences. It includes 21 research units in the faculties of biology, biophysics–biochemistry, chemistry, mathematics and physics. A staff of 1,800 researchers, engineers and technicians are involved in some 800 basic and applied research projects.

Each summer, some 75 outstanding science students (high school graduates) from Europe, Asia, the Americas and Israel have the opportunity to work alongside top researchers and to use sophisticated scientific instrumentation. Applicants are selected on the basis of previous experience in laboratory research (e.g. competitions), high motivation, interest in pursuing a career in scientific research, recommendations from their home school and interviews. The participant can choose a subject in accordance with their own interests. At the end of the three-week-long laboratory period the students are required to present their findings to a seminar and to write a thesis on the completed work. Additional parts of the programme are a four-day visit to a field-school in the Negev desert, with introduction to desert ecology, a tour of Jerusalem and other places in Israel, as well as lectures given by senior Institute scientists.

Further north, in the Upper Galilee, the MIGAL Ecological Research Institute offers bright motivated pupils the chance to work on real-world ecology problems – without pre-selection (Pyryt et al., 1993). They do original work which has no pre-set answers, and are in the charge of a working researcher, who acts as a mentor. This expands beyond the classroom to the community, not least as schools could neither afford the equipment, nor provide the expertise. Because the programme requires many hours of work and dedication, less able or motivated pupils do not apply.

COMPETITIONS

Another avenue that almost ideally combines Weinert's desiderata (described above) are competitions. They are relatively easy to administer and organize, they can be made accessible to a wide variety of participants, and they can be differentiated to suit any level of ability. Competitions are an excellent tool to elicit, stimulate and challenge talents in many different fields. They are intended to activate and strengthen the inclination for the subject matter and thus to improve knowledge and ability. Struggling with the tasks of the competition enhances the ability to work autonomously, while experimenting, problem-solving, learning and practising set free energies and enhance perseverance.

By taking up the challenge of a competition, the participants gain insight into their abilities and their position in comparison with peers beyond the confinement of their classroom and school. By coming together with other participants they may meet similarly interested and able peers. Attractive prizes like scholarships, summer programmes or money are additional incentives.

The UNESCO General Conference on Education in October 1989 recommended that: 'Member states should promote out-of-school activities such as the international and regional Olympiads (that is, mathematics competitions) in the sciences and mathematics in order to encourage scientific talent and initiative among young people.'

Competitions can be arranged for nearly any field of human endeavour, and are widespread. In Germany alone, for instance, there are more than 20 nationwide competitions, not to mention several dozen smaller competitions organized on regional or state level (Bundesminister, 1991). Annually, more than 100,000 pupils participate in disciplines such as mathematics, science (biology, chemistry, physics, technology, computer science, environmental studies), foreign languages, social studies, history, creative writing, music, composing, drama, film and video production. Most of these competitions are subsidized by the Federal Government to a total amount of more than 7.1 million DM in 1994 (Bundesministerium, 1994b, p. 37). In addition, a considerable further part of the cost is covered by sponsoring foundations and industrial companies.

Worldwide, competitions in mathematics seem to be far the most popular. A recently published compendium (O'Halloran, 1992) lists 231 competitions at regional, national and international level with a total of more than four million participants.

Pupils with outstanding achievements might enter one of the international olympiads which are held annually in mathematics, physics, chemistry, biology and computer science (informatics). More than 30 European countries run competitions for young researchers in the sciences (e.g. *'Jugend forscht'*, 'Science Fair'). Up to three entries from each country may participate in an international European competition for environmental studies initiated in 1990 by *'Jugend forscht'* and Deutsche Bank.

FOSTERING HIGH ABILITIES IN THE VOCATIONAL DOMAIN

Support programmes for the highly able are usually exclusively directed towards those who seemingly have talents in traditional academic subjects, music, the arts or sports.

Only recently has public and scientific attention turned to highly able persons in vocational education and in non-academic occupations.

In 1991 the Federal Ministry of Education and Science in Germany initiated a programme *Begabtenförderung berufliche Bildung* (Promoting Giftedness in Vocational Education) which supports continuing in-service training for young workers and craftspeople. The programme aims

- to develop individual abilities;
- to help gain qualifications that may improve chances on the labour market;
- to enhance the attractivity of the dual system of vocational education (apprenticeships and vocational schooling);
- to upgrade vocational education, striving for an equivalence to academic education;
- to foster the continuous development and supply of skilled personnel.

The programme offers a scholarship of up to 3,000 DM per annum for three consecutive years to applicants who are under 25 years of age and who have been employed for less than three years. They should have passed their final vocational examinations with superior results or participated successfully in one of the vocational or crafts competitions. The decision over the grant rests with their local guild or chamber of commerce or industry.

In 1994 approximately 9,200 scholarship holders were supported with a total of 28 million DM. The scholarships may be used to attend courses to acquire additional qualifications e.g. foreign languages, electronic data processing, planning and organization, technology, communication or personality development (Bundesministerium, 1994b).

DEVELOPMENT OF POTENTIAL IN LATER LIFE

The development of potential is not confined to childhood and adolescence. For many professions, life-long learning and continuous studies have already become self-evident (von Ardenne, 1990). Many people with inadequate schooling will only discover their aspirations later in life, and find means to mobilize the necessary energies to go in for them. Educational opportunities should therefore be provided for the development of any potential at any age towards appropriate occupational position and personal satisfaction. Some 'late bloomers' come out only after retirement or during a phase of unemployment. With the rapidly growing proportion of senior citizens in Western societies, provision for the education of people of the 'third age', that is over 50, will become increasingly important. In Germany, for instance, by the year 2000 one out of four inhabitants will be older than 60 years. It is estimated that this proportion will have grown to one out of three by the year 2020. Marjoram (1986) reported on the opportunities available in the United Kingdom; open learning systems, flexi-studies (offering a variety of routes to mature qualification with individual timetables, working at study centres or at home, making use of correspondence courses, advanced technical media and tutorial support) and the Open University have been successfully in existence since the early 1970s.

In Germany, according to a report by the Federal Ministry of Education and Science, in 1991 nearly 30,000 senior citizens with an average age between 60 and 70 years attended university lectures and seminars as guest students. The usual entry requirements are not necessary – as long as the guest students do not strive for academic examinations and diploma. Guided mainly by interest in the subject area, most mature guest students choose subjects from the humanities and social sciences. The main motives for these activities seem to be the wish to stay mentally fit and to avoid loneliness. Most of them claim to feel healthier while studying.

Some universities already offer special studies for seniors. About 1,500 senior citizens attend the University of the Third Age which is attached to the Johann Wolfgang Goethe University in Frankfurt, attending lectures on 'Social history of the aged' or 'Political perspectives in old age'.

The Technical University in Berlin qualifies adults beyond 45 years of age within four semesters for voluntary social work in charities by instructing them in subjects such as ecology, nutrition and social communication.

In the autumn of 1995 the first private university for senior citizens is to open near Lörrach in southern Germany, near the Swiss city of Basel – a seemingly unique endeavour in Europe. The academic programme will start with lectures and seminars on the aesthetics, theory and practice of artistic production. Within a few years the 'student body' is expected to grow to 100 (*Der Spiegel*, 47/1994, p. 83).

CONCLUSIONS

Within the space limitations of this chapter it has only been possible to indicate some of the most effective non-school provisions for highly able individuals. Additional ones may be found in the comprehensive Richardson Study (Cox *et al.*, 1985). The major benefit of the great variety of special programmes seems to be that they provide opportunities for interaction with equally able and motivated peers. Pupils feel accepted (often for the first time in their lives), and many of them are astounded how easy it is to communicate and make friends within their ability peer group. The results are frequently long-lasting relationships and communication networks.

Encounters with excellent instructors provide valuable role-models for an academic orientation. These experts can be helpful in career counselling and might open perspectives into previously unconsidered professional areas. The intense atmosphere of residential programmes is capable of activating and stimulating dormant potentials. Many of the pupils relate with amazement what they were able to achieve in the short time. In total, these programmes have a tremendous impact on the young persons' lives. It would be highly desirable to increase the number of residential programmes because the demand far exceeds the existing places.

For adults and senior citizens open learning systems provided by institutions of higher education seem suitable for continuous studies and to take care of the needs of 'late bloomers'.

REFERENCES

Albert, R.S. (1983) *Genius and Eminence: The Social Psychology of Creativity and Exceptional Achievement*. Oxford: Pergamon.

Ardenne, M. von (1990) 'Facilitating the development of talents', *European Journal for High Ability*, **1**, (1/2), 127–35.
Benbow, C.P. and Stanley, J.C. (eds) (1983) *Academic Precocity. Aspects of Its Development*. Baltimore: Johns Hopkins University Press.
Bundesminister für Bildung und Wissenschaft (ed.) (1991) *Begabte Kinder finden und fördern [How to Find and Foster Gifted Children]*. Bonn: Bundesministerium für Bildung und Wissenschaft.
Bundesministerium für Bildung und Wissenschaft (ed.) (1994a) *BundesSchülerAkademie [Federal Academy for the Talented. Concept and Report on Experience Gained]*. Bonn: Bundesministerium für Bildung und Wissenschaft.
Bundesministerium für Bildung und Wissenschaft (ed.) (1994b) *Begabtenförderung im Bildungsbereich [Promoting the Gifted in the Educational Domain]*. Bonn: Bundesministerium für Bildung und Wissenschaft (= Schriftenreihe Grundlagen und Perspektiven für Bildung und Wissenschaft, Band 42).
Bildung und Begabung e.V. (Hrsg.) (1994) *Schülerakademie. Programm 1994*. Bonn: Bildung und Begabung e.V.
Cox, J., Daniel, N. and Boston, B. (1985) *Educating Able Learners*. Austin: University of Texas Press.
Cropley, A.J. (1995) 'Actualizing creative intelligence'. Chapter 8, this volume.
CTY (Center for Talented Youth) (1992) *Young Students Summer Programs 1992. A Liberal Arts Education for Highly Able Youth Grades 2 through 6*. Baltimore: Johns Hopkins University, CTY.
CTY (Center for Talented Youth) (1994) *Summer Programs 1994. A Liberal Arts Education for Highly Able Youths*. Baltimore: Johns Hopkins University, CTY.
Curtiss, S. (1977) *Genie: A Psycholinguistic Study of a Modern-day 'Wild Child'*. New York: Academic Press.
Czikszentmihalyi, M., Rathunde, K. and Whalen, S. (1993) *Talented Teenagers: The Roots of Success and Failure*. Cambridge: Cambridge University Press.
Elkind, D. (1987) *Miseducation: Preschoolers at Risk*. New York: Knopf.
Freeman, J. (1991) *Gifted Children Growing Up*. London: Cassell.
Freeman, J. (1995) 'Where talent begins'. Chapter 2, this volume.
Heller, K.A. (1991) 'The nature and development of giftedness: a longitudinal study', *European Journal for High Ability*, **2**, 174–8.
Kulieke, M.J. and Olszewski-Kubilius, P. (1989) 'The influences of family values and climate on the development of talent', in J.L. VanTassel-Baska and P. Olszewski-Kubilius (eds), *Patterns of Influence on Gifted Learners. The Home, the Self, and the School*. New York: Teachers College Press.
Marjoram, T. (1986) 'Better late than never – able youths and adults', *Gifted Education International*, **4** (2), 89–96.
Maoz, N. (1993) 'Nurturing giftedness in non-school educative settings – using the personnel and material resources of the community', in K.A. Heller, F.J. Mönks and A.H. Passow (eds), *International Handbook of Research and Development of Giftedness and Talent*. Oxford: Pergamon.
Ochse, R. (1990) *Before the Gates of Excellence: The Determinants of Creative Genius*. Cambridge: Cambridge University Press.
O'Halloran, P.J. (ed.) (1992) *World Compendium of Mathematics Competitions*. Canberra: Australian Mathematics Foundation.
Olszewski-Kubilius, P. (1989) 'Development of academic talent: the role of summer programs', in J.L. VanTassel-Baska and P. Olszewski-Kubilius (eds), *Patterns of Influence on Gifted Learners. The Home, the Self, and the School*. New York: Teachers College Press.
Pyryt, M.C., Masharov, Y.P. and Feng, C. (1993) 'Programs and strategies for nurturing talents/gifts in science and technology', in K.A. Heller, F.J. Mönks and A.H. Passow (eds), *International Handbook of Research and Development of Giftedness and Talent*. Oxford: Pergamon.
Sloane, K.D. (1985) 'Home influences on talent development', in B.S. Bloom (ed.), *Developing Talent in Young People*. New York: Ballantine Books.

Wagner, H. and Zimmermann, B. (1986) 'Identification and fostering of mathematically gifted students', *Educational Studies in Mathematics*, **17**, 243–59.
Weinert, F.E. and Wagner, H. (eds) (1987) *Die Förderung Hochbegabter in der Bundesrepublik Deutschland: Probleme, Positionen, Perspektiven [Educating the Able in the Federal Republic of Germany: Problems, Positions, Perspectives]*. Bad Honnef: Bock.

Chapter 12

Talent, Plasticity and Ageing: A Behavioural Management Approach

Peter G. Heymans and Gerard M. Brugman

Ageing is a process which can be described in terms of a changing relationship between gains and losses (Baltes and Willis, 1982; Baltes, 1987). In ageing there are well-documented losses in several relevant functions, especially in the cognitive domain, supposedly caused by a reduction of cognitive resources, such as the capacity of working memory, attention and speed (Salthouse, 1990; 1991a). In order to maintain a satisfying performance level, the ageing person has to make use of his or her available reserve potential. In this context, every person, most notably the high-performing individual, can be seen as a behavioural manager who compensates for resource reduction to minimize losses and maximize gains. Ample evidence exists that high performance in old age is possible, although less probable (Beckerman, 1990; Pritikin, 1990; Simonton, 1990; Charness, 1992). The central question is how, despite their losses, high-achieving individuals manage to preserve an acceptable level of performance when they grow old.

There are several research traditions which are obviously relevant to behavioural management. We will point at four of them:

- There is a small but growing body of literature documenting changes over the life-span in high-level performance in the arts, sciences and leadership. Simonton's work (1988; 1991), for example, suggests a non-linear relationship between age and outstanding performance, and confirms the findings of earlier researchers such as Sward (1945), Lehman (1953) and Dennis (1966). Although there are considerable differences within and between the different scientific disciplines and art domains, there seems in general to be fast growth in the quantity and quality of output up to the age of peak performance, usually between 35 and 40 years of age, which is followed by a slow and gradual decline in high-quality output, due to a reduction in quantity as predicted by chance-configuration theory (Simonton, 1988; 1991). This yields an inverted backward-J curve. Nevertheless, high performance in later life is possible. There are even individuals who are primarily recognized for achievements made in their late years, e.g. the Czech composer Janáček, whose last years before his death at 74

were his most productive ones: his creative power continued unabated to the end of his life (Grout, 1960).
- A large body of research on the effects of training provides evidence of some plasticity in the performance of older people, especially in cognitive performance. The evidence about the extent and long-term effects of the training gains is equivocal, though (Willis, 1990; Baltes and Kliegl, 1992; Klauer, 1992; Poon et al., 1992).
- Research on metacognition (Weinert et al., 1983; Schneider and Uhl, 1990) and self-management (Skinner, 1983) shows a positive, if weak, relationship between metacognitive competency and cognitive performance. This suggests that individuals can in fact manage their cognitive resources to optimize their performance (Hebb, 1978).
- There is some research into social factors in cognitive functioning, asking how adult thinking is affected by the individual's position in the social structure (Schaie and Schooler, 1989). Ecogenic and/or epogenic factors associated with ageing, i.e. factors associated with the normal ageing process (ecogenic) and factors associated with specific conditions of ageing in a specific historical period (epogenic), like less challenging surroundings, obsolescence or negative expectations, might be partly responsible for the differences found in cognitive performance by groups at different points in the life-span. However, considerable counter-evidence for this hypothesis is found (Sward, 1945; Salthouse, 1990, 1991a).

In summary, there are some indications that high performance can be preserved at an acceptable level throughout the whole life-span. Some talented individuals are apparently effective behavioural managers with enough reserve potential to counteract the losses associated with ageing.

The Behavioural Management Model (BeM-model) which describes the way in which individuals, especially those with a high initial performance-level, manage their behaviour in order to maintain that level, will be presented below (Heymans and Brugman, 1990). We will start with a brief conceptual analysis before relating the BeM-model to ageing, talent and behavioural management. Plasticity can be described as the potentiality to regain shape after deformation by pressure. This potential can be accomplished if impediments are removed, certain conditions are met, and individual efforts are made. In other words, plasticity depends on the availability of the appropriate resources, and how they can be brought into action, when either internal and/or external changes take place which threaten performance levels (see Figure 12.1).

The model presented in Figure 12.1 comprises four components:

- component 1: factors that nurture the reserve potential, e.g. experience, training (Salthouse, 1985, 1991b);
- component 2: external constraints and biological limits;
- component 3: factors that trigger the reserve potential, e.g. awareness of loss of perceptual speed (Horn and Hofer, 1992; Salthouse, 1990, 1991a);
- component 4: the potential itself, e.g. untapped resources, reallocation of resources.

The model can be illustrated with the well-known transcription-typing example (Salthouse, 1985), in which older typists equalled younger ones on a global level

160 *Actualizing Talent*

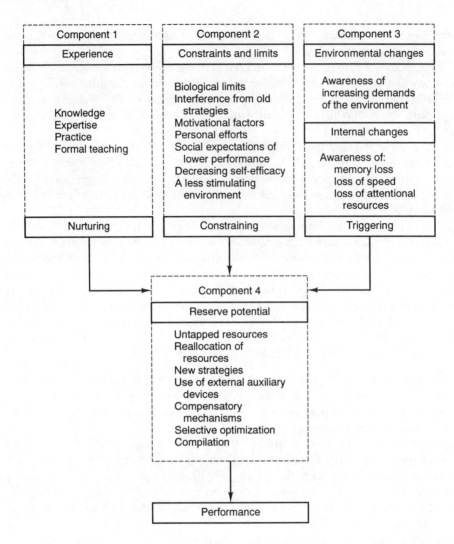

Figure 12.1 *A conceptual model of plasticity*

(performance), despite declines on the level of specific skills, such as higher reaction times (component 3), and, perhaps, despite environmental expectations of lower performance (component 2). Their experience (component 1) had enabled them to compensate (component 4) for this disadvantage in using preview: they looked further ahead in the text to be typed than the younger typists, thus anticipating the next typing operations. Other examples concerning high-level performance are to be found in research on, for example, chess (Elo, 1965; Charness, 1991), bridge (Charness, 1983; 1992), management (Taylor, 1975; Streufert *et al.*, 1990), computer programming (Keithen *et al.*, 1981), scientific productivity in general (Heeringen, 1983; Simonton, 1988), physics (Chi *et al.*, 1981), and medicine (Cijfer, 1966). In all these examples, there is evidence of some plasticity operating to make high-level performance possible later in the life-span.

Applying this model to performance over the whole life-span and using the gains and losses approach of Baltes (1987), we can expect that when later-life losses become more prominent in relation to the gains, triggering (internal) factors will become more active. In other words, there will be a greater need to rely on one's available reserve potential, because of the constraints and biological limits which become more conspicuous with ageing.

There is also some empirical and theoretical evidence of an increase in the nurturing factors with ageing: experience increases as a function of age and is positively correlated with performance. Salthouse (1985, 1991a, 1991b) mentions four 'benign' functions of experience for performance: maintenance, compensation, compilation and accommodation. Several theories about cognitive ageing have stressed the positive role of experience in cognitive functioning, e.g. the theories of crystallized intelligence (Cattell, 1963; Sternberg, 1984), encapsulated thought (Rybash *et al.*, 1986), and neo-Piagetian conceptions of adult thinking (Labouvie-Vief, 1985, 1992; Commons *et al.*, 1989). Finally, concerning the reserve potential itself: there is ample empirical evidence about the use of reserve potential to preserve the previous level of performance. An excellent example can be found in a study of Charness (1983) in which he investigated different strategies used by younger and older chess players. Although older chess players were clearly inferior when speed of computation of several variants was concerned, they equalled the younger players in strength, i.e. their ELO-rating, because of their computing less but more promising variants in given positions. Their experience guided them in the choice of those more promising variants.

PLASTICITY AND HIGH-LEVEL PERFORMANCE IN LATER LIFE

Given that high-level performance in later life is in fact possible, a fact which is underexposed if not overlooked in most of the theories on cognitive ageing (Salthouse, 1990; 1991a), perhaps with the exception of neo-Piagetian theories (Commons *et al.*, 1989) and theories about wisdom (Sternberg, 1990), alternative theories must be formulated to solve the paradox of the mainstream cognitive theories stressing decline with ageing and the possibility of high-level performance in later life (Talland, 1965; Charness, 1991, 1992). Several hypotheses are possible:

- The high initial level may prevent the individual from dropping below the critical point at which task-demands would normally outweigh the available capacities, resulting in impoverished performance. The distance between available capacities and task-demands is assumed to be smaller in the less gifted individual.
- Metacognitive skills make high-performing individuals more efficacious in cognitive self-management. Although the empirical evidence concerning the relationship between metacognition and cognitive performance is equivocal, probably partly due to conceptual obscurities, an excellent example of this metacognitive management (which is elaborated later as an illustration of the proposed Behavioural Management Model) can be found in Hebb's 'On watching myself get old' (1978). He describes the measures he took to preserve his performance as an outstanding scientist, after discovering a threatening decline in his memory-performance when

he was only in his forties. When he was confronted with a memory black-out he decided to change his reading strategy: instead of trying to read as much psychological literature as possible, he adopted a more selective strategy. Enabled by his experience he could choose the most relevant publications, thus keeping up with the professional literature without overloading his memory. Furthermore, he took more rest, stopped working at night and avoided working lunches. In that way he managed to keep his head above water.

- Because highly achieving individuals usually engage in more challenging activities, they will get more relevant experiences, thereby building up a bigger reservoir of potential. In terms of the conceptual model presented in Figure 12.1, the older high-level performer has both more triggering conditions (self-management and/or challenging i.e. more demanding conditions) and more nurturing ones, i.e. more relevant experience, and therefore a bigger reservoir of reserve potential. The talented individual also is less likely to encounter constraining conditions which might impede optimal performance, as indicated by research on the biological limits of plasticity. For example, there is empirical evidence for Edelman's notion of 'neural Darwinism', in that the dendritic density and the frequency of alpha-rhythms in the brain increase as a function of experience (Buell and Coleman, 1979; Craik and Trehub, 1982; Cohen, 1988). Viewed in that light, the more challenging activities and broader experience of the high-performing individual imply less liability to biological constraints. Finally, high-performing individuals might be less liable to the environmental constraints of social expectations of lower performance with ageing.

A more detailed, quantitative analysis by means of the Behavioural Management Model will be given below: in particular an analysis of the self-management component (triggering) and the external constraint component of the conceptual plasticity-model (Figure 12.1). This will be illustrated by examples of two fictitious individuals.

APPROACHING THE CONSTRUCTS OF COMPETENCE AND PLASTICITY ON THE BASIS OF THE BEHAVIOURAL MANAGEMENT MODEL

The constructs of 'competence' and 'plasticity' are presented as a model-based conceptualization and assessment-procedure. Starting from the developmental theoretical work on competence by Waters and Stroufe (1983), both constructs are mapped onto a model borrowed from Operations Research. The Behavioural Management Model (BeM-model) is proposed to describe an important aspect of human action: goal-directedness under environmental and/or internal constraints. Parameters of the BeM-model are then used to come to terms quantitatively with the constructs of competence and plasticity. Several non-intuitive predictions are derived from the BeM-model. A real-life situation of a student and of an older scientist will be described below to demonstrate the approach.

Progress in psychology has been seriously hampered by what is known as 'the operationalization approach' to measurement. In this, a direct correspondence is sought for a verbal term describing some capability of an individual; behaviours are then grouped together on the assumption that they directly index some 'underlying construct'. In this way numerous constructs 'explaining' behaviour are produced and proliferate, mainly through the intermediate material of published tests. However, the results of empirical research show mainly the poor predictability of human behaviour, even in situations only slightly different from the test situation. What is more, even good predictions are not necessarily signs of a good understanding of the mechanisms explaining human functioning. Explanation and understanding can only be achieved on the basis of models which map observed behaviours onto some explanatory mechanism. Measurements are a side-product of such mapping.

Recently, there has been renewed interest in the construct of competence (Sternberg and Kolligion, 1990), which unfortunately is often equated with ability or skill. As Waters and Stroufe (1983) point out, following Goldfried and D'Zurilla (1969) and also Freeman (1992), it is better to take the lead already given by Socrates, who described competent individuals as 'those who manage well the circumstances which they encounter daily, and who possess judgment which is accurate in meeting occasions as they arise and rarely miss the expedient course of action'. Proposing a developmental perspective on the construct of competence, Waters and Stroufe (1983) define the competent individual as 'one who is able to make use of environmental and personal resources to achieve a good developmental outcome'. Competence is not equated with any particular trait or pattern of personal resources. Rather, they see it as an integrative and coordinative capacity, tied to what the environment will allow, and showing itself in 'good' developmental progress. The proximate criteria for what is 'good' are defined in terms of specific developmental periods (Waters and Stroufe, 1983). Thus, in a talented person, competence in old age will continue to present a high standard of achievement within the individual's circumstances.

This can be taken to indicate that goals which the individual is supposed to pursue at a certain period of life are relevant to the assessment of competency. These goals can be either self-chosen or externally imposed. It is generally agreed that adults have goals in their lives, and that these goals are somehow related to behaviour and emotion. It is only in the last decade, however, that academic psychology has gradually become willing to treat individual goals as a possible factor in explaining emotion and behaviour (Palys and Little, 1983; Brandstädter, 1984; Brandstädter *et al.*, 1986; Emmons, 1989).

Some features which are essential for a fruitful model of competence

- The goal-directedness of human action must be taken into account.
- Coordination of actions, rather than merely the actions themselves, must be described. This coordinative capacity must not only show attunement to the goal(s), but also reflect the resources which the individual uses in approaching the goal. The model must allow for the mapping of the individual's managerial skill, using his or her finite resources in achieving a goal.
- The conceptualizations of both the constructs of competence and plasticity must be recognized together. When the individual comes under pressure, due to changes in circumstances, one with considerable plasticity adapts his or her behaviour in such a way that the goal can still be met without a fundamental change in the

organization of this person's behaviour, while at the same time allowing for surface changes in behaviour, stemming from the competent pursuit of the goal in new circumstances.
- Modelling and testing the model must be at the level of the individual. That is, it should allow the use of idiographic, personal information, without losing the possibility of nomothetic, scientifically based statements, a feature required for clinical decisions.

The Behavioural Management Model (BeM-model)

The previous section sketched a framework in which an individual's competence is judged on the basis of specific performances, showing that one is able to coordinate one's resources in a controlled manner in order to achieve a goal in the best possible way. This performance was termed 'managerial skill'. The BeM-model, which will be described below, allows for the mapping of this managerial skill. A formal description will be given, followed by an explanation of its internal dynamics, with fictional but close-to-real-life data, and finally by the formulation of the model for competence and plasticity.

In its formal structure, the BeM-model belongs to a class of models in Operations Research where the problem is one of maximizing a goal-function under the simultaneous observance of a number of constraints, and where the optimal solution of this problem can be found with a technique known as 'linear programming' (LP) (Ignizio, 1985). This optimal LP-solution can be calculated with inexpensive computer programmes (for PC) which remove the burden of hours/days of calculations (Kalvelagen and Tijms, 1990). For simple problems, a graphical method of finding this optimal solution can be followed, as will be demonstrated in the examples below.

The BeM-model assumes that in the area of their competency, competent people find (nearly) the same optimal solutions as LP. In other words, the more the behavioural configuration of an individual in a problem-situation resembles the one indicated as optimal by the BeM-model, the more competent this individual is. Because plasticity is nothing other than proven competency when facing the same problem under changing conditions, an individual acting in accordance with the BeM-model in changing conditions has not only been displaying high plasticity, but also high competency: plasticity and competency are two sides of the same coin. Note that there is no assumption that processes postulated by the BeM-model are consciously accessible to people.

Two case studies of the BeM-model approach

Example 1: the student Mary

The performance of Mary, a graduate student, will be analysed with the BeM-model. The approach is demonstrated in the process of translating data from Mary's problem situation into formal quantitative BeM-model statements. Firstly Mary's situation is

Talent, Plasticity and Ageing

described, followed by the translation into BeM-language, and then the graphical procedure is outlined for finding Mary's goal-optimal behavioural configuration.

Mary is an eager graduate student; she wants to spend as much of her time as possible on her coursework and assignments. However, she does not have enough money to survive without extra income from part-time jobs. She regularly babysits, which pays $4 per hour, and also sometimes works in a factory, which brings in $10 per hour. However, factory work for Mary is five times as tiring as babysitting: one hour of factory work costs her ten energy units, against two energy units per hour for babysitting. Mary wants to spend not more that 40 energy units a week on work, as otherwise she feels too exhausted to study. Moreover, Mary wants to keep the amount of time spent on jobs to a minimum, but she badly needs a weekly additional income of at least $60. Mary's problem is: how can I best spend my money-earning time?

BeM-modelling: first step, looking for goal(s) and constraints

The BeM-analysis first looks for the goal Mary is pursuing. Apparently, Mary wants to minimize the number of hours spent earning money. Secondly, BeM-analysis looks for a description of constraints in her situation. Constraint 1 has to do with money: Mary has to earn at least $60 a week. Constraint 2 has to do with energy expanded on jobs: Mary wants to spend at most 40 energy units a week. At this point, any questions about the units must be postponed: it will turn out that units are rather unimportant.

BeM-modelling: second step, formal description

Next, both the goal and the constraints are specified more precisely on the basis of the information in the situation (see above). These specifications generally result in linear functions and equations. Mary's goal is translated into a goal-function in the following way: each hour of babysitting (B) costs one hour of Mary's study time. The same is true for one hour of factory work (F). Let B indicate the number of hours a week spent on babysitting, and F the same for factory work: the number of hours a week which Mary spends on earning money (irrespective of the type of job) equals [B + F], or more precisely [1∗B + 1∗F] (the symbol ∗ is used to indicate multiplication). The number 1 indicates the amount of time which one hour of each job activity takes away from Mary's study time. If Mary could study for half the time while on duty as a babysitter, the amount of time taken away from study time by jobbing would be [0.50∗B + 1∗F]. In the present example, Mary wants to minimize the weekly time spent on jobbing. So the goal-function to be minimized is [1∗B + 1∗F].

Constraint-equation 1: constraint 1 (money) will now be formulated as a linear inequality. Each hour of babysitting (B) brings Mary $4, and each unit of F (hour of factory work) brings $10. So, as Mary works B-hours a week on babysitting, she earns the amount of $[4∗B]. For F-hours of factory work, Mary earns $[10∗F]. The total weekly income from both jobs sums up to $[4∗B + 10∗F]. This amount should be at least $60 a week. So constraint 1 can be written as:

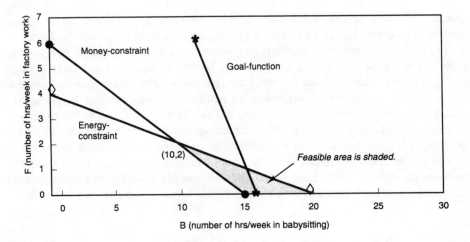

Figure 12.2 *Minimization of the time spent by Mary at work while bound to study under two constraints (money and energy)*

$$[4*B + 10*F] \geq \$60.$$

Constraint-equation 2: constraint 2 (energy) can be specified in a similar way as the inequality:

$$[2*B + 10*F] \leq 40 \text{ energy units.}$$

The complete BeM-modelling of Mary in her situation can now be summarized in the following three lines:

Minimize the goal-function [1*B + 1*F] under the following two constraints:
  money-constraint : [4*B + 10*F] ≥ $60
  energy-constraint : [2*B + 10*F] ≤ 40 energy-units

BeM-modelling: third step, finding the optimum

The third step consists in finding the optimal solution, if there is one. When using a computer program to find this solution, one simply types the above three lines into the slots of the program and in a few seconds, the solution appears. Here, a graphical procedure will be used, as this gives insight into the dynamics of the BeM-model.

Both functions in the above three-line BeM-description of Mary's problem-situation, as depicted in Figure 12.2, represent a two-dimensional space, its dimensions corresponding to the 'decision-variables' B and F. This space is also called the 'feasibility space'. Each constraint-function divides the space into two parts. Actions satisfying all constraints are located in the 'feasibility-area'. In Figure 12.2, this is the triangular (shaded) area in the lower right-hand part. Mary cannot 'produce' acceptable combinations of hours on both jobs {B,F} outside this area.

The goal-function has some indeterminacy, in that only its direction is specified; knowing its precise location is the same as knowing the optimal solution. The location of the goal-function is graphically determined by moving it parallel to itself, until it crosses the feasible area. Figure 12.2 shows this intermediate state of the location of the goal-function. Then, as we are looking for a minimization of the value of the goal-function, the line indicating the goal-function is moved as far as possible to the left, without ever leaving the feasible area. The reader is requested to perform this translation mentally. The ultimate point where this is possible is the point whose coordinates {B,F} signal the optimal configuration; the optimum is always located at one of the corners of the feasible area.

For Mary, the optimum is located at the point {10,2}. This means that she will work 10 hours on babysitting (B) and two hours on the factory (F). It will cost her minimal time (12 hours a week), without her becoming too tired, and generates sufficient additional income ($60).

It is perhaps now easier to see that the units used to describe the constraint-components are somewhat irrelevant for the solution. The same solution will be found if Mary was paid in English pounds or in Dutch guilders, rather than in US dollars as in the example. The same is true for the energy units: if they were further specified in, e.g. calories or in kilo joules, or in any other metric or unit, it would not have affected the solution to the problem of which combination of babysitting and factory work was best for Mary. The units are here used only to conceptualize the situation in BeM-terminology.

Suppose now that we have observed the actual performances of a student like Mary in a similar situation to the above. We could observe the (eventual) discrepancies between the behavioural combinations of hours on the two jobs, as predicted by BeM-Mary who acts optimally and the behaviour of the observed student. From these observations in situations which differ qua goals, action-contingencies and/or qua constraints, a chi-square can be calculated indicating the degree of discrepancy from the BeM-ideal. The lower this discrepancy measure, the higher the degree of competency of the observed person in the problem area under consideration. When the data come from successively changing situations then this discrepancy measure indicates the lack of plasticity in the individual under observation.

A brief non-intuitive illustration of such a lack of plasticity will now be given. Let us assume that Mary, as she becomes experienced in babysitting, succeeds in studying during 50 per cent of the time she is on duty as a babysitter. All other aspects of her situation remain unchanged. Should she therefore spend more time on babysitting (B) than the 10 hours per week which are part of the optimum in her previous situation? Mary's overall goal is unchanged, but her goal-function is now $[0.50*B + 1*F]$. However, the optimal action-configuration remains unchanged $\{B,F\} = \{10,2\}$. If Mary-with-experience increased her number of B-hours, she would contribute to the discrepancy from the BeM-optimum. Therefore, here, unchanged behaviour in a changed world is regarded as contributing to plasticity!

Example 2: Professor Clever

As the principles of the BeM-model and linear programming are given in the first example, the second example (using some of Hebb's (1978) anecdotal information) will be presented in a less elaborated way.

168 Actualizing Talent

Professor Clever, a 50-year-old leading scientist is confronted with a heavy load of management tasks in her department. Yet, as a research manager she has to keep up to date with the developments in her scientific field in order to protect her high scientific reputation. She has two styles of reading the scientific literature: a quick-scanning strategy (Q) and an in-depth strategy (D) (*note*: the following analyses are per week). The quick-scanning strategy takes 15 minutes per article and has a profit per article of 2 'scientific units'. The in-depth reading takes 1 hour per article and has a profit of 12 scientific units. So, the goal-function she has to maximize is [12D + 2Q]; if she fails to reach this goal her scientific reputation is at stake. There are, however, several constraints which she has to take into account. First of all, Professor Clever has only 12 hours a week available for reading: her management tasks swallow up almost all of her time.

Constraint 1 (Time): $(1D + 0.25Q) \leq 12$ hours

Constraint 2 (Prophylaxis Retrieval Problems): $(D + Q) \leq 30$ articles

This second constraint has to do with age-related changes in cognitive resources. As an older woman Professor Clever has discovered that too much reading results in retrieval problems. She can handle 30 articles a week at a maximum; to prevent memory problems she has stuck to this maximum.

Constraint 3 (Condition): $(D \leq Q)$ or $(D - Q) \leq 0$

In order to decide which article is qualified for in-depth reading, she has to scan it first. So, the number of articles scanned must be greater than the number of articles read in-depth.

Constraint 4 (Scientific urge): $(D + Q) \geq 7$

As a good scientist Professor Clever has a strong scientific urge: she can't sleep without reading at least one article a day. This leads to the fourth constraint; Professor Clever has only a restricted amount of energy resources, which unfortunately decrease with age. Reading is tiring and although at time 1 she may have 54 energy units at her disposal, at time 2 the situation has grown worse: she has only 36 energy units available. She has found out that reading articles in-depth costs three times as much energy as the quick method.

Constraint 5 (Energy time 1): $(3D + 1Q) \leq 54$ energy units

Constraint 5 (Energy time 2): $(3D + 1Q) \leq 36$ energy units

In Figure 12.3 the feasible areas with the corresponding optimums at the two points in time (t1, t2) are depicted. Notice that in this example the values of the other constraints are held constant over time for the sake of economy of presentation. It is, however, conceivable that the other constraints also vary over time, thereby changing

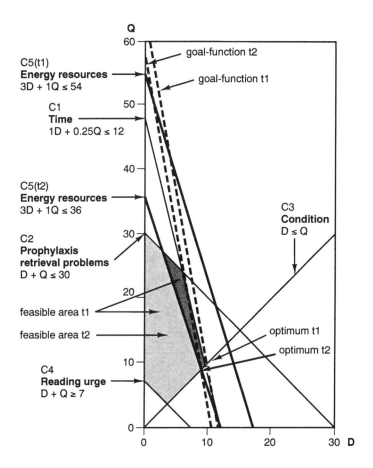

Figure 12.3 *Feasibility space for Professor Clever, optimizing reading profit under five constraints and on two points in time*

the feasible area. Moreover, conditional upon job characteristics, the goal-function may change too. For instance, some scientific functions, such as research manager, require only a broad overview of the field, whereas other functions require more in-depth knowledge. This implies different goal-functions, and eventually different optimums in the feasible area.

THE TALENTED FROM A BeM-PERSPECTIVE

Starting from conceptual analyses of competency and plasticity, their manifestations as organizational or managerial skills have been discussed. Then, a model was presented which can serve as a formal structure on which to map observable actions: the Behavioural Management Model or BeM-model. The degree to which real people in concrete situations act and change their actions as a function of changing circumstances in accordance with the BeM-model, is indicative of their competency and plasticity. Quantitative estimates of competency and plasticity can now be based on the discrepancies between an individual's observed action-pattern and the one ascribed to the BeM-individual. The BeM-individual optimizes his action-pattern in order to reach the goal(s) under the given constraints. The fictitious examples of Mary and Professor Clever have been used to illustrate the workings of BeM-competency and BeM-plasticity.

The BeM-model conceptualizes competency and plasticity in the same way for people over the whole ability range, while allowing for inter-individual differences and/or intra-individual changes. At this stage in its empirical testing, however, only informed guesses can be made about aspects in which the talented differ from 'normal' people. Seven such aspects can be listed; the talented individual:

- is more sensitive to resource-constraints and their changes;
- is able to take into account more constraints simultaneously;
- is more sensitive to environmental and/or internal changes necessitating behavioural changes;
- has more experience/expertise available to nurture the reserve potential;
- is able to find a use for 'slack' (unused resources) by aiming also at additional goals, in addition to the main one;
- explores new strategies for the 'production' of one unit of a decision variable, which use less resources. Such a production strategy is quantitatively described by the column-vector attached to that decision-variable in the set of constraint-equations. For instance, Mary in Example 1 uses the strategy [4,2] with regard to babysitting and the strategy [10,10] with regard to factory work;
- looks for the possibility of minimizing deviations from the multiple goals he is aiming at simultaneously, instead of searching only for an optimal solution for the single-goal situation at hand. In BeM-terminology, this amounts to goal-programming to find the optimal solution.

CONCLUSIONS

What can our approach contribute to actualizing talent? In the development and application of the BeM-model of competence and plasticity, it has become clear that competence is exercised in problem-solving situations, and that plasticity is called for in problem-solving under changing or changed circumstances, e.g. circumstances associated with ageing. Thus, situations where routine, standard procedures are supposed to be applied at all times are detrimental to talent. In this sense, ageing might be conceived as beneficial for talent, though this would be too daring a hypothesis because of the increasing likelihood of an increasing impact of constraints. Fortunately, recent theoretical and empirical work becomes increasingly directed towards the study of ageing individuals, engaging in behavioural planning in situations of decreasing resources and eventually enforced accommodation of goals, i.e. changing goals if they fall outside the feasible area (Lachman and Burack, 1993; Brandtstädter et al., 1993).

In any case, tolerance for deviations from the 'normal way' of acting, and pressure for justification for the new way are both important ingredients of a talent-friendly environment. Despite this tolerant attitude, though, the constraints within which a solution must be found should be clearly visible. Clearly, change and variety should be present in an environment that is supposed to be beneficial to the actualizing of talent.

REFERENCES

Baltes, P.B. (1987) 'Theoretical propositions of life-span developmental psychology: on the dynamics between growth and decline', *Developmental Psychology*, **133** (5), 611–26.
Baltes, P.B. and Kliegl, R. (1992) 'Further testing of limits of cognitive plasticity: negative age differences in a mnemonic skill are robust', *Developmental Psychology*, **28** (1), 121–5.
Baltes, P.B. and Willis, S.L. (1982) 'Plasticity and enhancement of intellectual functioning in old age', in F. Craik and S. Trehub (eds), *Aging and Cognitive Processes*. New York: Plenum Press.
Beckerman, M.B. (1990) 'Leoš Janáček and "The Late Style" in music', *Gerontologist*, **30** (5), 632–5.
Brandtstädter, J. (1984) 'Personal and social control over development: some implications of an action perspective in life-span developmental psychology', in I.P. Baltes and O. Brim (eds), *Life-span Development and Behavior* (Vol. 6). San Diego: Academic Press.
Brandtstädter, J., Krampen, G. and Heil, F. (1986) 'Personal control and emotional evaluation of development in partnership relations during adulthood', in M. Baltes and P. Baltes (eds), *The Psychology of Control and Aging*. Hillsdale, NJ: Erlbaum.
Brandtstädter, J., Wenture, D. and Greve, W. (1993) 'Adaptive resources of the aging self: outlines of an emergent perspective', *International Journal of Behavioral Development*, **16** (2), 323–49.
Buell, S.J. and Coleman, P.D. (1979) 'Dendritic growth in the aged human brain and failure of growth in senile dementia', *Science*, **206**, 854–6.
Cattell, R.B. (1963) 'Theory of fluid and crystallized intelligence: a critical experiment', *Journal of Educational Psychology*, **54**, 1–22.
Charness, N. (1983) 'Age, skill, and bridge bidding: a chronometric analysis', *Journal of Verbal Learning and Verbal Behaviour*, **22**, 406–16.
Charness, N. (1991) 'Expertise in chess: the balance between knowledge and search', in K.A. Ericsson and J. Smith (eds), *Toward a General Theory of Expertise*. Cambridge: Cambridge University Press.
Charness, N. (1992) 'Age and expertise: responding to Talland's challenge', in L.W. Poon, D.C. Rubin and B.A. Wilson (eds), *Everyday Cognition in Adulthood and Late Life*. Cambridge: Cambridge University Press.
Chi, M.T.H., Feltovich, P.J. and Glaser, R. (1981) 'Categorization and representation of physics problems by experts and novices', *Cognitive Science*, **5**, 121–52.
Cijfer, E. (1966) 'An experiment on some differences in logical thinking between Dutch medical people, under and over the age of 35', *Acta Psychologica*, **25**, 159–71.
Cohen, G.D. (1988) *The Brain and Human Aging*. New York: Springer.
Commons, M.L., Sinnott, J.D., Richards, F.A. and Armon, C. (eds) (1989) *Adult Development*. Vol. 1. New York: Praeger.

Craik, F. and Trehub, S. (eds) (1982) *Aging and Cognitive Processes*. New York: Plenum Press.
Dennis, W. (1966) 'Creative productivity between the ages of 20 and 80 years', *Journal of Gerontology*, **21**, 1-8.
Edelman, H. (1987) *Neural Darwinism: The Theory of Neural Group Selection*. New York: Basic Books.
Elo, A. (1965) 'Age changes in master chess performances', *Journal of Gerontology*, **20**, 289-99.
Emmons, R. (1989) 'The personal striving approach to personality', in L. Pervin (ed.), *Goals Concepts in Personality and Social Psychology*. Hillsdale, NJ: Erlbaum.
Freeman, J. (1992) *Quality Education: The Development of Competence*. Geneva and Paris: UNESCO.
Goldfried, M. and D'Zurilla, T. (1969) 'A behavioral-analytic model for assessing competence', in C. Spielberger (ed.), *Current Topics in Clinical and Community Psychology* Vol. 1. New York: Academic Press.
Grout, D.J. (1960) *A History of Western Music*. London: J.M. Dent.
Hebb, D.O. (1978) 'On watching myself get old', *Psychology Today*, 15-17.
Heeringen, A. van (1983) *Relaties tussen leeftijd, mobiliteit en productiviteit van wetenschappelijke onderzoekers*. Den Haag: Staatsdrukkerij.
Heymans, P.G. (1991) *Lifespan Development: Management. Part 1: Behavioral Management*. Utrecht: Intern rapport vakgroep ontwikkelingspsychologie, no 3.
Heymans, P.G. and Brugman, G.M. (1990) 'Plasticity and ageing: at the nexus of person and context', in W. Koops, H. Soppe, J. van der Linden, P. Molenaar and J. Schroots (eds), *Developmental Psychology Behind the Dikes*. Delft: Eburon.
Horn, J.L. and Hofer, S.M. (1992) 'Major abilities and development in adults', in R.J. Sternberg and C.A. Berg (eds), *Intellectual Development*. Cambridge: Cambridge University Press.
Ignizio, J.P. (1985) *Introduction to Linear Goal Programming* (Sage University Paper Series on Quantitative Applications in the Social Sciences). Beverley Hills: Sage.
Kalvelagen, E. and Tijms, H. (1990) *Exploring Operations Research and Statistics in the Microlab*. Englewood Cliffs, NJ: Prentice Hall.
Keithen, K.B., Reitman, J.S., Rueter, H.H. and Hirtle, S.C. (1981) 'Knowledge organization and skill differences in computer programmers', *Cognitive Psychology*, **13**, 307-25.
Klauer, K.J. (1992) 'Entwicklung eines Trainingsprogramms zur Förderung des induktiven Denkens bei älteren Menschen', in J. Klauer and G. Rudinger (eds), *Kognitive, emotionale und soziale Aspekte des Alterns*. Opladen: Westdeutscher Verlag.
Labouvie-Vief, G. (1985) 'Intelligence and cognition', in J.E. Birren and K.W. Schaie (eds), *Handbook of the Psychology of Aging*. New York: Van Nostrand Reinhold.
Labouvie-Vief, G. (1992) 'A neo-Piagetian perspective on adult cognitive development', in R.J. Sternberg and C.A. Berg (eds), *Intellectual Development*. Cambridge: Cambridge University Press.
Lachman, M.E. and Burack, O.R. (1993) 'Planning and control across the life span', *International Journal of Behavioral Development*, **16** (2), 131-43.
Lehman, H.C. (1953) *Age and Achievement*. Princeton: Princeton University Press.
Palys, T. and Little, R. (1983) 'Perceived life satisfaction and the organization of personal project systems', *Journal of Personality and Social Psychology*, **44**, 1221-30.
Poon, L.W., Rubin, D.C. and Wilson, B.A. (eds) (1992) *Everyday Cognition in Adulthood and Late Life*. Cambridge: Cambridge University Press.
Pritikin, R. (1990) 'Marcel Duchamps, the artist, and the social expectations of aging', *Gerontologist*, **30** (5), 636-9.
Rybash, J.M., Hoyer, W.J. and Roodin, P.A. (1986) *Adult Cognition and Aging*. New York: Pergamon Press.
Salthouse, T.A. (1985) 'A theory of cognitive aging', in G.E. Stelmach and P.A. Vroon (eds), *Advances in Psychology*, vol. 28. Amsterdam: New Holland.
Salthouse, T.A. (1990) 'Cognitive competence and expertise in aging', in J.E. Birren and K.W. Schaie (eds), *Handbook of the Psychology of Aging*. 3rd ed. San Diego: Academic Press.
Salthouse, T.A. (1991a) *Theoretical Perspectives on Cognitive Aging*. Hillsdale, NJ: Erlbaum.
Salthouse, T.A. (1991b) 'Expertise as the circumvention of human processing limitations', in

K.A. Ericsson and J. Smith (eds), *Toward a General Theory of Expertise*. Cambridge: Cambridge University Press.
Schaie, K.W. and Schooler, C. (eds) (1989) *Social Structure and Ageing*. Hillsdale, NJ: Erlbaum.
Schneider, W. and Uhl, C. (1990) 'Metagedächtnis, Strategienutzung und Gedächtnisleistung: vergleichende Analysen bei Kindern, jüngeren Erwachsenen und alten Menschen', *Zeitschrift für Entwicklungspsychologie und Pädagogische Psychologie*, **22** (1), 22–41.
Schooler, C. and Schaie, K.W. (eds) (1987) *Cognitive Functioning and Social Structure over the Life Course*. Norwood, NJ: Ablex Publishing Company.
Simonton, D.K. (1988) *Scientific Genius: A Psychology of Science*. New York: Cambridge University Press.
Simonton, D.K. (1990) 'Creativity in the later years: optimistic prospects for achievement', *Gerontologist*, **30** (5), 626–31.
Simonton, D.K. (1991) 'Career landmarks in science: individual differences and interdisciplinary contrasts', *Developmental Psychology*, **27** (1), 119–30.
Skinner, B.F. (1983) 'Intellectual self-management in old age', *American Psychologist*, **38**, 239–44.
Sternberg, R.J. (ed.) (1984) *Handbook of Human Intelligence*. Cambridge: Cambridge University Press.
Sternberg, R.J. (1990) *Wisdom: Its Nature, Origins, and Development*. Cambridge: Cambridge University Press.
Sternberg, R.J. and Kolligion, J. (eds) (1990) *Competence Considered*. New Haven: Yale University Press.
Streufert, S., Pogash, R., Piasecki, M. and Post, G.M. (1990) 'Age and management team performance', *Psychology and Aging*, **5**, 551–9.
Sward, K. (1945) 'Age and mental ability in superior man', *American Journal of Psychology*, **58**, 443–79.
Talland, G.A. (1965) 'Initiation of response, and reaction time in aging, and with brain damage', in A.T. Welford and J.E. Birren (eds), *Behavior, Aging, and the Nervous System*. Springfield: Charles C. Thomas.
Taylor, S. (1975) 'Age and experience as determinants of managerial information processing and decision-making performance', *Academy of Management Journal*, **18**, 41–74.
Waters, E. and Stroufe, L.A. (1983) 'Social competence as a developmental construct', *Developmental Review*, **3**, 79–97.
Weinert, F.E., Knopf, M. and Barann, G. (1983) 'Metakognition und Motivation als Determinanten von Gedächtnisleistungen im höheren Erwachsenalter', *Sprache und Kognition*, **2**, 71–87.
Willis, S.L. (1990) 'Introduction to the special section on cognitive training in later adulthood', *Developmental Psychology*, **26** (6), 875–8.

Chapter 13

Towards a Policy for Actualizing Talent

Joan Freeman

Education and learning is a lifelong process, so a policy for the talented should take a wide approach to include individuals of all ages. Such a policy, whether aimed at potential or actualized achievement, would encourage the recognition of the talented and help them to access appropriate resources and learning situations. However, in most of the world, special provision for the development of exceptional ability is patchy, not only for economic reasons, but because of negative attitudes (Reis, 1989). Too often, extra help is limited to the fashionable talents such as sport and music, or only accessible to those who can afford it (Ojanen and Freeman, 1994). There are three primary reasons for this: the difficulty in identifying potential for excellence, the uneasy balance between competition and egalitarianism, and élitism – appearing to provide more for those who already seem to be privileged by, for example, birth or wealth. In fact, very few authorities anywhere have designed a specific educational policy for the talented. Although the top few per cent are certainly a minority, they are in most ways like other people, and so must be seen in the context of human development. But since it is their abilities which distinguish them, special concern must focus mainly on opportunities for learning along with concern for emotional balance. Given appropriate opportunities, throughout their lives the talented will learn more quickly and in greater depth than others. But without them, such as access to materials, high-level teaching, and emotional support, this potential will remain unrealized.

The talented are defined here as those who either demonstrate exceptionally high-level performance, whether across a range of endeavours or in a limited field; or those who could demonstrate this level, given the chance. They are not a homogeneous group e.g. in terms of learning style, creativity, speed of development or social behaviour. Almost all advocacy efforts are aimed at 'gifted' schoolchildren who show advanced achievement in school subjects, with relatively little regard given to what happens in non-school activities. Since most schools tend to be keenly aware of examination results, they may push their brightest pupils to high academic achievements, sometimes to the detriment of all-round emotional and creative development (Freeman, 1994). Specific counselling care for their problems is rare, although advice is available (e.g. Milgram, 1991; Deslisle, 1992). Even educational enrichment, where it is provided, usually occurs outside school hours, such as at weekends, thus leaving the critical time in the classroom unchanged.

Everyone should have the right to aim for excellence (Coe, 1990; HMI, 1993), and a supportive, advancing society will foster the various aptitudes and enthusiasms of its individual people. But recognizable talent can never be seen in isolation; it is a product of the conditions provided by a particular society. All abilities need to be nurtured, both psychologically and materially, and to be seen in terms of what a person *could* do, rather than what he or she *can* do now. It is not only ease of access which is important in this provision, but the quality of what is provided, which requires an approach that focuses on the process, rather than the product. Were this approach to be widely spread through society, it would greatly increase the proportion of children and adults who would today be seen as talented. But since even basic educational provision is inadequate in much of the world, special facilities for the brightest, as well as further education for those who have missed out in childhood, are often dependent on individual efforts and charitable organizations (Freeman, 1992; Wagner, 1995).

A life-span view

There is abundant evidence that social and economic influences affect individuals' development and opportunities (e.g. Stapf, 1990; Archer, 1992; Collier, 1994), both in the family (Schneider, 1993), and by a school's ethos and provision (Rutter *et al.*, 1979). A rich educational environment can benefit the talented relatively more than the average because of their capacity to abstract more learning from their environments (Freeman, 1983; Span, 1995). Childhood has long been the dominant focus of empirical research and theories because of the belief that it is the most significant growth period, while adulthood serves only to refine existing capacities. In recent years, however, significant phases of change have been identified in adulthood (Berger, 1988; Alexander and Langer, 1990).

Learning in infancy is vital for future high-level achievement (see Freeman, 1995). Certain aspects of advanced development, measured in the first three years of life, provide indications of life-long attributes, such as physical control (Lewis and Louis, 1991), cognition (Slater *et al.*, 1989; Colombo, 1993), mastery motivation (Messer, 1993), and verbal ability (Fowler, 1990). Even in infants, intellectual development can be thought of in terms of problem-solving skills, which not only depend on the knowledge they have accumulated and how well they can retrieve and use it (Mayer, 1992). It follows that the earliest psychological help should begin as near birth as possible, to be offered along with child-care teaching in clinics and during home-visits by health workers; this contact should continue in the first years of school. The first teaching materials should develop fine-motor skills, enhance sensory learning experiences – seeing, feeling, and listening – so that infants practice discriminating between shapes, textures, colours, and sounds etc. (see Freeman, 1991b). This growing ability to see differences and be selective underlies later, more abstract levels of productive thinking in science, engineering and industry.

However, not everyone can demonstrate their abilities when they are young. There are many instances of people who have contributed greatly to the benefit of knowledge and the improvement of life, who were failures at school; well-known examples being Winston Churchill and Albert Einstein. Those who are late in development, for whatever reason, need further provision when they have left school. A flexible continuing education system, providing the opportunities to find help where and when it is needed may be specifically designed for particular age-groups. Examples are the University of the Third Age for older people, or systems using 'distance learning', such as the Open University or the Open College, which use television and radio to provide part-time teaching for adults who have other demands on their time.

Some reasons for a policy for the talented

- Efforts to improve education throughout life need to be clearly directed if they are to be effective. For example, individuals who are not able to fulfil their promise in the school years should be enabled to do so later.
- Provision for the talented can both improve their own achievement and motivate others' efforts in both school and workplace. Special attention for the talented in schools has been seen to improve results all round (HMI, 1993).
- Given the means to reach their potential, in an atmosphere of acceptance and encouragement, the talented can make an exceptional contribution at school and later to their society.
- Expert observation and measurement is important in the identification of high potential, as well as in forming guidelines for subsequent action. Parents need information from authoritative sources, and schools may have to improve their record-keeping and assessment, for example, when a child is passing academic and other 'milestones' at an advanced rate. Such good habits of observation of development and performance, including discussion with parents, have a generally beneficial effect.
- In the competition among the many good causes asking for help from limited resources, the case for special attention for the talented must be made clearly, which would be present in a policy. There is always concern to avoid taking provision away from other children, such as slow learners, who are usually seen as having greater needs.

THE DESIGN OF A POLICY

A policy for the promotion and actualization of talent should be applicable in many places, including those where money is in short supply. This is especially pertinent where parents and teachers may feel satisfied if their children are merely receiving a basic education, and those who have left school may feel themselves for reasons of time and money not to be in a position either to enrich their learning or make up any that is missing. Ideally, it should thus be flexible enough to serve many cultures, and yet sufficiently well structured to provide the basis for a single community. But it will be adaptable to local conditions. Educational policy should not only be concerned with school, but rather with promoting a life-span and community approach to learning. It should be based on clear principles, such as the suggested list below, which is adaptable to local conditions.

Specific policy principles

- Learning and being creative is continuous throughout life
- Learners will take responsibility for their own progress
- Assessment confirms progress, rather than identifies failure
- Shared values and team-working are recognized equally with the pursuit of knowledge
- The efforts of parents and schools are coordinated with those of vocational training, adult education and community.

Policy aims

Education is adequate only when it is suited to the needs of the individual. But the idea that adequate provision for individuals with high potential ability demands considerable funding at the expense of others has to be rejected in favour of the view that it is part of fair education for all. Nor should formal education always be seen as responsible for the highest levels of human endeavour; it can even be detrimental, as when creativity is inhibited by the obligation to memorize and reproduce (Freeman, 1994; Cropley, 1995). The most useful aspects of education are concerned with its continuation throughout life. The aim of any policy which promotes talent should be to enable each individual to attain knowledge in a manner which is meaningful, and which can then be used in a creative manner in different situations. Flexibility in education, concern for the individual, the provision of free, high-quality education, as well as non-school educational provision for all who want it – all these are facilities which enable excellence to develop in people from all walks of life. However, one must recognize that it is not possible to legislate for excellence, to pass edicts that people should love learning, or to require teachers to be enthusiastic about their work and their pupils. There are limits to the effects of any policy.

Specific policy aims

- Heightening awareness of the needs of the talented
- Identifying and recognizing high-level potential
- Making provision for advanced learning and creative endeavour, both within and outside educational establishments
- Promoting research in this area of human development

A research-based policy

A policy for the talented should not only be based on evidence but also aimed at promoting further research, while passing on new information and conclusions to teachers, student-teachers, and parents. However research standards in this area vary widely, with samples being biased, very small, without control groups or consisting of retrospective studies of eminent people. Alternatively, research can sometimes be overly 'scientific', which means focused on testing, with little regard for the subjects' overall lives. Research into high-level intellectual activity is particularly complicated because of the considerable number of cognitive operations involved in problem-solving, such as the combined use of both convergent and divergent thought processes in creativity, so that reliable prediction of adult success is limited, even when potential is recognized in adolescence (Heller, 1991). There are several (mostly American) theories and models about the development of talent which are yet to be put into international action (e.g. Renzulli et al., 1981; Sternberg, 1985; Simonton, 1990; Gardner, 1993).

Even where educational policies for the talented exist, though, they may bear little relationship to research findings. So far, there has been little evaluation, outside the USA, of the effects of special educational provision (e.g. Cox, 1985; Subotnik et al., 1993), and what there is shows that it has had marginal effects. Very little controlled experimental work is being undertaken to evaluate the effects of any special provision for the talented, e.g. in different cultures (see Wallace and Adams, 1993), mixed-ability teaching, instruction within school hours compared with that given outside them, or the effects of different kinds of organization at the workplace.

Some questions for research

- How to convert research findings about the development of high ability into practical action, especially for the socially disadvantaged and individuals with learning difficulties, e.g. dyslexia or perceptual dysfunction.
- How to improve the flexibility of school-teaching in all subjects, to enable children in mixed-ability classes to flourish.
- Is it better for talented children to be identified and educated separately, or managed within a mixed-ability situation?
- Do talented individuals need special counselling and vocational guidance to achieve their potential?
- Should educational help for the talented be of a general nature, such as training in thinking or imagery skills, or should it focus on specific areas of learning, such as skills in foreign languages or science?
- How do the talented perceive and think?
- Should the talented spend most of their energies building on their outstanding strengths – be these individual or cultural – for high-level achievement, or should they spend the time improving their weaker areas, for a balanced education?

TEACHING THE TALENTED IN SCHOOL

The talented benefit particularly from a flexible teaching style, and from competent, imaginative teachers. These teachers should also be aware of their pupils' emotional development, because creative excellence comes from self-confidence to use learning in new ways. Sometimes, the intellectually gifted can be too keen on study. Because of the danger of too much memorizing, they need encouragement to think independently (autonomously), maybe at a tangent to the syllabus. For the enhancement of their creativity, many need encouragement to take a more playful approach to their learning (Gardner, 1991), an attitude which many great minds, such as Einstein and Linus Pauling, have claimed as the basis for their success. They also need to be in contact with their ability peers, especially those of the same age, who will help them to feel more at ease within their own areas of interest, either during the school day or at specialist courses and on social occasions.

Because the intellectually gifted think and learn differently from others, it is important for their development to teach them appropriately, particularly with guidance in thinking skills. These include the encouragement of attitudes such as curiosity, persistence and confidence, and general strategies including planning, monitoring and evaluation. 'The equation is relatively straightforward, the more able an individual the more self-regulation will be needed for high achievement; the less able the individual the more teacher regulation is needed' (Span, 1995, p. 65).

In teaching the talented, the professional competence of the classroom teacher is paramount. To be successful, teachers must have both a positive attitude towards the special needs of these pupils, and expertise in using individualized learning techniques. To educate such children towards autonomy and intellectual maturity, rather than just informing them, teachers have to create the atmosphere in which rational and reflective thinking can take place. This means that they too must be able to use those abilities in their own teaching. With teachers' enthusiasm, special help can be offered to talented children in ordinary schools, sometimes in unusual subjects. The teacher is in a position to enhance creative thought with an open, questioning, and challenging style, providing a safe atmosphere in which the talented might try out their intellectual wings.

Some specific educational needs

- A consistent challenge. There is a great variety of ways in which this can be provided by using the resources which already exist, such as those provided by local authorities in parks and libraries (Freeman, 1991b). Challenge may also come through contact with experts in particular fields, such as mentors, people who act as guides to individual children, spend time with them in a learning relationship and challenge them to make the most of their capacity (Daloz, 1986).
- The opportunity to work at their own rate of learning, to pursue their own interests to a high level, and to practise their skills for the required length of time to produce expert performance.
- Help with their special vocational problems, because the many talents that some possess cause difficulties for them, sometimes for many years, in choosing how best to direct their lives.
- Regular communication and interaction with others of like mind, through, for example, science networks or out-of-school activities.

Organizing the teaching of the talented

There is disagreement on how to educate the talented, which reflects some cultural bias: the American outlook tends to favour giving bright children some form of separate education and/or advancing children by a class or two (Gallagher, 1991), whereas the European outlook is rather to provide a rich environment in the normal classroom (see Mönks et al., 1992).

In Britain, Her Majesty's Inspectorate of Schools (HMI) investigated provision for the talented in normal schools and concluded that: 'It should be possible to cater for the majority of very able pupils within the context of the normal school curriculum, if proper consideration is given to their particular special needs, and some flexibility is introduced into both organisational and teaching strategies' (HMI, 1992, 26). Formal education, though, should not be seen as the only route for developing the highest levels of expertise. If promotion of the skills and talents needed by society are limited to an élite, however that élite is selected, there will inevitably be talented individuals whose potential contributions are not developed, and so are lost. Moreover, because it is not possible to predict the kinds of talents that will be needed in the future, there has to be a wide variety of skills and outlooks available in any society.

The following three major organizational strategies have been advocated to help children with high potential; each has advantages and disadvantages, both educational and social, but all can be enhanced with enrichment techniques, which are described after them. (For a fuller review of these matters see, e.g. Dar and Resh, 1986; Freeman; 1992; Southern et al., 1993; Rogers and Span, 1993.)

Acceleration. The cheapest and easiest form of special provision, and consequently the one most frequently used, is to move a bright child up a class or two above his/her age-group, preferably followed by continuous monitoring. The problems which come from this move arise because it is usually done in terms of age, so that the accelerated child is normally less mature, both physically and emotionally, than the rest of the class. It is often assumed that age-acceleration brings content-acceleration with it, but the child may merely be working along the same lines as before, the academic challenge being provided by the difficulty of making up the missing year; a broader, deeper view of the subject matter would therefore still be missing. However, acceleration may be the only option, and when care is taken of possible emotional problems by a sympathetic approach, it has been seen to be successful, even at university level.

Selective education. This involves children's identification and placement in special education. This selection may be made on the basis of IQ scores or other forms of high achievement, using an agreed cut-off point. Allowance may be made for home circumstances and language difficulties in an attempt to overcome bias against recognized disadvantaged groups. However, subjective nomination of children as talented by teachers is unreliable, and bright children who are not achieving highly in the regular classroom are unlikely to be chosen. Furthermore, the features on which children might be selected may change with circumstance and time, and as the number of places in special educational programmes is inevitably limited, an ability which would give admission in one district may not be successful in another. Selection could be for full-time education (e.g. for academic aptitude or music), for a separate class, or for part-time groups which are withdrawn from normal classes. Because of this identification as talented or gifted, there is the danger of psychological changes in the children's self-concept and outlook; they may feel themselves to be superior to others, and so become less willing to relate easily with less able people. Schools which specialize, teaching certain subjects to a high level, are called 'magnet' schools because they aim to attract (rather then select) talented children to an area of excellence.

Mixed-ability classes. In every part of the world, almost all talented pupils are taught in mixed-ability classes in neighbourhood schools. Teachers, being wary of any form of 'élitism', whether of wealth or ability, usually prefer to keep them in the normal classroom. There is consequently widespread commitment to mixed-ability teaching, which calls for special skills to cater for a sometimes widely disparate collection of children's abilities in one class. Though all children, especially the culturally deprived, are very dependent on school for an adequate education, the brightest are relatively more restricted by inadequate provision there, because their potential (and therefore their relative loss) is greater. Bright children's learning can not only be disrupted by the presence of unwilling classmates in an unstimulating environment, but also by the time taken up by too many non-academic school activities, such as sports practice, team meetings, school fairs, etc., which in some schools eat heavily into study and thinking time.

In mixed-ability teaching, although all the pupils in the class should be following the same theme to different depths, most classroom teachers tend, in fact, to pitch their level of lessons to the middle range of ability. Some even use their brightest children to teach the others, though this means that the talented do not get the teaching and stimulation that they should. However, the major problem is that teachers are not specifically trained for mixed-ability teaching, which requires a high level of skill and planning if it is to be effective.

A big problem for the talented in a mixed-ability class is in adapting socially with classmates, yet remaining intellectually alive and different from them. Expecting a child to think at a level of brilliance, while others around are behaving 'normally', demands exceptional maturity, since a high level of performance needs to be shown at some times and conformity to social norms at others. The talented are particularly vulnerable to the 'three times problem', identified by Freeman (1991a), which comes from the common teaching habit of presenting information three times – to introduce it, to remind the children, and a third time to summarize and reinforce. Since the talented hear it and remember it the first time round, they may daydream on the second two times to avoid tedium, and so may also miss other parts of the lesson. Their learning can thus seem erratic, and if some content is missing, they can reach wrong but firmly held conclusions.

Differentiation in mixed-ability teaching is helped by grouping the pupils. This is often by ability, but a more fluid (e.g. vertical) grouping, based on a learning rather than a teaching approach, enables individual children to develop at their own pace. An example is in musical instrument playing, where a group, of, say, brass players of all ages will be gathered together to form a band because of their shared ability and interest. This is also possible in more academic subjects, where children may be allowed to proceed at their own pace and style. However, there can be problems with small group work, such as the dominance by one or two pupils, or reaching conclusions too quickly so that some will not follow the steps by which these have been reached. Reciprocal teaching (Palincsar and Brown, 1984), in which pupils, or pupils and teachers, take turns to be teacher, is useful in mixed-ability situations.

Enrichment

Educational enrichment is the deliberate rounding out of the basic curriculum subjects with ideas and knowledge that enable a pupil to be aware of the wider context – not a supplementary diet which depends on whether there is enough money for 'extra' material and tuition. It is a particularly important aspect of the education of talented youngsters who have the potential to go well beyond the elements of any particular area of study, relate it to other areas, and play with ideas so as to come up with new ones. The teacher's task is to provide the groundwork, and to guide and encourage pupils to explore further. Enrichment is possible in all kinds of schools, helping each child to learn what they need within the limits of timetabling. (There is, after all, no restriction of high-quality television to those who might best appreciate it; programmes are provided at all levels, and people can select for themselves.) It can take place in the school classroom by using extension learning materials, in the school or public library, in the community, or even through a correspondence course in which the student and the instructor never meet.

In schools which have a policy of providing enriched education, teachers are encouraged to develop their skills through in-service courses and workshop activities. During the school day, they can enrich different subjects by coordination, e.g. relating the basic material in one area to that of others; this is usually more beneficial to the learner than further detailed study of the same subject. An example would be when history and geography specialists, whether in their own classrooms or together, coordinate their teaching about the Second World War, which would give a more enriched picture of events than either one working alone.

There are many ways to loosen up the rigidity of formal teaching, where each child is locked by age or school-class into the same lessons, timing and homework, regardless of ability and maturity. Many human aptitudes are better developed outside the classroom than in it. Bright children, especially, can benefit through contact with professionals – artists, performers, agricultural and industrial scientists, scholars, craftspeople and others who are not primarily educators. It is not always lack of money which prevents them doing this; it needs a fresh outlook, a real concern, and a willingness to alter routine – to think differently. The wider gains for the child lie in the advantages of improved understanding, relating, and forming new ideas, along with the positive personal rewards of enhanced self-concept and improved ability to cope with life.

Specialist groups of talented pupils can meet outside school time, e.g. in an extended lunch break, short courses, exploratory groups on special interests, such as ancient history or jazz, or for debating. Provision for them can be made by restructuring the school timetable to include periods of independent learning, which can also be supervised less formally by individual teachers. This need not necessarily be a problem, though, if it is acknowledged that such help is not entirely dependent on teachers. Parents can contribute to specialist subjects in which they are experts, and with due care taken that their own education is not being affected, volunteer older pupils can be very helpful if the school has the kind of atmosphere in which cooperation rather than competition is encouraged.

Talented children usually like a challenge, and enjoy thinking creatively round a subject: they need access to special enriched curricular materials, even if these are not directly related to the lesson, for times when they finish assignments early. This extra material could be shared by a group of schools, or it could be housed in the school library, with the child being given permission to go out of the classroom to use it. Commercial toys and games, many of which are designed to increase children's skills of observation and planning, are helpful in this respect. Enrichment support systems in the community will obviously vary; there may be local associations, or clubs and societies which run activities and would welcome school groups, such as those for talented children or young mathematicians. There may be museum and library courses, such as art classes for children at weekends. Competitions that are open to everybody present the opportunity of discovering so far unnoticed talents. Colleges or other higher-level educational establishments may be persuaded to allow bright children to use their facilities, while businesses and places of production may also be willing to help.

Some specific teaching strategies for the talented

- Guiding children to coordinate the principles found in different texts
- Teaching research skills so that children can round-out basic material for themselves
- Encouragement to question as a part of every-day learning, to stimulate thinking and creative problem-solving.

Teacher training

Faced with pupils who read voraciously, reason and absorb information rapidly, ask questions, invent problems, provide creative solutions, and cope with concepts and abstract ideas at a young age, many teachers feel inadequate. But teaching talented children does not imply that the teacher has to be super-knowledgeable, rather than interested and keen to learn along with the pupils. It is as much as anything a matter of a positive attitude, as well as specific understanding of the situation and the techniques to deal with it. There are many ways of improving teachers' ability to deal effectively with their talented pupils, either during first-level training, or as in-service courses – and without heavy expenditure. More contact and coordination between different education authorities, to share resources and knowledge, would also help. Teachers can be helped to take a wider view of education, seeing it in personal and social contexts, which could involve obligatory experience outside the classroom, freedom to innovate within their own sphere of influence, with credit being given for doing so.

Any course of training for future or practising teachers of the talented should cover at least the following four elements:

Managing the curriculum. For talented pupils, the curriculum is too often based on an inadequate model of knowledge, and needs to be enriched with more stimulating and complex cognitive demands. To do this, teachers not only require a sound knowledge of cognitive development, but also a grasp of the aims, intentions and objectives of the whole curriculum, as well as familiarity with individual schemes of study and lessons. At present, only too often the quickest students are obliged only to do more work of the same kind.

Using language appropriately. For teachers of talented pupils, certain skills, especially verbal interactions between teachers and pupils, are particularly useful on a lesson-by-lesson basis. Intellectually bright children often love playing with words, especially using proverbs and idioms. The spoken language of classrooms revolves around three main transactions – teachers' talk, teachers' questions, and pupils' responses or initiations. The cognitive demands of a lesson – a significant factor in the satisfaction of the able pupil – can be recognized by the level, speed, and quality of the verbal interactions that go on in it.

Improving task demand. Intellectually talented pupils are capable of enhanced cognitive stimulation beyond that offered in most mixed-ability classrooms. So, for example, new knowledge should not be presented in isolation as facts to be remembered, but given in the context of a conceptual framework. The talented should also use the appropriate technical language, rather than a simplified version, and the teacher should take a problem-posing as well as a problem-solving approach, to stimulate thinking about the study area. Tasks emerging from a study that was planned in this way would be likely to have both immediacy and a relevance.

Recognizing underachievement. Underachieving bright pupils are especially difficult to identify, but it is important for teachers to be aware of both the current emotional and potential educational problems of such children (Deslisle, 1992; Butler-Por, 1993). Signs to watch for are children who are bored, restless, orally fluent but poor in written work, friendly only with older pupils or adults, or excessively self-critical yet apparently also quick-thinking. Some who do poorly in tests are nevertheless creative, able to solve problems, ask searching questions and think in abstract terms. Others may have been bullied by their schoolmates into mediocrity. The overriding reason for underachievement in the talented is the lack of provision for learning, whether in materials, teaching or emotional support (Butler-Por, 1993). High ability in underperforming children can be discovered by a sensitivity to the way they are handling language, and their general knowledge, problem-solving, and personal interests. Some, who keep a low profile in class, can be discovered through standardized tests. The teacher can help the underachieving talented child by appropriately designed procedures, such as making the material relevant to the child's interests (Feuerstein and Tannenbaum, 1993).

School policy for the talented

The stated goals of the school will influence the staff who are attracted to work there, and so will influence the less tangible ethos of the school. A school's policy for their brightest pupils is an indication of how it attends to the different needs of all its children, which is an essential part of mainstream education. The following points focus on practical aspects of a policy which a school can incorporate for the encouragement of high-level performance in both pupils and teachers.

The commitment of the head of school. The person in charge of the school, and the leadership he/she gives in the education of the school's brightest pupils, should provide an immediate incentive for teachers. But to offer more than fine intentions, the headteacher has to make practical support available in the distribution of resources, and be concerned with, for example, flexibility of timetables, response to noise levels in the classroom, quality and quantity of work that is completed and attitudes to parents. The influence of the head will spread to teaching strategies, such as providing encouragement and backing for innovations.

A whole-school approach. All the school staff should be involved in presenting a policy, because otherwise bright children might spend more time with uninterested teachers than with those motivated to help them. Teachers should be aware of their own attitudes to the talented, and be helped to understand why they may feel that such children can look after themselves. They may need reminding that a school should cater fairly for the needs of all its pupils, and that the talented need interaction at a higher level of challenge. The school climate has to favour excellence in all its pupils' efforts, extended where possible and acknowledged (say, in exhibitions or school publications).

It is useful to have one or more staff members, preferably with some extra status, who can act as cross-curricular coordinators for the talented across the whole curriculum, as when an appointed teacher coordinates multicultural education or language. The danger in this, though, is that the designated person or group may be seen as fulfilling the school's obligation in that area, so relieving the other teachers of any responsibility for it. At very least, there should be one person on the school staff appointed to care for the talented, to monitor and evaluate the education they receive; this should be a position of special responsibility, coordinating with heads of departments.

The school pastoral system should be aware and able to take steps to cope with the special vulnerabilities and stress, not only of being unusually capable, but of working at an exceptionally high level. The school counsellor, or the year tutor in a secondary school, would fill this role. Such concern would have to involve the teachers in awareness of potential problems of the talented, and maybe the style of teaching of subject teachers. Such matters as self-confidence and personal relationships can be as important in education as the often well-taught command of skills and knowledge. The problems of being able to do a great number of things extremely well arise when vocational choices have to be made, and skilled attention is needed for young people in that situation (Deslisle, 1992).

A challenging curriculum. Liberating the talented from the demand for only average performance is likely to entail changes to the curriculum, for example, enabling talented pupils to progress through a series of competencies at their own speed, rather than accelerating them through age-related school classes. In that way, they would not waste so much time waiting for a challenge, but could continue to make progress at the more advanced level which suits their abilities. Teaching that is standardized with the 'average' child in mind is less likely to take account of individual differences, and can disappoint the talented by offering only an inadequate challenge. Additionally, if the basic subjects are to take up, say, 70 per cent of school time, then there is relatively little time left for wider-ranging education and the study of areas not normally catered for. At present, most curricula are based on content – on acquiring knowledge. It would be much more suitable and valuable if, in addition, children were to be taught the skills of data acquisition and analysis, as well as the processes of independent self-directed learning and self-selected study.

Resources. One of the main ways in which a school can serve all its pupils is the good management of its resources. Too often, though, such ability is lacking; this leads to wastage and erosion of funds. The 'less urgent' causes, such as special provision for the talented, suffer. Some funds should be set aside for enrichment materials, which will not, of course, benefit only the talented. The resources should also include a list of local experts, who can share their ideas and skills, and possibly act as mentors. Such a data bank will also include peripatetic teachers, and local centres of interest, institutions, clubs and workshops. All pupils, but especially the talented, should also be encouraged to find out these things for themselves, as an aspect of self-motivated extracurricular work.

Quite apart from the financial benefits of parents' involvement, schools which work closely with parents as resources are often able to use the educational assistance which they are often glad to give. A parent who can listen to children read, take a class around a factory, or describe how a car engine works is bringing the real world through the school gate. Schools which deny the role of parents as educators or who fear that by opening the door to them the status of their teachers will drop, appear to have little faith in their own expertise, which may become apparent in a greater degree of rigidity and control. Teachers can help parents improve the educational impact of the way they bring up their children by sharing their educational knowledge; in this way, the development of the child's learning and thinking can be promoted in everyday life.

Monitoring. Special care should be taken, via such methods as record-keeping, discussions, samples of work and a tutor system, to make sure of the continuity of education for the talented, so that they are not subject to different treatment and attitudes from each new teacher. In other words, involvement of the whole staff and close communication between them is essential in raising awareness about these children and in forming the school's policy. This includes regular reviews of present and future provision for them.

Questions to ask about a policy for the talented

Policy. Has the education of the talented ever been raised in discussion of school policy, and has the school made a specific policy statement about them?

Differentiation. Is some differentiation of teaching a requirement in all subjects? For example, are all children given the same tasks, to be assessed according to the same standards? If so, what happens when some finish much sooner than the rest of the class? Does every child start at the same point and go through the same number of stages at the same speed? Is homework differentiated by ability? Are pupils grouped by ability in different subjects, and if so, how are they selected? How much use is made of individual acceleration through year groups? To what extent are the talented pushed to their limits?

School atmosphere. To what extent do the pupils in the school applaud excellence in academic learning, creativity, all-round ability, leadership skills, sport and extra-curricular activities?

Parents. Do many parents choose the school for the recognized success of its talented pupils? Does the school provide support for parents of talented pupils?

Outside school. On behalf of its talented pupils, does the school have good relationships with industry, centres of higher-level learning, commerce, administration, etc.?

In some places, the idea that some children may be talented courts accusations of élitism, and schools there are likely to oblige all pupils to conform to the average (Ojanen and Freeman, 1994). But the local education authority can help schools to cater for all their pupils by encouraging an atmosphere in which attention and provision for able pupils is regarded as a normal part of school life. Although individual teachers may be well motivated to help the talented, unless there is clear concern about it from 'above', that help is unlikely to be enough. The alternative dilemma is sometimes to choose between government requirements for what are seen as 'high standards' in schooling, which usually implies high examination marks, and what the talented actually need. For example, they do not need as many hours in school as the less able, but they do need greater flexibility. Flexibility enables innovation and diversity to be carried out in schools for all pupils, so that they can change their routines with circumstances. An example of flexible education is open-plan construction, e.g. quiet and carpeted areas for reading, or where experimenting with sand and water can take place and where a wet mess is acceptable. However, while this system is seen to work well with extrovert children, it is less productive with the introverts, who prefer a more structured environment (Bennett, 1976). There is a limit to the amount of differentiation in teaching that any system can present.

Planning a policy for the talented involves recognizing and using whatever facilities are available – no matter how few of these there seem to be. And because all educational systems exist within a society, they must to some extent reflect it, so that attempts at change must necessarily take such influences as religion, tradition, level of resources and social discrimination into consideration. Details of how local education authorities might be most effective are given below, followed by suggestions for national governments.

Specific actions for education authorities

- Appoint specialist advisors to schools in the education of the talented, perhaps forming a team; schools might jointly contribute to funding the post. The authority could establish a separate body to train and promote specialist 'super-teachers', who would go into schools and liaise between pupils and teachers. They would monitor the objectivity of teachers' assessments, and yet be able to take a view of the child as a whole. Assessment must take into account what a pupil is being assessed for, e.g. a master class in mathematics does not call for the same level of social maturity as overall acceleration to a higher age-group.

- Provide opportunities for talented pupils to meet and interact with others like themselves. For example, local education authorities could arrange a flexible system of part-time withdrawal of talented children from normal classes, and/or offer summer schools, where the youngsters can exchange ideas and gain emotional support with like-minded peers.
- Offer courses for teachers on the education of the talented, both before qualification and on an in-service basis.
- Provide open learning centres in school or community buildings for all who want to use them – without selection – which could be used by pupils, teachers and parents. They should be available either in or out of school hours, be well coordinated, and integrated with school life. They would not just have material about the basic school subjects; each one could focus on areas such as technology and enterprise, with help and equipment available and they could include numerous variations, such as puppetry or anthropology. They could also be used to provide teachers with specialist practice in teaching talented pupils. Funding could come from either education and/or outside.
- Team teaching could be encouraged. For example, using the image of the spokes of a wheel, the teaching team could take a theme in history as the 'hub' and divide it into different 'spokes' from the central point, with teachers working together, integrating their ideas, and teaching through each age-level. This avoids locking the talented into the same level as their less-able classmates, giving them the freedom to take their interests further.
- Some extra resources are required to make differentiation of the curriculum really possible. This may be money to pay extra adults, such as university students, to act as mentors who can give more intensive support to individual pupils or small groups, for, say, one half-day a week. Specialist teachers are also needed for individual work with pupils. Teachers also need access to extra materials for enrichment and extension of the curriculum; they are unlikely to have either the time or the expertise to test and develop these for themselves, and it is decidedly inefficient for them to keep 'reinventing the wheel'. Schools can combine forces to develop a bank of such resources.
- Help to coordinate contacts and cooperation with sources of extra education in specific areas, such as institutions of higher education and the workplace. Teachers are not always familiar with business and industry, and they would benefit from knowing more about it, such as by means of short-term placement in work outside school, which would also help them guide their pupils in vocational choice. It is important for educational bodies to invite people, whether managing directors or trade union leaders, into schools, and to take pupils into the workplace for visits or work experience. Companies usually have materials and know-how which can be used by schools. They may also help to finance special school projects and competitions.

GOVERNMENT ACTION

Although individuals and even local education authorities may be well motivated to help the talented, unless there is clear concern from the government at all levels, that help is unlikely to be enough to make a measurable difference to a community, because impetus for change is heavily influenced by those who hold ultimate power. There are several ways in which this can be done:

How national and state governments can help

- Establish a government office responsible for the care and education of the talented, which would provide encouragement and resources to local education authorities or to schools directly.
- Authorize, say, three per cent of the education budget to cater specifically for talented individuals. This implies recognition of their needs, both in and out of school.
- Present specific plans for enabling talented individuals to move towards realizing their potentials.
- Establish a nationwide centre to distribute information and approved materials for teachers and parents, aimed toward educating the talented.
- Because family life is the basis of future high ability, governments can make extra help available to parents when their children are born, such as free information in clinics on children's psychological development, early learning centres offering advice, toy libraries etc. (described in detail in Freeman, 1991b): these could also be subsidized by private enterprise. Health workers could be trained to look at families from an educational point of view, paying attention to the earliest developmental stages.
- Provide readily available and inexpensive opportunities for challenge and fulfilment in continuing education, especially for late developers and those who have missed out on earlier educational provision. These may be designed for school-leavers or could be taken up by any age group.
- Cooperate with other national governments to bring in foreign experts or arrange teacher exchanges.

CONCLUSIONS

A policy setting out the philosophy and aims for the education of the talented has to be clear to everyone concerned, because efforts to change attitudes are unlikely to be effective without their involvement and agreement (Timar and Kirp, 1988). To some extent, limited knowledge about the effects of education on high ability is explained by shortage of funds for research and poor planning, but it is also the result of political antagonism. Yet a policy cannot be effective which is not firmly supported financially and administratively by the public authority. Pupils, too, need an accurate picture of what is provided and expected of them if they are to be motivated to aim for appropriate goals. They also need the freedom to negotiate for what they feel is right for them.

The prime aim of a policy for the talented is to provide opportunities to fulfil the potential of individuals. This implies promotion of life-long independent learning, based on strengths and abilities, and the discovery and recognition of the great diversity of human potential for the cultivation of hidden talents. To do this means changing educational systems. For children, these changes are most valuable during the school day, with teachers who are trained to recognize and educate talented pupils, providing more individualized educational provision for them. There is a need for more research designed to find reliable ways of providing what the talented need, being aware of the most effective existing current provision.

The partnership of parents, teachers and the children themselves is essential in devising the means to help each child. Of course, education authorities have to be involved, not least in the provision of educational services out of school hours, such as competitions, summer camps and further education classes. This is essential not only for children, but also for adults who may either have missed their educational chances or who are late developers. Voluntary action by parents and teachers can be effective in changing administrative policy.

Education is not only a matter of passing exams; it is a feeling for learning and speculating. Although life can be lived on a basic level with no sustenance for the spirit, that is not the way of choice. Creativity is the dynamic of human society – not a luxury, but a necessity. A policy for the talented is vital to ensure that all aspects of their education throughout life are considered. It asks for a creative, caring approach for individual development as a human right, blended with concern for the greater good of society.

REFERENCES

Alexander, C.N. and Langer, E.J. (eds) (1990) *Higher Stages of Development*. New York: Oxford University Press.
Archer, J. (1992) 'Childhood gender roles: social context and organisation', in H. McGurk (ed.), *Childhood Social Development: Contemporary Perspectives*. Hillsdale, NJ: Earlbaum.
Bennett, S.N. (1976) *Teaching Styles and Pupil Progress*. London: Open Books.
Berger, K.S. (1988) *The Developing Person through the Life Span*. New York: Worth.
Bryant, P.E. (1992) 'Arithmetic in the cradle', *Nature*, **358**, 712–13.
Butler, N.R. and Golding, J. (1986) *From Birth to Five: A Study of the Health and Behaviour of Britain's Five Year Olds*. Oxford; Pergamon.
Butler-Por, N. (1993) 'Underachieving gifted students', in K.A. Heller, F.J. Mönks and A.H. Passow (eds), *International Handbook of Research and Development of Giftedness and Talent*. Oxford: Pergamon.
Coe, S. (1990) 'The public's responsibility to promote excellence', *European Journal of High Ability*, **1**, 7–10.
Collier, G. (1994) *Social Origins of Mental Ability*. New York: Wiley.
Colombo, J. (1993) *Infant Cognition: Predicting Later Intellectual Functioning*. London: Sage.
Cox, J., Daniel, N. and Boston, B.A. (1985) *Educating Able Learners: Programs and Promising Practices*. Austin: University of Texas Press.
Cropley, A. (1995) 'Actualizing creative intelligence'. Chapter 8, this volume.
Daloz, L.A. (1986) *Effective Teaching Mentoring*. San Francisco: Jossey-Bass.
Dar, Y. and Resh, N. (1986) *Classroom Composition and Pupil Achievement*. London: Gordon and Breach.
Deslisle, J.R. (1992) *Guiding the Social and Emotional Development of Gifted Youth*. London: Longman.

Elshout, J. (1995) 'Talent: the ability to become an expert'. Chapter 7, this volume.
Feuerstein, R. and Tannenbaum, A.J. (1993) 'Mediating the learning experiences of gifted underachievers', in B. Wallace and H. B. Adams (eds), *Worldwide Perspectives on the Gifted Disadvantaged*. Bicester: AB Academic Publishers.
Fowler, W.F. (1990) *Talking from Infancy: How to Nurture and Cultivate Early Language Development*. Cambridge, MA: Brookline Books.
Freeman, J. (1983) 'Environment and high IQ: a consideration of fluid and crystallised intelligence', *Personality and Individual Differences*, 4, 307–13.
Freeman, J. (1991a) *Gifted Children Growing Up*. London: Cassell.
Freeman, J. (1991b) *Bright as a Button*. London: Optima.
Freeman, J. (1992) *Quality Education: The Development of Competence*. Geneva: UNESCO.
Freeman, J. (1994) 'Some emotional aspects of being gifted', *Journal for the Education of the Gifted*, 17, 180–97.
Freeman, J. (1995) 'Where talent begins'. Chapter 2, this volume.
Gallagher, J.J. (1991) 'The gifted: a term with surplus meaning', *Journal for the Education of the Gifted*, 14, 353–65.
Gardner, H. (1991) *The Unschooled Mind*. New York: Basic Books.
Gardner, H. (1993) *Creating Minds*. New York: Basic Books.
Heller, K.A. (1991) 'The nature and development of giftedness: a longitudinal study', *European Journal for High Ability*, 2, 174–8.
HMI (1992) *Education Observed: The Education of Very Able Children in Maintained Schools: A Review by HMI*. London: HMSO.
HMI (1993) *Exceptionally Able Children: Report of Conferences*. London: Department for Education.
Lewis, M. and Louis, B. (1991) 'Young gifted children', in G. A. Colangelo and G.A. Davis (eds), *Handbook of Gifted Education*. Boston: Allyn and Bacon.
Mayer, R.E. (1992) *Thinking, Problem Solving, Cognition*. Oxford: Freeman.
Messer, D.J. (1993) 'Mastery, attention, IQ, and parent-infant social interaction', in D.J. Messer, *Mastery Motivation in Early Childhood: Development Measures and Social Processes*. London: Routledge.
Milgram, R.M. (ed.) (1991) *Counselling Gifted and Talented Children*. Norwood, NJ: Ablex.
Mönks, F.J., Katzko, W. and van Boxtel, H.W. (eds) (1992) *Education of the Gifted in Europe: Theoretical and Research Issues*. Amsterdam: Swets and Zeitlinger.
Ojanen, S. and Freeman, J. (1994) *The Attitudes and Experiences of Headteachers, Class-Teachers, and Talented Pupils Towards the Education of the Talented in Finland and Britain*. Savonlinna: University of Joensuu.
Palincsar, A.S. and Brown, A.L. (1984) 'Reciprocal teaching of comprehension: fostering and monitoring activities', *Cognition and Instruction*, 1, 117–75.
Reis, S.M. (1989) 'Reflections on policy affecting the eduction of gifted and talented students', *American Psychologist*, 44, 399–408.
Renzulli, J.S., Reis, S.M. and Smith, L.H. (1981) *The Revolving Door Identification Model*. Storrs, CT: Creative Learning Press.
Rogers, K.B. and Span, P. (1993) 'Ability grouping with gifted and talented students: Research and guidelines', in K.A. Heller, F.J. Mönks and A.H. Passow (eds), *International Handbook of Research and Development of Giftedness and Talent*. Oxford: Pergamon.
Rutter, M., Maughan, B., Mortimore, P. and Ouston, J. (1979) *Fifteen Thousand Hours*. London: Open Books.
Schneider, B.H. (1993) *Children's Social Competence in Context. The Contributions of Family, School and Culture*. Oxford: Pergamon.
Simonton, D.K. (1990) *Scientific Genius: A Psychology of Science*. Cambridge: Cambridge University Press.
Slater, A.M., Cooper, R., Rose, D. and Morison, V. (1989) 'Prediction of cognitive performance from infancy to early childhood', *Human Development*, 32, 137–47.
Southern, W.T., Jones, E.D. and Stanley, J.C. (1993) 'Acceleration and enrichment: the content and development of program options', in K.A. Heller, F.J. Mönks and A.H. Passow (eds),

International Handbook of Research and Development of Giftedness and Talent. Oxford: Pergamon.

Span, P. (1995) 'Self-regulated learning by talented children'. Chapter 6, this volume.

Stapf, A. (1990) 'Hochbegabte Mädchen: Entwicklung, Identifikation und Beratung, insbesondere im Vorschualter [Talented girls: development, identification and counselling, especially at pre-school age]', in W. Wieczerkowski and T.M. Prado (eds), *Hochbegabte Mädchen.* Bad Honnef: K. H. Bock.

Sternberg, R.J. (1985) *Beyond IQ: A Triarchic Theory of Human Intelligence.* Cambridge: Cambridge University Press.

Subotnik, R., Kassan, L., Summers, E. and Wasser, A. (1993) *Genius Revisited: High IQ Children Grow Up.* Norwood, NJ: Ablex.

Timar, T.B. and Kirp, D.L. (1988) *Managing Educational Excellence.* (Stanford Series on Public Policy.) New York: Falmer Press.

Wagner, H. (1995) 'Complementary approaches to talent development'. Chapter 11, this volume.

Wallace, B. and Adams H.B. (eds) (1993) *Worldwide Perspectives on the Gifted Disadvantaged.* Bicester: AB Academic Publishers.

Name Index

Abroms, K.I. 27, 28, 50
Ackerman, P.L. 63
Adams, H.B. 13, 178
Adey, P. 10
Albert, R.S. 104, 146
Alexander, C.N. 175
Alexander, P. 47
Allison, M.T. 131
Amabile, T.M. 100, 103
Amano, I. 8
Ambrose, D.C. 64
Anderson, C.C. 103
Andrae, J. 73
Anthrop, J. 131
Anzai, Y. 89
Archer, J. 175
Ardenne, M. von 154
Ari, B.A. 14
Arnold, K.D. 6, 7, 49
Arnold, L.E. 23
Atkinson, J. 26

Bakker, D.J. 8
Baldwin, A.Y. 99, 108
Baltes, P.B. 48, 158, 159, 161
Balzac, H. de 34
Bamberger, J. 47
Bandura, A. 28, 44
Barron, F. 92
Barton, B.L. 74
Bassock, M. 59
Baum, S. 47
Beavis, N. 129, 130
Beckerman, M.B. 158
Beittel, K. 115
Benbow, C.P. 8, 49, 148
Bennett, S.N. 187
Benton, D. 26
Bereiter, C. 62, 64, 65, 66, 67
Berger, K.S. 175
Berlin, I. 3
Berry, C. 107
Beukhof, G. 72
Bhaskar, R. 89
Bidder, G. 35–7
Biermann, K.-R. 102
Blagg, N. 78
Bloom, B.S. 5, 11, 108, 130
Boekaerts, M. 10, 51, 61
Boerlijst, G. 52
Bordouin, C.M. 51
Borkowski, J.G. 75
Borms, J. 128, 129, 130
Bornstein, M.H. 24
Boshuizen, H.P.A. 90
Bouchard, T.J. Jr 8
Braddick, O. 26
Brandstädter, J. 163, 171
Brook, D. 119, 126
Brooks-Gunn, J. 23
Brookshire, W.K. 45

Brower, J.J. 136
Brown, A.L. 79, 81, 182
Brown, J.S. 63
Brugman, G.M. 159
Bryant, P. 26
Buell, S.J. 162
Burack, O.R. 171
Butler, K.A. 51
Butler, N.R. 21
Butler-Por, N. 13, 47, 61, 108, 184
Butterworth, G.E. 23
Byrne, B.M. 44
Byrne, J.P. 10, 74, 80

Callahan, C.M. 7
Campbell, S. 140
Carr, M. 12
Cattell, R.B. 161
Ceci, S.J. 6, 35
Charness, N. 60, 87, 158, 160, 161
Chase, W.G. 93
Cheng, P. 60
Chessor, D. 44
Chi, M.T.H. 10, 25, 59, 70, 83, 87, 93, 160
Chomsky, N. 21
Christensen, H. 4
Christensen, P.R. 103
Churchill, Winston 176
Cijfer, E. 160
Clampit, M.K. 50
Clark, E.F. 36
Clark, R.E. 78, 81
Clark, R.W. 21, 30
Cobb, P. 62
Coddington, R.D.S. 137
Coe, S. 141, 175
Cogill, S. 28
Cohen, G.D. 162
Cohen, L.M. 64
Cohen, R. 47
Colangelo, N. 47
Colburn, Z. 36
Cole, M. 76
Coleman, P.D. 162
Collier, G. 8, 175
Collins, A. 80
Collins, W.A. 27
Colombo, J. 9, 22, 23, 175
Commons, M.L. 161
Copernicus 102
Cornell, D.G. 45, 51
Council of Europe 130
Cox, C.M. 5, 102
Cox, J. 13, 155, 178
Cox, T. 26
Craik, F. 162
Cratty, B.J. 137
Craven, R. 44
Crombach, H.F.M. 91
Cronbach, L.J. 78

Cropley, A.J. 59, 60, 100, 101, 103, 104, 106, 108, 109, 146, 177
Csikszentmihalyi, I.S. 39
Csikszentmihalyi, M. 6, 7, 39, 43, 46, 145
Curie, Marie 3
Curtiss, S. 144
Czeschlik, T. 11, 43, 45

da Vinci, L. 13
Daloz, L.A. 49, 179
Dar, Y. 180
Darwin, Charles 3, 6, 34, 35, 102, 106
Dauber, S.L. 49
de Bono, E. 78, 79
De Corte, E. 10, 51, 59, 60, 62, 65, 68, 93, 100
de Groot, A.D. 89
de Jong, F.P.C.M. 62, 81, 83
Deci, E.L. 43
Del Ray, P. 131
Dekker, R. 60
Dennis, W. 158
Denton, F.C.J. 12, 109
Derain, André 123–4
Deregowski, J. 117
Deslisle, J.R. 13, 51, 175, 184, 185
Detzner, M. 45
Dickens, Charles 34
Dochy, F.J.R.C. 62
Doyle, W. 81
Dreyfus, E. 119, 124
du Pré, Jacqueline 11
Dudink, A. 130
Dujardin, K. 8
Duquin, M.E. 131
D'Zurilla, T. 163

Easton, C. 11
Eccles, J. 6
Edelman, H. 162
Einstein, Albert 3, 5, 35, 46, 106, 176, 179
Einstein, Mileva 46
Elkind, D. 146
Elliot, C.D. 8
Elo, A. 160
Elshout, J. 5, 10, 25, 38, 60, 80, 83, 99, 100, 107
Emmons, R. 163
Ericsson, K.A. 5, 38, 60, 87, 93, 130
Eysenck, H.-J. 11

Facaoaru, C. 101
Faraday, Michael 13
Farisha, B. 102
Feger, B. 51
Feldhusen, J.F. 13, 45
Feldman, D.H. 4, 5, 43, 47

Name Index

Feuerstein, R. 9, 27, 77, 78, 79, 82, 184
Fisher, R.J. 128, 129, 130
Fitzgerald, Zelda 46
Flynn, J.R. 8
Foddy, M. 103
Fowler, W.F. 9, 25, 130, 175
Fox, L.H. 63
Freeman, J. 7, 9, 11, 12, 13, 14, 21, 25, 27, 29, 43, 45, 46, 47, 48, 69, 78, 83, 103, 106, 110, 128, 129, 130, 136, 140, 141, 144, 146, 163, 174, 175, 177, 179, 180, 187, 189
Freeman, N.H. 122, 123, 124
Freud, Sigmund 3, 5, 21, 30, 106
Freudenberger, H.J. 44
Frisby, C.L. 78
Fromm, E. 103
Fucigna, C. 115, 118
Fullick, J. 125

Galileo 102
Gallagher, J.J. 180
Galluci, N.T. 45
Galton, F. 5
Gardner, H. 5, 8, 43, 49, 104, 121, 122, 178, 179
Gebart-Eaglemont, J.E. 103
Gibson, J. 101
Glaser, R. 59, 62, 72, 75, 80
Glaserfeld, E. von 62
Glick, M. 11
Globerson, T. 62
Goertzel, M.G. 5, 102
Goh, B.E. 45
Goldfried, M. 163
Golding, J. 21
Golomb, C. 120
Gombert, J.E. 9, 26, 84
Goodman, N. 120
Goudas, M. 130
Graham, Martha 5
Greeno, J.G. 63
Gross, M.U.M. 6, 130
Grossberg, I.N. 45
Grout, D.J. 159
Grover, L. 23
Grubar, J.-C. 8
Gruber, H.E. 5, 6, 10, 14, 43
Guilford, J.P. 101, 103
Gunnar, M.R. 27
Gustafson, S.B. 106

Hall, L.K. 101
Hany, E.A. 4, 12
Hargreaves, D.J. 120
Harlow, H.F. 21
Harlow, M.K. 21
Harris, A. 126
Harris, P.L. 10, 27, 121
Harsanyi, L. 129
Haskey, J. 133
Hassenstein, M. 102
Hayes, J.R. 5, 38, 60
Hebb, D.O. 159, 161, 167
Hebbelinck, M. 128
Heeringen, A. van 160
Heinelt, G. 102, 103
Heller, K.A. 6, 11, 46, 49, 146, 178

Henderson, A.S. 4
Hermann, D. 80
Herrmann, A. 73
Herrnstein, R.J. 3
Hershey, M. 48
Heymans, P.G. 159
HMI 82
Hofer, S.M. 159
Hoffman, M.L. 42
Hollender, M.H. 44
Honzik, M.P. 48
Horn, J.L. 103, 159
Hospers, J. 120
Howe, M.J.A. 6, 7, 36, 75, 106, 107
Humphrey, G. 73
Hundeide, K. 28

Ignizio, J.P. 164

Jackson, N.E. 59
Jacobs, J.E. 7
Janos, P.M. 47
Jensen, A. 78
Jobagy, S. 11
Johnson, N.R. 124
Johnson-Laird, P.N. 116, 118
Jones, E.D. 14
Jung, C.G. 21, 103

Kagan, J. 24
Kail, R. 5
Kalvelagen, E. 164
Kane, J.E. 129
Kanevsky, L. 10, 60
Karmiloff-Smith, A. 119
Karnes, F.A. 44
Karpati, A. 125
Kaufman, F.A. 11
Kavanaugh, R.D. 121
Keithen, K.B. 160
Kepler, J. 102
Kerr, B. 48
King, G. 125
Kirp, D.L. 7, 189
Klauer, K.J. 159
Kliegl, R. 159
Kluver, H. 120
Knopp, T.B. 133
Kogan, N. 101
Kohn, A. 50
Kolligion, J. 163
Kozulin, A. 9
Kroll, M.D. 13
Kulieke, M.J. 146
Kurtz-Costes, B.E. 12

Labouvie-Vief, G. 161
Lachman, M.E. 171
Laird, J.E. 88
Landau, E. 103
Landrum, M.S. 51
Langer, E.J. 175
Lask, B. 137
Lave, J. 63
Leboyer, F. 20
Lehman, H.C. 106, 158
Lehwald, G. 10, 23, 42, 76, 77, 78
Leslie, A.M. 121
Lewis, M. 9, 23, 25, 128, 175
Light, P. 101

Link, F.R. 77
Little, R. 163
Lobsien, M. 73
Loeb, H. 125
Louis, B. 9, 23, 128, 175
Lowyck, J. 74
Lubinski, D. 8
Luria, A.R. 26
Luthar, S.S. 7, 10, 84
Lynn, R. 8
Lytton, H. 27

McCartney, K. 25
MacGregor, R.N. 125
Machlowitz, M. 44
Macintosh, D. 131
MacKinnon, D.W. 103
McLeod, J., 108, 109
McNemar, Q. 103
McPherson, B.D. 131
McQuattie, S. 129
Mahler, Gustav 3
Maker, C.J. 47, 82
Mann, B.J. 51
Mansfield, R.S. 111
Maoz, N. 152
Marjoram, T. 154
Marjoriebanks, T. 5
Marsh, H.W. 44
Marton, F. 63, 75
Mascie-Taylor, C.G.N. 9, 26
Maslow, Abraham 42
Mayer, R.E. 175
Maziade, M. 28
Meijboom, G. 52
Messer, D.J. 10, 24, 28, 175
Michalson, L. 25
Milgram, R.M. 13, 51, 101, 175
Mill, James 37
Mill, John Stuart 34, 35, 36, 37
Milstein, Nathan 11
Mischel, W. 10, 27
Mönks, F.J. 42, 180
Montessori, M. 21
Morris, D. 120, 121
Motamedi, K. 103
Mozart, Wolfgang Amadeus 33, 34, 35, 38, 107
Mumford, M.D. 106
Murray, C. 3
Muthukrishna, N. 75

National Council of Teachers of Mathematics 61
Necka, E. 102
Neff, G. 103
Newell, A. 88
Newton, Isaac 102
Nisbet, J. 42
Nolan, M.F. 134

Ochse, R. 146
Oehler-Stinnett, J.J. 54
Ogilvie, B. 137
O'Halloran, P.J. 153
Ojanen, S. 12, 174, 187
Okagaki, L. 60
Oliver, E. 48
Olszewski-Kubilius, P.M. 11, 45, 146, 149

Name Index

Overtoom-Corsmit, R. 60
Owen, S.V. 47

Paganini, Nicolò 38
Pagliari, C. 8
Palincsar, A.S. 79, 81
Palys, T. 163
Papousek, H. 9
Paris, S.G. 10, 74, 80
Parsons, M.J. 123, 125
Passow, A.H. 50
Pauling, Linus 179
Pelegrino, J.W. 5
Perkins, D.N. 61, 80
Perleth, C. 6
Piaget, J. 6, 22, 26, 84
Pickering, J. 26
Pinker, S. 21
Plato 5
Plomin, R. 8
Pollins, L.D. 47
Poon, L.W. 159
Post, F. 5, 12
Postlethwaite, K. 12
Prado, T. 51
Prins, F.W. 74
Pritikin, R. 158
Proctor, T.B. 47
Pusch, L.F. 46
Pyryt, M.C. 152

Rabinowitz, M. 80
Radford, J. 5, 25, 43, 47
Reis, S.M. 6, 81, 174
Reith, E. 118
Renner, M.J. 8
Renzulli, J.S. 4, 81, 178
Resh, N. 180
Resnick, L.B. 63
Rich, Y. 14
Risemberg, R. 10
Roberts, R. 136
Roche, L. 44
Rogers, Carl 42
Rogers, K.B. 180
Rose, D.H. 24
Rosenblith, J.F. 20, 21
Rosenzweig, M.R. 8
Rost, D.H. 11, 43, 45
Rowley, S. 47, 99, 130, 136, 137, 140
Rump, E.E. 111
Runco, M.A. 104
Ruskin, John 34
Rutter, M. 175
Ryan, R.M. 43
Rybash, J.M. 161

Sage, G.H. 137
Säljö, R. 63, 75
Salomon, G. 62, 63, 80
Salthouse, T.A. 158, 159, 161
Sand, G. 73
Sanger, D. 123
Sapon-Shevin, M. 48
Satie, Erik 38
Savell, J.M. 78
Sayler, M.F. 45
Scardamalia, M. 62, 64, 65, 66, 67

Scarlett, C.L. 131
Scarr, S. 25
Schaie, K.W. 159
Schiller, P. 121
Schmidt, M.H. 45
Schneider, B.H. 175
Schneider, W. 60, 61, 159
Schoenfeld, A.H. 80
Schooler, C. 159
Schunk, D.H. 44
Sears, R.R. 46
Secondary Heads Association 140
Selye, H. 44
Selz, O. 73
Shakespeare, William 33
Shaughnessy, M.F. 100
Shavelson, R.J. 44
Shaw, G.B. 34
Shmukler, D. 119
Shore, B.M. 10, 108, 109
Shostakovich, Dmitri 38
Shuell, T.J. 62
Sidis, W. 11
Sierwald, W. 101
Sigman, M.D. 24
Silver, S.J. 50
Simon, H.A. 88, 89
Simons, P.R. 62, 72, 75
Simonton, D.K. 4, 10, 102, 104, 106, 107, 158, 160, 178
Sisk, D.A. 50
Skinner, B.F. 159
Skinner, M. 26, 47
Slater, A.M. 9, 24, 175
Sloane, K.D. 146
Smith, J. 87
Smith, N. 115, 118
Smith, R.E. 137
Smoll, F.L. 137
Snow, R.E. 78
Socrates 163
Sofranko, A. 133
Sommers, R. van 125
Southern, W.T. 14, 47, 180
Span, P. 10, 51, 60, 62, 100, 175, 179, 180
Spear, M.G. 46
Spearman, C. 3
Sports Council 140
Stanley, J.C. 148, 149
Stapf, A. 7, 46, 175
Stedtnitz, U. 92, 100
Stephenson, George 34, 35, 36, 37
Stephenson, R. 37
Sternberg, R.J. 4, 8, 60, 75, 79, 100, 161, 163, 178
Streufert, S. 160
Strip, C. 51
Stroufe, L.A. 162, 163
Subotnik, R. 6, 7, 8, 12, 49, 178
Süle, F. 100, 130
Sward, K. 158, 159
Sylva, K. 7

Talland, G.A. 161
Tannenbaum, A.J. 9, 27, 50, 184
Taylor, B. 123, 124
Taylor, C.W. 92

Taylor, S. 160
Terassier, J.-C. 12, 47
Terman, L.M. 6, 35, 42
Thistlewood, D. 122
Thompson, L.A. 8
Thomson, R.W. 129, 130
Tijms, H. 164
Timar, T.B. 7, 189
Tinbergen, N. 21
Tizard, B. 9
Torrance, E.P. 74, 101, 111
Trbuhovic-Gjuric, D. 46
Treffinger, D.J. 74
Trehub, S. 162
Trevarthen, C. 9
Troxell, J.R. 137
Tsiamis, A. 108, 109
Tulkin, S.R. 24
Turner, P. 123

Uhl, C. 159
Urban, K.K. 10, 45, 50

van der Sanden, J.M.M. 78
Vermunt, J.D.H.M. 62
Volkov, S. 11
Vosniadou, S. 62
Vrugt 44
Vygotsky, L.S. 14, 26, 63, 76, 77, 81, 83, 84

Wagner, H. 14, 148, 175
Walberg, H.J. 6, 43, 49
Walker, B.A. 46
Wallace, A. 11, 43
Wallace, B. 13, 178
Wallace, D.B. 5, 6, 10, 14, 43
Wallach, M.A. 101
Washington, J. 63
Waters, E. 28, 162, 163
Watt, James 34
Weinert, F.E. 144, 153, 159
Weisberg, R.W. 10, 102, 107
Weisz, V. 7
Wellman, H.M. 122, 123
Wenger, E. 63
Wertsch, J.D. 9, 14, 26, 76, 77, 78
West, T. 13
White, B. 21, 28
White, K.R. 13
Whitmore, J.R. 47
Wilkinson, S.C. 50
Willats, J. 117
Williams, J.M. 10, 27
Willis, S.L. 158, 159
Winch, C.W. 9
Winner, E. 118, 120
Wolf, D. 121, 122
Wolf, D.P. 118
Wordsworth, Dorothy 46

Yaffe, M. 137
Yewchuk, C. 11

Zigler, E. 11
Zimmermann, B. 148
Zimmermann, B.J. 10
Zuckerman, H. 35

Subject Index

ageing 4, 154, 158
  experience 161
  metacognition during ageing 159, 161
  of talented individual 170
aptitude-treatment-interaction 78
artistic talent 115, 116, 120
attention 23, 24, 149

Behavioural Management Model (BeM) 159, 162, 163
'burn-out' 130

child prodigy 36, 37, 93
cognitive apprenticeship 80
competence 162
Computer-Supported Intentional Learning Environment (CSILE) 64, 65, 67
convergent vs divergent thinking 101, 104
cooperative learning 80, 81
counselling 51, 145

definitions of giftedness 4, 100, 106
  advanced language 9
  advancement 25, 174
  concentration 9
  creativity 100, 104
  curiosity 23, 42, 76
  IQ 4, 6, 9, 15, 23, 24, 35, 43, 93, 101, 147
  memory 9, 25, 149
  tenacity 118
denotations 117
development over the life-span; in sport 137
Discipline-Based Art Education Movement (DBAE) 122
domain-specificity 79, 94
drugs 20

education of the talented 12, 109, 144, 179
  acceleration 14, 47, 63, 68, 110, 129, 180
  challenge 14, 145, 179
  competitions 153
  early admission 47
  enrichment 63, 68, 110, 175, 182
  gifted programmes 13
  guidance 14
  long-term courses 148
  mentorship 49, 108
  residential programmes 149
  special education 180
educational concerns 13–14
  critical periods 21, 47, 144
  underachievement 13, 47, 61, 184

eminent people, see genius
emotional influences on cognitive development 27, 47
  mediation of emotion 27
  motivation 43
  perfectionism 44
  self-esteem 27, 92, 107
  stress 28, 44
emotional vulnerability 11, 136

gender and talent 45
genius 33, 43
  attributes 33
  chance-configuration model 102
  family background 34, 39

Hamburg model of finding and fostering mathematically able pupils 148
heuristic methods 60, 88

identification 108, 174
  by performance 108
  by provision 109
  of talent in sport 128–30
insight 118
Instrumental Enrichment (IE) programme 77–8

Johns Hopkins University's Center for Talented Youth (CTY) 150

knowledge-telling vs knowledge-transforming 65

'late bloomers' 154
leisure-time activities 49, 130
life-span perspective 48, 175

Management coaching 51
mastery motivation 24, 175
mathematical disposition 61
mental models ('as-if') 122
metacognition (intellectual meta-activities) 23, 60, 65, 73, 100
  development of meta-activities 76

National Child Development Study 21, 25
nature vs nurture 7, 20, 25, 34, 38, 42, 73, 84, 107
novices vs experts 25, 59, 80, 87
  training (practice) 38, 93, 107, 139

operators 89
out-of-school provision 145, 188
outward and inward cognitive development 26

pattern recognition 90
peak performances 109
physical talent 128
plasticity 159, 162
policy for actualizing talent 174
  aims 177
  principles 177
  school policy 184
potential 88
problem-solving 88

research methodology 5, 39, 42, 112, 162
  biographical research 43, 107
  idiographic information 164
  longitudinal studies 6, 22, 68, 92
  retrospective view of adults 5

schemata 90, 91
Schülerakademien 151
self-efficacy 28, 51
self-help groups 146
self-regulation vs teacher regulation in learning 9, 51, 62, 72, 78, 179
  'high road' of learning 80
  training programmes for self-regulated learning 77–80
  transfers of training 79
social giftedness 50
Socratic teaching 81
stereotyping/labelling 12, 48
Study of Mathematically Precocious Youth (SMPY) 149
surface vs deep learning 63, 75
symbols 26

teacher training 183
teaching–learning process 74, 81, 82
  learning environment 59, 63, 82
tests 23, 100, 108
  Bayley 23
  form-board 29
  Gesell 23
  SAT 149
  WISC-R 50
theories of giftedness (intelligence) 4, 49, 75, 115, 178
theory
  of art 122–4
  of intervention 63
  of learning 61
Training of Young Athletes Study (TOYA) 130–6

University of the Third Age 155, 176

zone of proximal development 83